Number 96

MAVIS BRAMSTON

and me

Number 96 MAVIS BRAMSTON and me

David Sale

Published by Vivid Publishing
P.O. Box 948, Fremantle
Western Australia 6959
www.vividpublishing.com.au

Cover Design – Andrew Foster

National Library of Australia Cataloguing-in-Publication data:
Author: Sale, David
Title: Number 96, Mavis Bramston and Me / David Sale.
ISBN: 9781922204080 (paperback)
Subjects: Sale, David.
Authors, Australian--Biography.
Television writers--Australia.
Dewey Number: A823.3

Photographs courtesy of ABC Archives; ATN Channel 7; Umbrella Entertainment and the TEN Network; leading photographer Susie Hagon; and from the author's private collection. If a credit has been overlooked, apologies are offered, and upon notification any omission will be rectified at the first opportunity.

To order further copies of this book or to contact the author, please visit
www.vividpublishing.com.au/number96 for further information.

I wish to dedicate this book to all the dear friends and talented colleagues who have enriched my life, both personally and professionally. They have helped to make the successes possible, the failures bearable, and this book a reality.

Foreword

The Hon. Michael Kirby AC CMG
Onetime Justice of the High Court of Australia

David Sale played an important part in Australia's social history. I know because I grew up during the Golden Age when two of the television programs he was associated with were all the rage. I refer to T*he Mavis Bramston Show* and the inimitable *Number 96.*

Australian society back in the 1960s and 70s was a pretty solemn, censorious, buttoned up place. Aboriginal Australians were denied respect and full legal recognition until the referendum of 1967. And even then land rights, to recognise their traditional lands, had not been upheld by Parliament. It took the High Court decision in the Mabo case in 1992 to reverse that shocking discrimination. White Australia was still in full swing until 1966. It was next to impossible, even for a married couple, to arrange for a person of Asian or other 'coloured' ethnicity to migrate to Australia. Many people thought that only Britishers should be allowed in and they looked with suspicion at Germans, Scandinavians and Netherlanders, let alone Greeks and Italians. The woman's place was in the kitchen. And as for gays, with their abominable conduct, they had to be entrapped by handsome young policemen, rounded up and put in prison. It was a pretty depressing time to grow up in Australia.

Into this complacent scene burst the amazing, challenging, entertaining, raucous series that David Sale helped to bring to fruition. Young Australians of today will not appreciate the courage, imagination and risks he took to push a reluctant Australia into the 20th century, before that century was finally out. *The Mavis Bramston Show* was terribly distressing to many decent, law abiding citizens. It was unerringly irreverent. It challenged all the sacred cows. It upset all the usual suspects. The studio was flooded with protests from 'ordinary' Australians who could not believe that such a program would be put to air in a decent society such as ours. But gradually, and shockingly, the show built up an enormous audience as Australians learned to laugh at themselves. Laughter and sharp observation are the ways to change society from self-righteousness to modernity. I pay tribute to David Sale and his co-conspirators for their magnificent contribution to loosening up the Australia in which I had come to maturity. We are still a somewhat self-satisfied and uncritical community. But we are a whole lot better than we were before the Mavis team took us to pieces.

Growing up homosexual in Australia in the 1950s and 1960s was not an easy journey. The animosity and hatred of the churches and public authorities bred an atmosphere of fear and stigma. In February 1969 I met my partner Johan and we are still together 44 years later. But it was not easy in those days. Imagine our delight to learn that one of the heroes in *Number 96*, Don Finlayson (played by the unforgettable Joe Hasham), portrayed a young self-confident, homosexual lawyer living in the apartment block whose stories delighted huge audiences every week. The character was not ashamed of himself. He was talented. Everyone in the apartments looked to him for wisdom, calm and leadership. Talk about challenging the stereotypes! I have always thought that this presentation of a gay hero to a mass audience did more for acceptance of sexual minorities in Australia than all the solemn speeches of judges and professors or the worthy talk programs on the ABC. Here was life in the raw. And sometimes *Number 96* showed too much raw for the taste of the censors. Coming home from a busy day in court, it was such a pleasure for Johan and me to sit on our lounge and watch our hero being the community role model that we did not dare to be.

So I want to thank David Sale and all the famous and unknown participants in those marvellous, challenging, circuit breaking programs that they created in the far-off days of youth. They were not just entertainment. They were instructive. They constituted a serious social commentary. They held up a glass, as it were, by which we could see ourselves. And what we often saw was not nice and needed to change.

For their contribution to entertainment and enjoyment, but also for acting as change agents in Australian national life, David Sale and his colleagues deserve our thanks. It is good that the record has now been presented in this book. It is more than a book about bestselling TV programs. It is a book about changing the ethics of a nation. We are not yet quite there. But we are much further along in the journey, thanks to David Sale and his friends.

Sydney, 11 February 2013
Michael Kirby.

Prologue

"If I have his baby, do you think they'll keep me on in *Number 96* - I mean, long term?"

I stared at her, this diminutive would-be actress who'd had a small part in the hit television series I'd created.

"*Whose* baby?" I asked.

She reeled off the names of several men connected with the show - Bill Harmon, whose production company was responsible for the series, and several others in important positions. It was like a shopping list of people she'd probably never even met.

"I think we've both had a little too much to drink," I said, unable to believe what I was hearing. "And anyway, they're all happily married."

She had cornered me in a lift after Logies Night in Melbourne had finally fizzled like a huge fire cracker drowned in alcohol. She was sweet, ordinarily quite shy. Now I saw something else.

Raw ambition.

I'd encountered it a number of times and it was scary; people verging on desperation to make it to the top. I didn't think I'd suffered from it myself, but only because I'd been lucky, whatever that might mean. My definition of luck is opportunity backed by ability and experience.

She was talking again.

"I want to stay on in the show. This is my big chance. It's a massive hit. I want the exposure. But I could be dropped any minute." She took a step towards me. "I need insurance. And I know I can talk to you about it. Which one do I go for? I'm not talking about the casting couch. I mean a long-time bond. A kid with someone powerful. Then they'd have to keep me in work."

I glanced at the control panel. Three more floors to go. Lifts, unlike starlets, were slower in the seventies.

She started to cry, to fumble at me for support, weeping in desperation. I held her, thinking: *This must be the weirdest moment in my show business career.* I felt embarrassed and inadequate.

Nothing in my life thus far, eventful though it had been, had prepared me for this kind of situation. Here I was faced by a rampant Lolita, thrusting her delusional desire at me like some malformed newborn and begging me, in effect, to be its Godfather

The lift doors opened. I gave the girl a hug then tried to extricate myself. She wouldn't let go. She clutched at me as if I were a long-term contract.

This was neither the time nor the place for a moralizing lecture. "Look on the bright side," I said stupidly as I bodily edged her out into the corridor.

And I thought of my own bright sides.

The hits. *Mavis Bramston* and *Number 96*. My two novels, published in London and already bought for the movies. And before that, whatever had brought me from the war-ravaged slums of Manchester to creative success in Australia. From blitz to glitz.

I held her firmly at arm's length and told her not to forget to leave her breakfast order outside the door. All around us, whispers of debauchery filtered from elsewhere in the hotel. She turned her face up at me, with an innocence that belied her words, blinked at me, the tears still visible on her cheeks. "I'm serious, you know. I want to be a star. And I'll do anything, fuck anyone, to get there."

"I know you will," I said.

And eventually, she did.

1

The premiere of *Number 96 – the Movie* had all the trappings of a Hollywood opening. The TV series had been launched in early 1972 and had immediately become a massive hit. Now, in mid '74 came the big screen version and this over-the-top opening night. It had the red carpet flanked by hundreds of jostling, excited fans. There were searchlights and police cordons. And if memory serves me correctly, someone had even managed to cram a brass band into the proceedings. The hairstyles were extravagant, the dressing flamboyant, the jewellery gold, chunky and heavy. And that was just the men. The cavernous Hoyts Regent in George Street, Sydney, now sacrificed to developers in the name of progress, was filled to capacity with a rapturous audience. The huge ripples of anticipation matched a heavy surf at Bondi.

I didn't share this excitement. I knew what was coming – three or four episodes of *Number 96* strung together on a miniscule budget.

Shot on 16 mm, blown up to 35 mm. I had already seen the result, and even on TV-size monitors it had a grainy, fuzzy texture not enhanced by abrupt editing and lousy sound. God only knew what this travesty would look like on a giant cinema screen.

It was one of the many show business events in my life. To the public, these occasions appear to represent the pinnacle of achievement. Fame. The ultimate reward. Perfumed and polished gods parading with the savage elegance of starved peacocks, all seemingly intent on having a fabulous time. And yet, to the participants there is usually no joy involved. It is work. Hard work. Any words uttered are banal and meaningless. It all has as much to do with real life as so-called reality television, which means none whatsoever.

By late 1973, planning for the movie version was under way, which basically meant that script supervisor Johnny Whyte and I were asked to collaborate on what was laughably called the screenplay. We realized immediately that absolutely no concessions would be made to the art of motion picture-making. The budget was set at $100,000, which wouldn't even cover the cost of catering on the set of today's massive blockbusters. Our cast were paid their regular ($400) salary for each of the two weeks work. There were no negotiations. The only actor approached for discussion was Pat McDonald (Dorrie Evans) who, carried away with her new-found star status, seemed perfectly happy to agree to anything. Her acceptance of the terms set the seal on the miserly sum everyone else was doomed to be paid. A few baulked. Elaine Lee (Vera Collins), because she'd have to do nude scenes, bargained and got a little more. So did Johnny (Aldo Godolfus) Lockwood. The rest got their basic rate which was ridiculous for a movie with such box office potential. The whole thing was to be shot on the regular studio sets on a production schedule of two weeks during our 1973 Christmas break. In an alarming departure from tradition, which usually kept the series studio-bound, two whole days were allotted to exterior location filming.

To the cast, director Peter Benardos and crew, it was business as usual. No-one was surprised when the project came in under time and under budget.

Johnny Whyte and I mapped out the storylines. Yes, Vera Collins had to be raped by a bikie gang even before the titles, just to reassure audiences they'd come into the right cinema. Pensioners Dorrie and Herb Evans discovered they might not be legally married, after Dorrie had instructed Herb to dig out their wedding certificate, telling him: "It's in the *Winning Post* chocolate box under our Last Will and Testicles." Dorrie's malapropisms had got that bad.

In a plot concerned with a husband driving his wife mad, a delectable but sadly inexperienced Rebecca Gilling was added to the lethal mix as an air hostess who was photographed more out of her uniform than in it. Interestingly, no airline would allow us to use their name or uniform, so we had to invent a fictitious airline and a specially-designed uniform. Qantas told us that our depiction of a sexually active member of their cabin crew would not only be unrealistic, but bad for their image. Hello?

The plots not only thickened, they congealed. Johnny Whyte and I approached the assignment with the careless aplomb that only success can generate, sharing batches of scenes, knowing our individual efforts would join seamlessly. By that time, we knew the characters as well as we knew ourselves. The script budget was set at $10,000 - $5,000 for each of us. Our contracts also stipulated that we were to receive ten percent of the producer's net profits, so we expected more payments along the way.

I look at that contract, which I still have, and I shake my head at our innocence. "Producer's Net Profits," is a joke in the motion picture industry. If you believe producers have net profits, you believe Saddam Hussein really *did* have weapons of mass destruction. It is now well known, though not by us at the time, that this term can be manipulated by 'creative book-keeping' to divest any expectant recipients of future payments. The movie was a smash hit all over Australia. Years later, it was listed in *The Bulletin* as one of the top money-making films in relation to budget ever made in this country. In his definitive book. *Super Aussie Soaps,* Andrew Mercado writes: "To this day, *Number 96 – the Movie* remains one of the most profitable Australian films ever made."

Johnny Whyte and I never received another cent.

We did not benefit financially from this major money-making hit, despite that clause in our contract. We all must accept some of the blame for letting it happen because, swept away in the euphoria of being involved in the most successful show on Australian television to that time, we were more than a little lax in claiming and pursuing our rights. That is the problem we trusting creative types face all the time. We expect others to match our standards.

But back to the premiere. Adding to my discomfort was the fact that seated directly behind me was legendary Hollywood screenwriter, Casey Robinson, newly resident in Australia. Casey was the remarkable talent whose scripts at Warner Brothers Studios during Hollywood's Golden Age included many of the Bette Davis classics such as *Dark Victory* and *Now Voyager.* The prospect of him breathing down my neck while our minor effort was unfolding held all the joy of anticipating a colonoscopy. Afterwards, the ever-diplomatic Casey waved away my embarrassment, saying: "You're giving the people exactly what they want."

Maybe he should have told that to rival TV production company, Crawfords. Needless to say, they followed our lead with a movie version of their answer to *Number 96 - The Box.* But they made the mistake of turning their turgid opus into a madcap comedy for the silver screen. It lasted about five days in cinemas and disappeared, never to be seen again except perhaps as a Midday Movie.

Despite my fears, our movie was more than enthusiastically received on that opening night. Even film critic Mike Harris, who tore it to shreds in *The Australian,* was forced to admit he had never seen a movie where each character's first appearance was applauded by the audience. Columnist Matt White also had his say in *The Daily Mirror*: "Just at a time when Australian movies are proving they are of world standard, along comes one that puts our film production quality back a decade. Translated from TV into colour and big screen, this chronicle of overcrowded love nests and raggle-taggle human behaviour is made even more glaringly repulsive. We have half-naked homosexuals touching each other in bed…full frontal nudity…rape…violence, slapstick comedy…tearless pathos. Sadly, I have no doubt this movie with all its faults will play to packed houses."

With publicity like that, why wouldn't it? Audiences didn't seem to mind the grainy look; they accepted Rebecca Gilling's nudity; they didn't even bat an eye at the kiss Joe Hasham exchanged with his romantic interest in the film, John Orcsik. Strange about that kiss. The first seriously passionate smooch between two males in screen history apart from one in *Sunday, Bloody Sunday,* it mysteriously disappeared from all prints after the Sydney season. Even copies now lodged in the National Film and Sound Archive no longer contain the footage. Funny about that…

The morning after the premiere, it came over the radio that queues had already formed along George Street, two hours before the first public session of the movie was to be shown at 11 am. And despite the Hallelujah chorus of disgust from the critics, it played to packed houses at the Regent, four sessions a day, for several weeks. In a smart move, members of our cast were rostered to mingle with the crowds at the evening sessions during the season. Meanwhile, on two Fridays later in the year, the cast stopped taping earlier than usual and hopped on a plane to appear at gala premieres in Melbourne and Brisbane. I never ceased to be amazed at the public's overwhelming reaction on these occasions. For the first time, we had made 'stars' out of television actors and actresses, not so-called personalities or rock singers, but everyday jobbing actors and actresses.

These unprecedented displays of acclamation had started during our annual treks down to Melbourne for the Logie Award Night. Soon, we were accustomed to estimates like: "Bigger crowds than turned out to greet The Beatles", and (in Perth) "More people lined the streets than during the Queen's last Royal Visit."

I was something of a veteran of the Logie Awards. Earlier in my career, as Executive Producer of *The Mavis Bramston Show,* I had accepted a Logie on behalf of my employers, Channel 7, during a brief ceremony in a suite at the then Chevron Hotel in Potts Point. No red carpet, no stage show, no crowds, no stars. I don't believe I was even given a drink or a sandwich. Compared to the hoopla that was to evolve in later years, this one was the equivalent of a one-night stand in a cheap motel.

Number 96 made its debut only a couple of months before the 1972 Logie Awards, but its immediate impact meant that everyone involved was invited to the big event. Everyone but me, that is. As usual, the writer was treated like a second-class citizen and ignored. I was furious. Without me, there would have been no show, at least not one called *Number 96* with that set of characters in those situations. Word of my displeasure got back to *TV Week,* the magazine sponsoring the event, and I was belatedly sent an invitation. I refused to go. "I am not going as an afterthought," I proclaimed, and tore up the invitation in a fit of anger. On Logie night, I didn't even watch. I went to dinner with a friend at the revolving restaurant atop Australia Square. It was like I was putting myself above all the crap that was going on.

My tantrum caused me to miss out on one of Publicity Director Tom Greer's magnificent brainstorms. He hired the Spirit of Progress or some other interstate train, loaded it with the cast and media, and turned the rail journey down to Melbourne into an all-night party. It was the mythical Gravy Train come to life, and it caused a sensation.

The following year, I was determined not to miss the repeat of this trip, particularly when I received my invitation to the Logies before anyone else. *TV Week* had learned its lesson.

We all boarded the train at Central Station in Sydney early evening. Train? It was more like a club on wheels. The dining cars were turned into bars, and there were movies like *Casablanca* showing on make-shift screens, a horrible waste of classics because everyone was too hyperactive or tipsy to settle down and watch movies. As the train roared into the night, the party atmosphere intensified. And then came the stops at country stations where the platform was crowded with fans, some carrying sleepy children in pyjamas. This was the middle of the night and they'd been waiting in the cold for hours. Members of the cast would descend from the train to chat briefly, before the train moved off again.

I witnessed the phenomenon of instant fame, and it rather scared me. I saw mothers thrusting babes-in-arms at Pat McDonald, pleading: "Touch her...touch my baby!" as if imploring a Papal blessing. And at tiny stations where no stop was scheduled, the train slowed down and we hung out of the windows and saw forlorn groups of people straggled along the platform, waving energetically despite the hour.

I remember one stop at dawn. Veteran actress Thelma Scott (Claire Houghton) stood on the footboard thundering to the advancing crowd: "Stand back! All books will be signed!" If there'd been a Red Sea, she would have parted it. She began grasping the nearest outstretched arms, scribbling her name in ballpoint on any bare flesh she could find. Johnny Lockwood christened her 'The Fastest Pen in the West.' Thelma, a well-known radio actress in her day, was relishing this resurgence of popularity and usually stayed on the platform until the last minute. On this occasion, the train started to move and I happened to glance out of the window. "Thelma's still out there – somebody grab her!" I yelled. Somebody did, and she was hauled aboard before the train picked up speed.

Nothing prepared me for our arrival at Melbourne's Spencer Street Station. The train pulled in, stopped, and we waited. We could hear the roar of the crowds. We huddled together like Christians waiting to be pushed out into the Colosseum. Security men came on board and assured us the mob was being held back by barriers. "Yeah," I replied, "but have the lions been fed?" After that stupid remark, nobody wanted to be first out.

Johnny Whyte grabbed me and said: "Let's make an example. Nobody knows us. We're writers. We'll be safe." We were not safe. A kind of cattle run had been set up from the train to the double-decker London bus that was to shunt us from the station to the Southern Cross Hotel where we were all billeted. Johnny and I descended from the train. The path seemed clear. There were excited crowds shouting on either side, but just as the security men had assured us, they were behind barriers. I turned and told Elaine Lee and the others on the train: "Just follow us. Stick close behind, keep moving and you'll be fine."

Famous last words. At first hand, I experienced the shattering impact of mass hysteria. As we walked, then hurried, then ran along the narrow walkway between the barriers, it became the bull-run or cattle-pen it appeared to be, with us as the farm animals headed for the abattoirs.

I dodged hands, tearing at me. "I'm nobody!" I kept yelling with forced laughter. It made no difference. They snatched at my hair, clawed at my jacket, pulled at my arms. Up ahead, I saw Johnny scramble onto the bus and as I followed him I heard an increase in the commotion behind me. I jumped onto the bus, turned and saw that the barriers were down, broken through by the crowd. Elaine was engulfed by people, as if by storm-tossed waves, both her arms raised high into the air, at the point of being swept away. I reached down, managed to grab one of her hands, then literally yanked her on board as if rescuing her from a whirlpool. We scrambled upstairs to the upper deck, wanting to distance ourselves as far away as possible from the crowds. We watched from the windows as other members of the cast somehow fought their way through to the bus. But when everyone was on board, the driver was unable to move off because we were surrounded by the crowd.

Like in all the best horror movies, it got worse. This was the moment flesh-eating zombies invade the village, the gargantuan alien monster bursts through the wall, Johnny Farnham announces another farewell tour.

In our case, with all of us crowded on the top deck, the bus started to rock from side to side. The momentum increased. There were wails of fright. Why would the fans do this to us? We clung together in a disarrayed bunch, fearing we were going to be tipped over, that we would actually topple and crash. The roar of the crowds drowned our cries of consternation. We couldn't keep our balance, staggering, clutching at seats and each other. It was beyond comprehension, beyond reason. We were popular. Why would they want to kill us?

The rocking subsided. Two of our younger actresses were on the floor, weeping. The bus moved off, and we all collapsed into seats, realizing for the first time that the price of fame can involve frayed nerves, extreme stress, and savage, dangerous, out-of-control behaviour by an adoring public. In retrospect, we had it lucky. These days, there's a lethal addition – the paparazzi.

Without further incident, like somebody throwing a bomb or themselves under the bus, we arrived at the Southern Cross Hotel where not only were we staying, but the Logie ceremonies would be held in the hotel ballroom. In a sane world, actually staying in the same building as the event should involve nothing easier than just taking a lift down to the ballroom. In the insane world of television, that was out of the question. Stars have to make an entrance. Therefore, our cast had to go through the ridiculous procedure of sneaking out through the kitchens, boarding limousines in the back alley and being driven around the corner to the main entrance of the hotel.

Yes, there was a red carpet, but none of the elaborate ritual that is a feature of such occasions these days. People just got out of cars, waved to the fans, and went inside. Nobody was waylaid by morons with mikes asking: "Who are you wearing?" Has there ever been a more idiotically-framed question? In those days, the ladies just got out their favourite dress or maybe splurged on a new one, went to the hairdresser, maybe had a manicure or a facial, and just turned up. The guys had a shower (maybe!) and wore their best suit. Now, award ceremonies appear to be more about dress designers and stylists vying for trophies than the people they groom. This started with the Academy Awards, of course, and needless to say has been copied in Australia up to the hilt. Aped ought be a more appropriate description. A troop of performing monkeys couldn't do better than the annual crop of simpering starlets and celebrity wannabees, twirling their way into ultimate oblivion. There is no journey more destructive than an ego trip.

Thank God back then it was into the ballroom and into the grog. A lot of heavy drinking went on at the start of the evening because no liquor was served during the actual televised proceedings. Everyone needed a little help from the bottle to get them through the boring and frequently embarrassing marathon.

Much to Johnny Whyte's outrage, we two writers were consigned to a private suite on an upper floor to watch it all on a monitor. I didn't mind one bit. We were not recognizable to the general public and it was a night for the 'stars' to be on show. Besides, this allowed us to drink all the way through it and make rude comments about what was going on. People seated in the ballroom managed to drink during the show by making frequent trips to strategically-placed bars. These days, someone goes to the toilet and returns as animated as a Disney cartoon. The coy term for the bathroom coined in the nineteen fifties – The Powder Room – now has a more sinister meaning. But back then, someone who said they wanted to pee actually wanted to relieve themselves and didn't come back with suspiciously frosted nostrils.

By the time the ceremonies were over and everybody staggered to the notorious after-show parties, most of the 'personalities' would be well and truly plastered. 'Personalities.' That was the label desperately stuck on people with no discernable talent and certainly no personality. Nowadays, 'personalities' have become the much grander 'celebrities', an equally desperate overused and in a lot of cases undeserved label stuck on publicity-grasping, pumped-up, cardboard cut-outs of what really famous people used to be like. They're easy to spot and I'll leave you to fill in the names.

But to get back to those post-Logie parties. These are where all the gossip and back-biting flourish, where feuds erupt or are resurrected, where the fist and cat fights flare up, and where the most unlikely sexual liaisons are initiated. The hair is let down, the true selves emerge, and for a lot of the time it's not pretty.

Being an amiable tippler, I tried to avoid areas of possible mayhem, the gatherings that mixed ex-wives and ex-husbands, current and former lovers, bitchy competitors from different networks and just plain old nasty drunks. I wasn't always fortunate. I remember the lesbian participant in a kid's show, tipsily scouting for a husband. After sounding out every male from Don Lane to the waiters, she eventually reached the bottom of the barrel and propositioned me.

"We could be a cover for one another," she burbled, swaying. "Whaddo they call it….a lavender marriage?" "I don't need any cover, I'm out," I told her. "Closets are for clothes."

Then there was the corner I turned and found myself witnessing a manly American actor shagging one of our local entertainment columnists. The local was not only male and gay but had a reputation for promiscuity, and so to rework the catch-phrase from a popular sci-fi series of the time, the visitor was *not* venturing boldly where no man had gone before.

More often than not I found myself being the shoulder to cry on. On one occasion, I had to placate a tearful Sheila Kennelly, our 'Norma Whittaker' who had been 'sacked' by a drunken Johnny Whyte. Johnny, a charming man when sober, became evil after too much alcohol. I held hands supportively with a despondent Paula Duncan who felt, wrongly, that she wasn't doing as well as she should in the important part of homosexual Don Finlayson's sympathetic sister.

Little did she or I know that she would go on to far greater fame in the long-running series *Cop Shop* and also become a vigorous worker for charity. And it was on another Logie night that I had my memorable encounter in a lift with the newcomer intent on trading her womb for stardom. Even more fascinating was the daytime sexual dexterity of one good-looking actor in our troupe. Idolised and mobbed by young and willing girls, he indulged himself – and them – by repeatedly taking the choicest ones up to his hotel room, at great risk not only to himself, but to the reputations of all concerned.

Number 96 won its share of Logies. When Gina Lollobrigida presented us with the award for Australia's most popular show, it was one time the voluptuous Italian star was eclipsed. The ovation that greeted our entire cast as they trooped up onto the stage was thunderous. Pat McDonald received the coveted Gold Logie one year. This gave the anti-Pat clique that now sat at the feet of Bunney Brooke fuel for much resentment, sneering that despite her feigned surprise, Pat had been carrying her acceptance speech in her bag for days. So? Wouldn't anyone who'd been nominated?

It all comes back…the bitter rivalries, the feverish competitiveness, and the inevitable starlet working the room, circling with the desperation of a Cessna trying to land in a fog.

It never changes, this war zone. Oh, yes. Forget ceremony. Forget celebration. Think war zone. Fortunately, I was used to wars. I grew up in one...

2

The air raid siren that heralded Nazi Germany's bombing of Manchester during World War Two is the most powerful of my childhood memories. This was back in the days when kids really did have a childhood and were not coerced into being adults from the moment they could pronounce the word McDonalds. There was no McDonalds in the 1940s, in fact there was very little food at all, thanks to rationing.

The siren would arouse us from sleep like the mournful wails of some nocturnal beast. Immediately, I'd start to shiver as I was hauled out of bed by my parents, bundled up and half-dragged, half-carried around the corner to my grandma's house in the next street. Already, the Ack-Ack guns would be warding off enemy planes with thunderous bursts of flack as searchlights probed the sky. It wasn't Manchester's legendary cold climate that gave me the shivers. It was sheer terror.

Grandma not only had Aunty Gladys and Uncle Geoff living with her; she had an air raid shelter in her backyard. And there we'd sit, in a huddled, rugged-up group around a tin bucket of glowing, smoky coals that had been tended all day by Uncle Geoff in an effort to keep the place warm. This small, square bunker had walls the thickness of three bricks and was topped with a slab of concrete. Add a couple of stone angels and a few curlicues and you'd have, depressingly, a mausoleum - and one already pre-packed with bodies!. The Government, which supplied these shelters on application, gave the assurance of utter safety except for the million-to-one chance of a direct hit. And certainly, it kept us safe. It shook and vibrated, and on one occasion when a bomb exploded close by it developed a large crack down one side, which was hastily bonded with cement the next day. This then was our claustrophobic bolt-hole, dreaded but valued.

The government had also built public shelters in some of the back alleys - elongated versions of our little bunker, but with nobody to tend them they became foul repositories for garbage, emergency toilets, and venues for all sorts of unmentionable goings-on, and even when bombs were dropping like hailstones, respectable people risked death rather than use them.

Grandma was paranoid about getting her brood into the safety of the shelter, sometimes neglecting her own needs in the process. One night, she got to the door of the shelter and stopped, crying "Oh Gladys, I've left my false teeth in the bedroom. Tell Geoff to go back and get 'em."

"You won't need 'em here, mother," Gladys replied, pushing her in. "They're dropping bombs not bloody meat pies!"

If we were lucky, the All Clear, a reassuring one-note wail, might sound after half an hour. At other times, we'd troop back and forth all night if the raids were repeated. Sometimes, it would be dawn before we emerged, blinking dry, sleepless eyes, into a world that stank with the acrid odour of explosives drifting on wisps of smoke, a world that sometimes greeted us with piles of rubble where houses had once stood, horrible toothless gaps where there had been a suburban smile. Rescue squads might already be digging for survivors or bodies. And I would pick up lumps of shrapnel as we went home, twisted bits of metal from shells or bombs, to add to my collection.

It didn't matter if the raids went on all night, kids were still required to attend school. No excuses. I'd toddle to All Saints Primary, only minutes from where we lived, my gas mask in a cardboard box slung over my shoulder. There were no high jinks in the playground. We just stood sleepily around, comparing notes on the previous night's raids, before being marshalled into our lines and marched into the classroom.

Some of my classmates would fall asleep during lessons. I know I did. But I'd stay awake if we had to write a story. It was the only part of school life I enjoyed, the English lessons. And reading. I devoured the tattered comic books that were in short supply. My mother asked one of the teachers whether such trash was healthy for me. The teacher told her: "It doesn't matter what he's reading, as long as he's reading. It'll become a habit that will last all his life." And teacher was right.

My stories were always the ones selected to be read out loud to the rest of the class. To express yourself in words is something that is born within you, and no amount of courses that purport to teach writing, be it literary, screen or television writing are worthwhile unless the talent is there to begin with. Suspiciously, some of these courses are presided over by individuals who - if you really dig into their credentials - have achieved little in the fields in which they claim to be experts. I can name names, and probably will, later, given a few drinks. They can teach you presentation and style, perhaps, but they cannot teach you how to write creatively unless you already have the gift.

Nobody was teaching me how to do it in school. The stories were my own, drawn from the fantasy world into which I regularly escaped. And not only from the war. Because while all my schoolmates regarded me as a storyteller, they also regarded me as a cheat..

There were contests at school, a ploy to keep us occupied, and keep our minds and fingers busy; contests that were initiated as to who could come up with the best model of (a) a seagoing vessel; and later (b) an aircraft.

I won them both.

But in no way did I deserve to. My father, an aircraft fitter, took over my early efforts. He fashioned the submarine. He put together the aeroplane. And each time, he put the model into my hands to take to school and pass off as my own work. I had no way of refusing him.

Nobody believed that I had done them. And I knew that they knew, and I was humiliated. Humiliation, abject humiliation, from classmates who suspected the truth but didn't say a word, was hard to take. They say kids can be cruel. I was lucky in a way, because nobody actually said: "You didn't make that". But I knew that's what they thought because with the surname Swindells (my birth name was Ernest Swindells), they'd been quick to call me *Swindler*, as a joke. But strangely in this instance they held off, maybe because the threat of being blown to bits by a bomb every night tends to trivialize minor cheating. It wasn't minor for me, it was too serious and too true. Now, I hated my father not only for pushing me into this embarrassing situation, but for the surname he had given me as well. Even though there were no taunts, I was about as popular with my schoolmates as a close relative of Adolph Hitler. I still feel the humiliation to this day.

Dad worked at an aircraft factory which is why he hadn't been drafted into the forces. He worked long hours in great danger. (The Nazi radio loudmouth, Lord Haw Haw, frequently said in his shortwave broadcasts to Britain, that the A.V. Roe factory in Manchester was a target for bombers and described its actual location) But I still feel it gave my father no reason to alienate his only son.

I'd be at home with my mother, dreading him to arrive home. There was no joy in his return from work each night. No warmth, just a strange freezing of the atmosphere. We had no personal contact whatsoever. I've since witnessed father-and-son-relationships and cried because it was something I never had. He wanted to promote me by forcing his own models on me as my own. Or maybe he didn't want to promote *me*, he wanted to promote me merely as his son who was so adept at making models. I cannot remember one personal or even fun conversation with him at that time. He was jovial in front of company and the reverse when there was just the three of us. He was skilled with his hands and made toys and furniture for young relatives and friends, but nothing for me except the deadly contest winners.

My parents quarrelled, incessantly. I just kept my head down over my comic books. And yet my mother would make excuses. "He's working long hours". And: "There's just this one chop, but your father's got to have it because he's the worker."

I didn't understand any of this. I didn't know what I know now, that all human beings have flaws. I escaped. First, into my imagination, crafting stories. Second, into the world of film.

My parents liked to go to 'The Pictures' as they were called in the forties. Apart from drinking in pubs, it was the only form of relaxation offering in war-torn England. My parents were teetotallers, so pubs were out. And as babysitters were as unheard of as astronauts in that era, they had to take me along to The Pictures with them.

We had two cinemas in Newton Heath, the suburb of Manchester in which we lived, the *Magnet* and the *Pavilion*. Each ran two programs a week, Monday thru Wednesday, Thursday thru Saturday. Sundays, there was a one-day showing of something very old. Each evening there were two sessions, from 6 'til 8, then 8-15 'til 10-15. Mostly, we went to the early sessions because there were unlikely to be air raids that early in the evening. If we went to the second show, we'd have to queue. Then, as the first show ended the cinema's side doors would open and clouds, literally clouds of cigarette smoke would billow out. Then we would go inside and everybody would find their seats, sit down, and light up, filling the place with smoke again. Is it any wonder the kids of that time started to smoke early? We'd already developed the craving, passively.

It was an incredibly unhealthy atmosphere, but what did we know? And the positive benefit was escapism, a brief chance to forget the war and - in my case - day-to-day unhappiness.

Oh, the movies. How I loved them, particularly the musicals in garishly wonderful technicolor. Nobody in our family had the slightest connection with show business, and yet some fanciful gene must have been there inside of me, lurking like the soft center in a chocolate. Still not out of short pants, I couldn't get enough of Betty Grable, Esther Williams, and Judy Garland. It got so that I lived for the movies. I'd go with my parents twice a week in the evenings, then sneak in a Saturday matinee and still feel deprived. British people have this reputation for never washing. Well, I have news for them. I at least was *brain*washed.

Woody Allen has expressed growing up in the era of double features, and I joyfully quote him and acknowledge the quote, because I could not put it better:

"...in the space of three hours you would be transported to some penthouse on Fifth Avenue and moments later to some pirate ship, from Casablanca to the Alamo. It was just astonishing, the overwhelming magic."

Woody got it right, and like him, I never recovered from movies. To me, reality was supposed to conform to what went on up there on that screen, not vice versa.

At that early age, courtesy of Hollywood movies, I developed a love of show business. And an understanding of what entertainment was all about, like keeping an audience at the most enthralled, and at the least amused.

Once or twice during the wartime years, we went away on a brief summer holiday. Betty Grable holidayed in South America, Esther Williams swam across turquoise pools in Mexico and Hawaii. I got as far as Blackpool.

We journeyed there by charabanc - forties-speak for motor-coach, and I think the travelling time was less than three hours but to me it was a safari into the unknown. An adventure.

I remember most strongly the salt air. You breathed it in and it was stinging and bracing. But let's face it, for a kid brought up in cinemas full of tobacco smoke, mustard gas would have been an improvement. Blackpool's beach was long and wide. What sand there was looked like damp ashes. Mostly, it was all pebbles and because the tide went way, way out, you'd be exhausted before you could get your feet wet. But there was the Blackpool Tower with its Zoo and its Ballroom, and whoever thought up that combination must have had a strong sense of irony. And the Pier, along which one could walk into infinity, or at least - if you had the stamina - until you could actually witness salt water splashing against its supports.

Back on the Promenade, there was this long line of deck chairs occupied by people rugged up as if they were experiencing the next Ice Age, all stoically facing the horizon where a distant strip of indigo indicated that there was an ocean out there.

Across a Promenade bisected by tramcars, there was this dazzling strip of amazing sideshows. 'The World's Largest Rat' was really enormous. In Australia, you'd mistake it for a wombat, which it may very well have been. There was also an abundance of freaks and amazing con-jobs. Much like Australian television as I would grow to know it.

My attention was most captured by the crowds strolling along the Promenade. This was wartime, so practically every young guy was in uniform. They looked good to me, like heroes. The girls seemed garish. Their legs were orange. Stockings of any description were unavailable, so they had to resort to smearing 'liquid stockings' on their bare legs. This product was an early forerunner of instant-tan, except an even more intense shade of orange that looked hideous, particularly with the knee-high skirts and the regimented styles of their 'Utility' dresses and suits. 'Utility' was the term given to the clothing that was available by surrendering clothing coupons, and was another form of rationing. Clothing coupons severely restricted any attempt to look smart; the materials were cheap and the cut nasty.

Blackpool was my first exposure to the outside world. The yellowish pancake the girls had smeared on had nothing to do with Betty Grable's smooth complexion. But then, none of the women in Newton Heath wore any make up at all, so I was only made aware of perfection by what I saw on the screen. What I was observing in Blackpool wasn't 'real life' as I knew it; real life, for me, was the movies. When we returned home, I felt as though I'd paid a visit to another planet, and couldn't wait to surrender myself to the smoke-infested dark of our local cinemas to see those wonderful *real* people up there on the screen in glowing colour.

The air raids began to peter out as the war turned in favour of the Allies. Manchester had survived despite an early bombardment that included a Christmas Eve blitz that flattened Piccadilly, the city's centre. The bombing continued in the surrounding suburbs for long afterwards, only to abate when victory was in sight.

Manchester was a city renowned for its achievements in science, technology and manufacturing, but not noted for its beauty. The sun rarely shone. Blow your nose and your handkerchief would turn black and viscous. Small, stunted houses clung together in rows on each side of the main roads, concealing the ugliness behind, the ugliness of narrow cracks of streets and back-to-back dwellings. Rows and rows of them, in lines broken only by the odd cinema, fish and chip shops, corner stores and, of course, the inevitable pubs. To be fair, there were garden suburbs on the far side of the city, but Newton Heath wasn't one of them.

If you've seen *Coronation Street,* that will give a vague idea of Newton Heath's squalor, - rows of houses with doors opening directly onto the pavement. Ours was on a corner, and like all the others was 'two up, two down'. This meant a narrow hallway from front door to kitchen, with a door opening off the lobby to a front sitting room, rarely used. Creaking, crippled stairs led up to the two bedrooms. And down below were dungeon-like cellars. Every Monday morning, my mother would do the washing down there, boiling the clothes in a wood-fired copper, squeezing them out afterwards using a huge old fashioned wringer with big wooden rollers that would have taxed the strength of Schwarzenegger, let alone my mam.

Then, the damp clothes would be hauled up to ground level and hung on a rack, lowered and raised by a rope, above the fireplace in our kitchen/living room. There was no point in hanging stuff outside to dry. Most of the year, it rained. We had no hot water in our house, and no inside toilet, just a lean-to in the dingy backyard. And no bathroom. Every Saturday morning saw me at the Public Bath House, sitting there in threepence-worth of tepid water, the tub ringed by the black, greasy legacy of the previous occupant's filth.

Every Saturday night, however, another means of escapism had presented itself, now that the Germans had stopped bombing us.

She wasn't 'The Girl Next Door', she was the little girl next-door-but-one, and she was the daughter of the licensees of *The Oddfellows Arms*, our local pub. Her name was Marion, and she became my first real friend. Every Saturday night, after The Pictures, I was allowed to hang out in their living quarters at the back of the pub. They'd buy us fish and chips from the shop opposite and snap open bottles of soft drink, and we'd gorge ourselves, enjoying the merry-making of all the locals, crowded into the bar parlour; lots of beer, lots of smoke and loud community singing to the accompaniment of Ernie Greenhalsh pounding the old piano. Conviviality of the highest order, never before experienced in my young life. The fact that I felt welcome in an establishment called *The OddFellows Arms*, could have been a forecast of some aspects of my future sex life. Certainly, Marion and I didn't play doctors and nurses. We put on little concerts in her backyard because it was marginally bigger than mine, and sometimes in the afternoons after school when the pub was closed, we'd sneak in and drink the dregs from the beer trays and I would try to emulate Ernie Greenhalsh on the piano. That piano. Its mahogany veneer was cracked like the skin of a prehistoric reptile. The keys were a vast array of yellowing teeth with ugly cigarette burns like badly-done fillings. Still, I sat down and started to pick out tunes that I knew.

Word of this must have got back to my parents. Being teetotal, they never set foot in the pub. But before I knew it, I was enrolled with a piano teacher called Mrs Sherlock at one guinea for a ten-week 'term'. And an old piano, marginally worse than the one in the pub, was moved into our kitchen.

I loved my piano lessons every Thursday afternoon and practiced diligently. My failings soon became obvious and I knew I had no natural ability. Still, I loved my music, and the practical knowledge of music those lessons gave me came in very handy, later in life.

The war in Europe ended. Trestle tables were put out for street parties and long-hoarded tins of spam, fruit and jellies came out of the larders for the celebratory feasts. It was on for young and old. Paper decorations were strung from house to house, diagonally across the narrow streets. Neighbours who hadn't smiled for years, beamed and danced and acted the fool, such was the all-pervading sense of relief that all the danger and the bloodshed was finally over.

Shortages continued. Britain, virtually bankrupted by the war, plunged into an economic crisis that led to draconian austerity measures. There was no end in sight to rationing. Peace brought more scarcities than less. We were still allowed only one egg per month per person and for the rest of the time it was powdered eggs that could only be cooked into rubbery omelets. I have a feeling they're still being used by airlines. Meat supplies were severely limited, butter non-existent, produce like onions and tomatoes were doled out in secrecy by greengrocers only to their best customers and a child given an orange for the first time played with it like a ball, not knowing that it could be eaten. I had my first banana at age 8 and had to be shown how to peel it.

To add to the general discomfort, there were power cuts and fuel shortages. Coal particularly was in short supply, a major problem in the bitterly cold Manchester winters. Similarly, in the bitterly cold Manchester summers! Coke was a substitute, and I'm not referring to either the soft drink or the drug. This coke is a by-product in the manufacture of gas, silvery, crisp lumps of burnable material that was sold on a first-come-first-served basis by the local Gasworks. Unfortunately, the local Gasworks was an hour away from where we lived. My mother and I would set out in the dark at 5 a.m. pushing a large barrow, a box on wheels, and it didn't matter if it was raining, snowing or just plain bleak, the journey had to be made if we were to have warmth in the house for the rest of the week. We would arrive at the Gasworks around 6am and join the inevitable queue. At 6-30, the large wooden gates would be thrown open, and orderly queues be damned, we'd all run across the vast cobbled yard like prospectors in the Gold Rush. Come to think of it, that coke *was* like gold to us. We'd push our barrow under a chute, and down would cascade our measured ration of about thirty kilos. Then came the hard part - hauling it home. Sometimes, like when the pavements were covered in ice, it was a nightmare. Other times, it was just plain hard. I was a skinny kid, no Atlas. I helped pull and shove as much as I could, but basically, it was my mother's efforts that got us and the coke home. We would both be in an exhausted sweat, despite the cold, but at least we could look forward to having a fire in the grate for the following week. And then we'd have to do it all over again.

I haven't said much about my mam up to now, but that does not diminish her importance to my well-being at that time. She did her best to make up for dad's failings. Lucy was good-hearted, a hard worker and I loved her. She also had an indomitable sense of humour, which I like to think I inherited from her.

So that was the Second World War from the limited perspective of a youngster. Uncomfortable, terrifying at times, but in reality just a mild distillation of the evil that was happening elsewhere in Europe.

I have no idea of the ramifications of the British education system as it was then, particularly as it had been thrown into disarray by wartime conditions. All I know is that I stayed at All Saints Primary School until I was almost eleven years old, and then I graduated to North Manchester High School for Boys. This drastic change in my life came with a school uniform - cap, blazer, pullover and tie, and other items such as soccer boots. These latter items made me nervous. I'd never played team sports.

The high school was situated in Moston, a bus ride away, in a newly-built 'posh' area. My first sight of the high school was a crude-ly-painted inscription in large letters on a long boundary wall, one which separated it from yet-to-be-built-upon open paddocks. The inscription read: "Jake is a Daft Swine." It was graffiti before it even had a name. I soon found out that 'Jake' was everybody's nickname for the headmaster, a tall, fearsome hulk of a man with a huge bald head and malevolently piercing eyes. His real name was Burnett, but Carol he was not! His chosen mode of punishment was a thick, flat piece of hardened leather which he continually fondled like a second cock. That is, of course, unless it was being brought down with tremendous force on some poor unfortunate's outstretched hand or backside. I saw boys keel over from the shocking pain that was inflicted, but being a goody-goody I never had to experience it myself, thank God. This may sound like something from Dickens, but it was the nineteen forties and England has always been slow to change.

Obviously, nobody had the guts to bring the graffiti to 'Jake's' attention. Certainly, nobody had the initiative to clean it off. It was still there four years later when I bowed out, and it could still be there for all I know.

Having been a loner, the story-writing and the movie-going all being solitary pursuits, I suffered a lot of nervous apprehension at the thought of being thrust amongst hundreds of other boys with the prospect of having to take part in all sorts of physical activities. Let's face it - I was a nerd before nerds were even invented!

Things sorted themselves out very quickly. On the soccer field, by today's Beckham standards, I was more Posh than David. So I stopped being picked for teams and - in that soccer-mad environment - I was again an outcast. Fortunately, a few weeks into the first term, swimming lessons at a local pool were introduced as an alternative to the field sports and so began my lifelong devotion to swimming for exercise and recreation. (Thanks, Esther!) I even made a few friends, classmates with the same shared interests such as films, music and books. In other words, more nerds.

By the second term of my first year, I'd been demoted to a lower grade. I couldn't understand it. I was a keen student and paid attention in class. I did my homework assiduously. But I kept getting things wrong, and that meant lower marks.

Nobody thought to test my eyes. I was slowly but surely becoming shortsighted and right from the start, placed at the rear of the class, I was copying what I thought I saw written on the blackboard, but it was flawed information. Finally, I was fitted with glasses. Voila! The nerd image was complete, and the enhanced appearance of vulnerability attracted bullying. On the daily walk from the bus stop to the school, the clutch of fellow students who boarded the bus at various stops included a lanky sadistic bully called Gordon Smith. He began the practice of grabbing me by the hair, practically yanking it from my scalp so that my body arched in pain and then proceeding to lead me along, contorted and twisted, like an animal. Now, I wish I'd had the guts to kick him in the balls. Bullying still goes on in our schools. Nothing has changed. I was small and vulnerable. He was the same age but taller, and stronger. I use his real name, and if that walking piece of filth is still alive, then I spit in his face. His cruelty, sitting atop my father's conduct, gave me complexes which have taken me a lifetime to overcome.

There were compensations. In the back bedroom where I slept, there was a bicycle. Yes, a bike in a bedroom. Don't ask why. I do not know. The bullying from bus stop to school gave me impetus. I fronted up to my parents and said I wanted to cycle to school and back.

Needless to say, my father was against it. Too dangerous. My mother took my side. They had rows, verbal shouting matches that were awful to sit through.

My father eventually capitulated. Suddenly, I was cycling to school and I loved the thrill of pedaling along. This way, I avoided the bully and had the wind in my face. And the week-ends! Now I had the means to get out of the house, I'd cycle to places that had greenery and space.

Now I could see properly, I started my crawl back in class. I studied hard because movies were showing me there were better things in life. My fantasies were extravagant and irrepressible.

The High School years passed quickly. English was still the subject in which I excelled. The final exam on graduating from High School was the School Certificate, but I really had no hopes of success because I was hopeless at maths.

A miracle happened. To this day, I cannot add up a grocery bill or decipher a bank statement. But somehow, I got my School Certificate. And what's more, I won the Year Prize - a book called *Van Loon's Lives* which I never read, because – forget about Van Loon - my life underwent a major upheaval.

The day after that final Speech Day, I contemplated myself in the damp-blackened mirror in my bedroom. Curly hair that refused to be controlled by combs full of water; plastic-rimmed glasses, pale, podgy face and body to match. Not a bit like Gene Kelly.

'Well?" I asked my image. "What now?"

My formal education was over at fifteen. There was no thought, no hope of continuing further. I knew I'd have to start looking in the

Manchester Evening News classifieds every night for an opening into what I wanted to do. I wanted to write. I wanted to become a journalist.

"Are you up there?"

It was my father's voice. I went downstairs and immediately sensed that something was wrong. He was standing there with his backside to the fire. Mam was just sitting, fidgeting with her hands.

I waited, dreading what he was about to say, simply because whatever he had to say was never very pleasant.

"We wanted to go to your Auntie Florrie in New Zealand, but there's a complication. So instead, we applied to migrate to Australia, and it's come through. Ten pounds each for your mam and me, a fiver for you. We'll raise the money by sellin' the furniture."

I felt my stomach churn. Australia? Not Los Angeles or New York or London or Paris. Not the palm-fringed boulevards of Beverly Hills. Australia.

I took a deep breath. " I don't want to go."

My father retaliated. "You didn't want to be evacuated, remember? When kids were being shunted off into the country where they'd be safe, you pleaded with your mam and me not to give permission. And we didn't. We kept you here with us because we're a team. Remember that? Remember how grateful you were? Well now the team's off to Australia."

I took a deep breath, but my voice still emerged weak and quavering. "I still don't want to go," I blurted out.

"Well you're goin'," dad replied. "We sail in three weeks."

I should have seen it coming.

All through the war years, if my father spoke at all, he revealed his obsession with migrating to another country as soon as the war was over. At one time, South Africa was favoured, but more and more

New Zealand seemed the most viable option, particularly as dad's sister Florrie, her husband and their two children, had gone there before the war and, in spite of being shaken like ice in a martini in the odd earthquake, were happily settled in Napier.

Then, with the war over, I hadn't heard any more talk on the subject. In those days, kids were not included in adult conversation, and certainly were not involved in any decision-making. And to be asked to give an opinion was unheard of.

So Australia had become the second choice. Its post-war migration boom had reached an all-time peak as we entered the 1950s, and we slid perfectly into the pipeline, as just the type of family group they wanted. No bureaucratic hold-ups, no fuss. Dad paid the ten pounds each for himself and mam and five pounds for me, and quick-smart, we were booked on the very next migrant ship. And that's when I was told.

Worse was to come, something far more wounding than the bombing and the bullying I had endured and survived.

There weren't just the three of us living in the little house in Newton Heath. There was a fourth member of the family - a loveable mongrel called Glen, who was white except for a brown head and a brown spot on his back. He'd been my dog for several years. And now he had to be dispensed with.

Even now, I cannot believe the insensitivity that led to my father, and even my much-loved mother, to force me to take him on his final journey to the dog pound. I'd been crying for days. But finally, I had to clip on his lead, and set off. Glen thought this was one of our walks, and he strutted and danced joyfully, his curly tail erect, sniffing and cocking his leg up for a squirt, without a care in the world. I was feeling physically ill by the time we reached the Pound, *The Dogs Home*, as it was erroneously and evilly titled. He heard the barking of other dogs and became uneasy, pulling at the lead. I coaxed him into the entrance where I had to explain to an attendant what the circumstances were. He told me Glen would be kept for a week, then if nobody took him, he'd be destroyed. Not 'put to sleep' as they say nowadays. Destroyed. That did it. I knew there was no other alternative. I couldn't even look at him. I thrust the lead at the attendant and made for the door. I was almost out when I heard yelping. I turned. Glen, being dragged in the other direction, slipped his head out of his collar and ran to me. I bent down and hugged and hugged him until the attendant lifted him bodily and took him away. Blinded by tears, I stumbled out the door and, never one for half measures, promptly tripped down the steps, landing on my face. Blood from my smashed nose mingled with the tears, but that was on the outside and it didn't matter. All I could feel was a terrible, choking ache inside.

I found a small park and sat under a tree. It started to rain. I must have sat there, numb, for a couple of hours.

When I got home, looking as if I'd been in a train wreck, nobody noticed. People were hauling away our bits of furniture. I went inside, and saw the piano had gone. Grandma had died, and Aunty Gladys and Uncle Geoff had stayed on in her house. We slept there for the few nights remaining before we sailed. Or rather, they all slept. I just lay there and wept for my dog.

I have successfully blotted out from my memory the name of the migrant ship which brought us to Australia. It was no *Luxury Liner*. There was no *Romance on the High Seas*. The voyage was more your *Two Years Before the Mast*. The former troopship was on its last, faltering trek across the seas before torn up for scrap iron.

Its air conditioning was faulty, its dispirited engines broke down night after night, and its indifferent crew couldn't be bothered with irrelevancies such as passengers, so impatient were they for new berths on slick liners.

The ship was heavily overcrowded, an indication of the persuasive influence Australia's immigration scheme was having on weary Britons.

The sexes were segregated. Dad and I were in a six-berth cabin, down on 'D' deck where there were no portholes because it was below the waterline. My mother similarly shared a cabin with five other women, but theirs had the added feature of a metal wall dividing the cabin from the ovens in the ship's galley on the other side. This wall practically glowed with heat, not an advantage with the air conditioning not working and the temperature rising as we hit the tropics.

A lot of shouting went on, as my father and the other husbands complained to the ship's officers, but nothing could be done. My mother ended up sleeping on deck for most of the voyage.

We didn't set foot off the ship in the five weeks it took to reach Australia. One distraction came as we edged along the Suez Canal and native vendors from Port Said came on board with their wares.

Our only scheduled stop was Aden. The ship dropped anchor offshore, and it was announced that small boats would take us to spend the day on dry land. This caused near-chaos as hundreds of bored passengers pushed and shoved to be first off. My father took one look at the restless crowds.

"Not for us," he said and began ushering us away.

"Aw, dad!" I protested, trying to hold back.

"Some bugger's going to get trampled to death in that crush," he said with his usual optimism. "Or else drowned when one of them boats gets overloaded and capsizes."

We stayed on board and looked glumly from afar at the dark slopes of Aden. I brooded on my future, dreading the moment when we would step off the ship in Melbourne. This was the early 1950s at the height of Australia's migration boom. And to a Lancashire lad with no experience of life, it was scary.

I felt exactly the same apprehension a few years later on making an unplanned move from Melbourne to Sydney. Let us jump ahead to that second drastic move, because on that occasion, it catapulted me to the very top of Australia's burgeoning television industry and planted me at the helm of the nation's most popular and controversial TV show.

3

The move from Melbourne to Sydney in the spring of 1964, indeed reflected the fears I felt when my parents and I first arrived in Australia. This time, I was accompanied by my partner, Roger, and again it was it not really my decision. Roger had left a life in England to join me in Melbourne. Now, he had the chance of promotion if he moved to Sydney. I figured it was my turn to make a sacrifice for him.

My trepidations ebbed as Melbourne retreated into the distance, and we drove further along the highway in the Mini-Minor I was still paying off. I can recapture now the sense of adventure we gradually felt as the future stretched before us like the highway. And those feelings were reinforced by the palpable excitement and promise that seemed to throb in the harbour city. Sydney, in these days more an elitist playground for the well-to-do and attitudinal, was one wide-open town back then. It was bursting with street life – and I'm talking about streets you could actually walk and drive through instead of having to negotiate tunnels and pay exorbitant tolls. The influx of American servicemen on R&R from Vietnam had restored some of Kings Cross's rough, tough vigour, but unfortunately also introduced the drug culture that is now the curse of that same area.

Elsewhere, there was a vibrant art and music scene. There were theatres like Her Majesty's and the Theatre Royal that actually looked like theatres, instead of being an adjunct to a gambling casino or buried underground…..and cinemas that had just one auditorium and featured just one movie. And there were the theatre restaurants, too; some in basements, like Frank Strain's Downstairs revues, some in converted shop-fronts like "The Bull and Bush" on William Street. There were also some in grand settings like the Menzies Hotel, where condensed versions of Broadway shows were lavishly presented while you dined. Homosexuality was still illegal, but there was a thriving network of clubs and bars where the big stars from overseas would head instead of frequenting the more respectable watering holes. The licensing laws were stringent and restrictive. I remember buying a bottle of gin on a Sunday from a pharmacy in Rose Bay, and drinking brandy from a coffee cup at a place in Challis Avenue in the Cross. There were still traditional delicatessens and greengrocers shops in Oxford Street, and chest hair was actually visible when a guy opened his shirt buttons.

Nightly parties overflowed into the streets of Darlinghurst and Paddington and there seemed to be students from NIDA whooping it up at every one of them.

Roger took up his new, more important post with the stockbrokers J.B. Were, and I headed straight for Gloria Payton at her International Casting Agency. Gloria, without doubt, was the best agent in town, a remarkable woman who, it was said, had survived the Holocaust as a child. She was kind, thoughtful and gentle in dealing with her clients. Unmarried and without a family, we were her children. And like a protective mother she would quietly but fiercely fight to negotiate the best deals for her brood.

Surprisingly, Gloria's first suggestion was that I audition for ABC radio, specifically for the very active educational department and their schools broadcasts. I auditioned at the ABC studios in Forbes Street, Darlinghurst and within a few days, Gloria rang with the news that I'd been accepted and put on their roster of actors. Another avenue of work was Frank Strain and his Copenhagen Restaurant revues in Kings Cross. He had another one in rehearsal and slotted some of my hastily-updated Melbourne material into it.

The only other contact I had in Sydney was an actor called Barry Creyton. All I knew about him was that he was having a successful run at the Neutral Bay Music Hall, which specialized in highly popular send-ups of Victorian melodramas, another aspect of the vibrant Sydney scene. I telephoned him. Immediately I mentioned the revue experience I'd stacked up in Melbourne, Barry invited me to a private preview the following day at the Channel 7 studios in Epping of a TV pilot in which he'd been involved. "It's a revue-type TV show," he told me, "and if it goes into a series we'll need all the topical original material we can get."

The next day, I found myself sitting on a plush divan in a viewing room at Channel 7, between two ladies. One was Carol Raye, and I was astonished at being introduced to her. I remembered vaguely that she had been a star in London's West End and I had seen her in a few British-made films during my schooldays, but I never expected to meet her in Australia. She looked sensational, and her vibrant personality was overwhelming. I had never met anyone quite like her.

On my other side was Noelene Brown, an attractive blonde with a laconic way of talking. I couldn't work out her involvement in the enterprise. There was also the ebullient actor Gordon Chater and, of course, Barry, with whom I'd only talked on the phone until then. He turned out to be immensely personable and charming.

The title of the pilot appeared on the screen. *The Mavis Bramston Show.* Then appeared an apparition, a gushing parody of a visiting English celebrity in a black A-line dress and a large black hat popped onto a bouffant hairdo that looked suspiciously like the one Joan Sutherland was featuring at the time. I latched onto the premise immediately. Owing to Australia's cultural cringe, it was believed no theatrical venture could succeed without an overseas star leading the local supporting cast. It meant that mostly no-name – and often no-talent – low grade performers and even mere understudies were imported to star, even though our home-grown artists were superior.

Everyone thought this practice had been dealt a death blow when Toni Lamond led a totally Australian cast in *The Pajama Game* in the mid-1950s. But old habits died hard. J.C. Williamsons and other managements were still inclined to ignore dazzling local talent and import lackluster nonentities. This character, Mavis Bramston, was a typical, if overblown, example of these imports.

Apart from the vacuous gushing, she also sang a cringingly off-key version of *"I Could Have Danced All Night,"* which was hilarious. Then came sketches and songs from Raye, Chater and Creyton, most of which I recognized as old stage revue material, but were very effective within the format of the show. Only when the final credits rolled did I discover that the cool blonde sitting next to me, namely Noelene Brown, had actually been playing the bizarre bee-hived brunette that was Mavis Bramston.

I was totally won over. The excitement in the room fairly crackled. Everyone was obviously aware that what we'd just seen was something very special. This was confirmed when the show's Executive Producer, Michael Plant, told me the studio had green-lighted six episodes, to be shot and screened before the end of the year.

Michael Plant, a short, dark-haired dynamic guy in his thirties was, like me, a former journalist. He told me they would be needing lots of topical, satirical material. "Every writer in Australia is going to be emptying their bottom drawers and sending us their old stuff." I had the grace to wince. It was just what I was planning to do, I confessed. Michael quickly put me at ease. "That's okay. Old material is fine as long as it's still relevant or can be updated. But for brand-new stuff, it's writers like you we'll be relying on."

I left the studio on a high. The people in that viewing room were the most professionally stimulating I had ever encountered. It was as if my life was just beginning and in a sense, professionally speaking, it was.

At the same time, I got my first radio assignment. It went well. In the year that followed I was in dramatizations of historical incidents and medical breakthroughs, biographical dramas (I played the legendary air pioneer, 'Smithy') and literary readings. I enjoyed it all, particularly as it involved working with radio greats, some of them hanging onto their careers as radio drama was being edged out by television.

As if all this wasn't enough, I was cast in a Christmas production of *The Wizard of Oz* at the Tivoli Theatre. The *Wizard* of Oz? I felt like I was *in* Oz, the one over the rainbow! Suddenly I was working in three mediums at once – television, radio and stage. I juggled my writing for *Mavis* with rehearsals for *The Wizard of Oz* and increasingly, more calls to do the schools drama broadcasts for the ABC. And, in one amazing week over Christmas, a B-grade movie I'd made during a return to England, *Crossroads to Crime,* was supporting some major blockbuster at the drive-ins, so that put me in four mediums at the same time.

The first *Mavis Bramston Show* went to air on November 11th, 1964.

Until then, only a few local TV shows like the pop-music showcase *Bandstand* and the Crawford company's *Homicide* had been making their mark nationally. Television was awash with American sitcoms and cop shows, all as bland as a vanilla milkshake.

The reaction to *Mavis* was amazing. The viewers and the press loved it. The religious right, already puffing its cheeks at the emergence of The Beatles, mini skirts and the Pill, exploded in a barrage of condemnation. After eight years of inoffensive entertainment, *The Mavis Bramston Show* finally shook Australian television free from the confining corsets of 1950s respectability. This was the new kid on the block – cheeky, vulgar, always irreverent and constantly demanding attention.

The most intriguing component of *Mavis* was that this was no protest from teenage rebels with bad skin and long, greasy hair. It involved no intellectualizing from anti-establishment undergraduate types. Fronting the show were three mature, elegant adults who were not only capable of delivering a sophisticated line, but could also get surprisingly raunchy in the best vaudeville tradition. Chater, Raye and Creyton. They were the trio that made the original concept work, and in doing so elevated themselves into household names.

In one of several wildly inaccurate publications about Australian television, I am credited as being one of the creators of *The Mavis Bramston Show.* This is incorrect. The perpetrators of this book, as is almost always the case, were either too lazy or too uninformed to bother to check out the facts. The bad thing is that these inaccuracies get into print and once in print they become matters of historical record unless challenged. Too many lies have been told, too many mistakes have been made in the retelling of Australia's television history. Maybe I can correct some of them.

I came into *Mavis* at the pilot stage, as I have written. I had no part in its creation. I rely on Carol Raye's account of how it came about. She was there right at the start.

Carol had come to Australia with her husband and three children in March, 1964. Previously, she had enjoyed a successful career in film, stage and television in England, but when her husband, a veterinarian and agricultural scientist transferred to Kenya, she packed up and followed. There, Carol went to work for the Kenya Broadcasting Corporation. Then, her husband's career prompted another move, to Australia, where she was hired by ATN Channel 7 as a producer and assistant to James Oswin, the General Manager.

Just to diverge from Carol's history for a moment, I'd like to credit Channel 7 with having a policy of appointing women to important positions. In the nineteen-sixties they were well ahead of their time.

Unfortunately, there are always those who look for excuses to explain their failures. One female performer employed by Channel 7 at that time applied for an executive position and was rejected. She has since blamed this rejection on 'the glass ceiling.' While this 'glass ceiling' did exist in those times, I know for a fact that in this case, the management disliked the applicant intensely and rightly considered she didn't have the ability for the job.

To get back to the real achievers, Carol soon justified the management's faith in her. Aware of the huge impact of British TV's *That Was The Week That Was*, a satirical comedy show based on current events, she suggested to Jim Oswin that Channel 7 do a similar show. Oswin gave her a budget of one thousand two hundred pounds and told her to go for it. Together with two consultants, James Fishburn and Jon Finlayson, both with theatrical backgrounds, they came up with a show that would satirize the existing cultural cringe and star a fictitious overseas actress called Mavis Bramston. This, Finlayson said, was a joke name, one used by the Melbourne show-biz fraternity to describe someone not at all talented.

Carol recruited Gordon Chater from Sydney's famous Phillip Theatre revues, and Barry Creyton from the Neutral Bay Music Hall. What came as a bonus was that Creyton was also a gifted writer. It was his composition, "Togetherness" that opened the show each week.

Now, a female member of the proposed trio had to be found. Various actresses were approached but were either unable or reluctant to participate. Finally Chater said to Carol: "Oh God, why don't you do the pilot yourself, and if it's a success we can find a replacement and you can go back to producing." So Carol did the pilot. And went on to do the first series because everyone conceded she was irreplaceable.

To be acclaimed by press and public was wonderful enough. To be condemned from the pulpit by a prominent religious leader was literally a gift from heaven. Breathing fire and brimstone, he exhorted his flock not to watch the sinful *Bramston* and to boycott the products of the show's sponsor, Ampol. His flock did neither. They watched the show in greater numbers and Ampol declared a profit. Another stage revue stalwart, June Salter guested on the first show and was asked to join the regular team. And from the studio's engineering department, they snatched Ken Shadie and made him a staff writer. What a find. An unassuming combination of ideas man and comedy scribe, Ken was everybody's favourite and I have a sneaking suspicion that if he had not been on hand, *Mavis* would not have survived. They were getting material from such established satirical writers as John MacKeller, Ray Beihler, Alan Kitson and the 'Oz' magazine boys, but – as I thanked God for in later times – Ken was always there to fill up any blank spots.

I was fortunate enough to have a lot of material used right from the start. Like the others, I began by recycling previously performed stuff, but soon Michael Plant began telephoning me and commissioning specially-written material. *Mavis* soon became an important part of my life, and the talk of Sydney. I say Sydney, because the first six shows were shown only in Sydney and Canberra. Then, when it returned in the New Year, it went national.

1965 saw me settle into a comfortably productive routine of writing at least two numbers each week for *Mavis*, usually commissioned by Michael Plant. This output, plus my radio work, provided a regular income. I was prolific and the pay was good. *Mavis* was topping the ratings, beating all opposition, both local and imported. Wednesday night had become undisputed *Mavis* territory. Years later, Carol Raye wrote: "It was like living on champagne, and it seemed like the whole of Australia was watching on Wednesday nights to see what *Mavis* was going to say." She went on: "The inimitable David Sale wrote sketches for us, but also wrote fantastic lyrics with amazing speed. Give him an idea, and half an hour later you had a script." Flattering as it is, I quote it quite unblushingly as it recalls one of the happiest periods of my creative life, and anyway, it will be balanced by less than complementary references to my efforts later on.

To the augmented original team of Creyton, Raye, Chater and Salter, there were others who made one-off guest appearances…performers like Hazel Phillips and Kathy Lloyd, who stayed on and were valuable stand-bys when Carol left the show mid-year. Noelene Brown had withdrawn from the show after playing the character of *Mavis* in the first six shows. Now, the mantle of *Mavis* was assumed by the redoubtable Maggie Dence who devoured the character with relish and skill. She actually grew out of the confines of the show and into the reality of everyday life, making public appearances and even delivering keynote speeches at conferences and conventions. Few of these were scripted, but Maggie actually became *Mavis* once she donned the wig and the outfit, and ad-libbed magnificently.

About mid-year, it was announced that the English actress/comedienne Miriam Karlin was coming to Sydney to star in a new stage revue under the Phillip Street Theatre banner. Her TV hit show *The Rag Trade* had been extremely popular with Australian audiences, together with her catch-cry "Everybody out!" She had once made a kind gesture to me on the set of the film *Crossroads to Crime* in England, and I resolved to submit some material for her. The new revue was called *Is Australia Really Necessary?* but my material was obviously deemed *un*-necessary, as it was all returned to me, much to my disappointment. When the show opened, Miriam got good notices, but generally the critics didn't think the revue was up to the usual Phillip Street standard.

I waited until long after the opening to go and see it. It was four years since I'd had the brief encounter with her on a movie set, and I was reluctant to go backstage in case she didn't remember me.

Amazingly, she did. When I opened her dressing room door, she gave a broad smile: "My little Teddy boy!" she exclaimed, with arms outstretched, "What in gawd's name are you doing here?"

I filled her in, and when I got to the revue writing, she pulled a face. "Why didn't you write something for this show? Half the material's crap!" I told her that what I'd submitted had been rejected, but not to worry, I'd recycled it into *The Mavis Bramston Show.*

At the mention of the name, she perked up. "Hey – they've asked me to be guest leading lady in that show when I get out of this. Will you write all my special material?"

It was like a repeat of an incident a few years before when Toni Lamond invited me to write for her *In Melbourne Tonight* shows. But Toni, at least had seen some of my work. Miriam or Mim to her friends – had no idea what kind of writer I was. But for some reason she had faith in me.

When the *Is Australia Really Necessary?* season ended, Mim went straight into *Mavis Bramston,* and I wrote every solo piece she did on the show, as well as my quota of other material. She was a joy to write for, and most considerate, too. If she wanted to change a single word, she would check it out with me first. This is in utter contrast to lesser lights, who automatically think their substitution is better and don't bother to consult the writer. Possibly that's why they remain lesser lights.

I continued doing my radio work and the odd voice-over for TV commercials. But one of my strangest jobs was to participate in the grand opening of Sydney's third commercial TV station, Channel TEN. This extravaganza, entitled *TV Spells Magic* was conceived by imported English revue writer, Peter Myers. Like me, he was a movie buff and adored MGM musicals. Therefore, he'd attempted to apply MGM production values to this launch. There were dance routines on the roof, choirs in the dressing rooms and chorus numbers in the executive offices....a cheesy overblown concept that sprawled idiotically over three hours.

In the midst of it all was yours truly, appearing briefly as a singing writer. Type casting!

After that opening night, Channel TEN's fortunes slid steadily downhill into the red. Ironically, that bit player who appeared as the singing writer, returned to TEN a few years later and created a series that saved the studio. It was called *Number 96*.

Meanwhile, *Mavis* was being as outrageous as ever. Gordon Chater uttered the word "Bum" at every conceivable opportunity, The Pill was referred to at a time when the word "pregnant" could not be used on the ABC. The subject matter of sketches was filled with naughty double entendres, and politicians and other public figures were lampooned unmercifully. We were all on a high. Everyone associated with the show rejoiced in its success. Australia had gone *Mavis* mad.

The euphoria lasted until mid-year. On Friday, July 9th, I drove out to Channel 7 to discuss some up-coming topics with Executive Producer Michael Plant. He was in his usual hurry, late for rehearsal, and suggested we continued our talk in his chauffeur-driven car on the way to the rehearsal hall, which was on the first floor of a retail block in the Eastwood shopping centre. He was so ill with what appeared to be a bad case of the 'flu, I was reluctant to share the back seat of the car with him for fear of catching it myself. I had to, of course, and our chat resulted in my promising to write a couple of numbers over the week-end, to be delivered Monday morning. "But I suggest you don't do a thing but rest over the week-end, and get over this terrible cold," I cautioned him.

First thing Monday morning, I had a radio call at the ABC. Afterwards, driving out to Epping, I noticed a poster outside a newsagent's shop, something along the lines of "Shock TV Death".

The Sun and the Daily Mirror, Sydney's afternoon tabloids of the time, were notorious for their exaggerated shock-horror headlines, so I paid little attention, thinking it probably referred to the demise of some little-known overseas bit player.

The studio seemed curiously subdued as I hurried through the foyer towards the administrative section. When I entered the *Mavis* office, I saw a sight I will never forget. Everyone was in tears. Maggie Dence, in full *Mavis* regalia, wailed the devastating news, then lapsed back into uncontrollable weeping.

Michael Plant was dead.

He had been found the previous day, Sunday, by his second-in-command, Jimmy Fishburn. He was lying on his bed, typically surrounded by scripts.

I sat in the office for a while, sharing the grief, unable to think of what to do next, my weekend's product of two songs forgotten in my satchel. Our happy-go-lucky world had stopped spinning. Maggie was dressed in costume, made up and ready to address a luncheon.

"I can't do it, I just can't do it!" she sobbed, mascara running down her cheeks. Whether she did or didn't has gone from my memory, numbed out by the shock of that day.

There were the usual rumours of suicide, a broken love affair with a well-known Rugby League player, and an all-revealing farewell note that had been found and subsequently destroyed by Fishburn. I prefer to believe the obvious, based on what I saw and what I knew. Battling the debilitating attack of 'flu, Michael washed down strong medication with a lot of alcohol, determined not to stop working. Unfortunately, in Michael's weakened condition, the combination proved fatal.

The show had to go on. Jimmy Fishburn took over in Michael's place, assisted by Peter Myers, the English revue writer responsible for Channel TEN's overblown opening. I continued my close creative relationship with *Mavis* through the new team. Fortunately, still on hand was virtuoso pianist, composer, conductor and arranger Tommy Tycho, the maestro who set *Mavis* wittily to music. When I wrote lyrics, I always had an accompanying tune in my head. It helped shape the lyrics and keep them in perfect coda. As I was unable to write music, I had to remember the tune until I got with Tommy. Painstakingly, he would listen to me sing the song line by line, and write it down, note by note. What patience he had. Within minutes, it seemed, he would have the tune polished and ready to go. Sometimes, when a tune failed me, he would come up with an alternative that fitted my lyrics perfectly. I think we made a good team.

1965 was coming to an end and with the exception of Michael's death, it had been an enjoyable, busy and fruitful year. Roger and I decided to drive down to Melbourne to spend Christmas/New Year with my parents. We had hardly settled in and swapped all the news when I received a surprise telephone call from James Oswin at Channel 7 in Sydney. He wanted me to fly back to Sydney for a meeting with Rupert Henderson. Mr Henderson, nicknamed 'Rags', was controlling head of the Fairfax empire which included the Sydney Morning Herald and the Seven network.

Needless to say, I complied. I found Mr Henderson an amiable old gentleman with a startling resemblance to Wilfred Bramble, TV's Steptoe. I spent half an hour with him in his palatial office, during which he did all of the talking. Unfortunately, I couldn't understand a word he said. For most of the time he was chewing on a pipe, his voice cracked with age, and he seemed to be rambling. I nodded here and there, anxious to please, and answered him when I detected questions about my career. We shook hands, and I flew back to Melbourne wondering what was going on.

Over Christmas, I got another call from Oswin. Could I fly back for another chat with Mr Henderson? He nominated a day during the following week. "But that's New Year's Eve," I protested. "I want to see in the New Year with my parents." I felt confused. "Look, what's this all about?"

"We want you to take over as Executive Producer of *The Mavis Bramston Show*," Oswin replied.

Happy New Year, David, I thought, as I picked myself up off the floor.

4

I have been extremely fortunate in my life that I have never had to chase after important jobs. They appear always to have come to me, as in the case of this surprise offer. The management of Channel 7 may have thought I was experienced enough to become Executive Producer of Australia's top-rated TV show, but I didn't feel qualified. I didn't even have a suitable agent to negotiate for such an exalted position. Gloria Payton at International Casting had handled my acting work, but on the writing side, I'd always coped by myself. This offer didn't fall into either category.

I told James Oswin that I'd accept the position, but because of my uncertainties I stipulated that I would not sign a contract. "That leaves us all freedom to move," I said. "If you don't think I'm up to the job, you can fire me. If I don't like the job, I can leave."

He agreed.

I was Executive Producer of *Mavis* for the next eighteen months with no contract, my association with Channel 7 based purely on this gentlemen's agreement, surely some kind of record in the treacherous waters of television. I didn't even have to haggle about money. That would have been churlish, given the salary offered was most generous. Or so it seemed in those days.

I stayed on in Melbourne with my parents for a few days into the

New Year. Roger had to fly back earlier as he had a much shorter break from his duties with J.B. Were.

And so it was that I drove back to Sydney alone, with a bad case of 'flu and filled with depressing thoughts of what had happened to Michael Plant. There were other worries on my mind during that journey, not the least the enormity of the job I'd taken on. Carol Raye had left the show. Gordon Chater was also gone. Of the immensely popular cast that had shot the show to the top, only Berry Creyton and June Salter remained. There would be no 'Mavis' figurehead. Maggie Dence, her entire professional and personal life having been taken over by her brilliant impersonation, needed a change and had declined a further season.

As I sneezed and snorted, and blinked at the highway through teary eyes, I wondered what I'd got myself into. To make matters worse, I was driving through heavy rain, one of those sultry, leaden-sky storms that happen in January.

Lost in thought, a sudden upswirl of gravel showering the car windows alerted me that I had veered off the highway and was swerving towards the bush. I hit the brakes and fortunately, the car stopped without hitting anything. Eventually, I eased my aching body out of the car and cleaned the grit off the windscreen. I noticed that about six feet, less than three meters in front of the car was a very substantial gum tree. If I'd hit that, this story would be ending right now, or obviously would never have been written.

I completed the journey to Sydney with a great deal of caution. And that word was the keynote of the lesson I had learned. Caution. For the first time in my life, I wasn't going to barge in all smiles and full of trust. Thank God for that near miss. It gave me a wariness that was extremely useful in coping with what I was about to face. It was like the preliminaries of one of those medieval jousts. I had eased into the armour, and now I was entering the arena.

First, I was greeted with the bizarre news that ATN was importing a new lead from England. What an ironic twist that was. The whole point of *Mavis* right from the start, was that it satirized the cringe-worthy tradition of Australian show business having to import leads because it was wrongly assumed local audiences would not endure shows with local stars. Now, the TV show that had made a laughing stock of this stupid practice and created its own stars – Raye, Chater and Creyton – was actually about to do what it had mocked.

I had to accept it. Facing Rupert Henderson across his enormous desk in my first session with him since my return to Sydney, I realized I was being entrusted with his 'baby'. I understood what he was saying a little better this time around. Rupert adored the show, was over the moon about its continuing success, and cared very much about what happened to it. I was flattered but uneasy that he was entrusting his precious infant to me.

"I have to tell you, I don't know one end of a camera from the other," I began. He waved a gnarled hand for me to shut up. He didn't want to hear what he already knew. I'm quite sure he'd had me checked out, right to the fillings in my teeth. "You'll be fine," he said benevolently. "But you've got to be ruthless." He repeated it, his quavering voice turning that one word into an arpeggio.

"Ru-u-u-u-u-uthless!"

I got the message that this was his own credo. "You do whatever you think best and don't let anyone stand in your way," he went on. "If they try to, and they give you trouble, come straight to me!"

This was a powerful statement of trust and backing. He was offering me a totally free hand while also pledging his support. I still didn't know why. It came to me later. Like Michael Plant, I was a former journalist with theatrical experience. I was also a proven writer of topical, satirical material. And if you're doing a topical, satirical show, who better as Executive Producer than a writer who'd be there to fill in any gaps?

The British import Rupert had personally hired – on the suggestion of Peter Myers, who was still bumbling around the studio – was Ronnie Stevens. I recognized the name. He wasn't a star. He wasn't even known in Australia. But he had done a lot of revue work in England.

Another addition to the cast was an Australian actor called Ron Frazer. "He's a lousy performer," Rupert confided with a sly nudge, "but he's a writer, so he'll be of help to you with material." Famous last words. In time, Ron Frazer became one of Australia's favourite comedy stars.

Johnny Lockwood was another newcomer to the cast. He had been recruited as a sort of knockabout vaudeville type to inherit the Chater mantle. Johnny was mainly a stand-up comedian, and while most stand-ups are accustomed to and prefer to work alone, I knew he had played Fagin in the West End production of *Oliver*, so he was obviously an actor, too. At our first meeting, Johnny said to me quietly: "Just tell me what you want me to do. I'm happy to learn." That, coming from a seasoned performer to a relative newcomer like myself, impressed me greatly. And Johnny was true to his word. He was always easy to work with, never any trouble, and provided he got his own spots to shine in the program was quite happy to support and 'feed' lines to others. It was his strong support for Ron Frazer in their sketches together that made Ron look good. Later, Johnny got his reward when I created the character 'Aldo Godolfus' specially for him in *Number 96*.

Ronnie Stevens turned up on the scene like a frisky poodle. Small and energetic, he had a wicked sense of humour and was a diligent worker, always word perfect. He was appreciative of good material, but had a sharp waspish side which only surfaced when he thought his new-found status was threatened. And he loved getting into drag.

June Salter had stayed on from the previous year. June had made rather a specialty of singing a number called *Something Cool* in earlier stage revues and had effortlessly assumed it as her image. She was so laid back, she was practically horizontal. The pose was there when I started, and I'll never forget the read-through of the first script assembled by me, when – in the middle of some explanation or other – I happened to glance back and caught her pulling a bored 'who-does-this-little-shit-think-he-is?' face. I just continued on. If I'd paid attention to those sort of actressy reactions, I'd have been quickly out of my mind. We did the whole of my first year with *Mavis* together, June and I. I stayed up nights and wrote her a solo number for every show, made sure with wardrobe that she always looked special, and attempted to ease the burden when she was upset by her private life. When, one production night, a phone call from her husband John Meillon just before we taped reduced her to an emotional wreck, almost incapable of performing, I ordered the studio switchboard to block any personal calls to artists after the dress rehearsal. In her autobiography, June didn't even mention my name. That's show business.

Noelene Brown returned, but not to take up her former role as Mavis. She had done her stint as that lady, and was back as one of the regular cast. The third lady in our team was, by a strange choice of management, an actress called June Thody. Mr Henderson referred to her as Thoddy. He referred to everyone by surname only, but in this case he got the pronunciation wrong. He'd got the casting wrong, too. She just didn't fit into the revue format. Mercifully, she only had a six-week contract. Her replacement was Arlene Dorgan, a dark, haunted world weary veteran of a couple of Phillip Street revues. She had a smoky, sexy delivery. She also had a disconcertingly enervated quality which caused her suddenly to collapse on the floor, no matter what the circumstance. Peter Myers, who had recommended her to the studio, whispered into my ear that she had a fatal kidney disease. Arlene demonstrated her contempt for the show by sitting at her first read-through and doodling an elaborate decoration across the cover page of her script. I caught a closer look as we finished the session. It was a beautifully rendered illustration, complete with florid swirls and whorls, of four giant letters.

F. U. C. K. Like her predecessor, she was there only briefly and I was glad to see the back of her.

Strangely enough, Peter Myers also whispered that same disturbing diagnosis about another lady on the scene, whom he pressured me to keep on "because she hasn't long to live." This time, the alleged cot-case was Gwen Friend, sister of renowned artist Donald Friend. She always dressed like an English public schoolboy in black pants and jacket and a white shirt. Dumpy with a slicked-back severely-cut Eton crop, she looked like an extra from *Goodbye, Mr Chips.*

I was so busy getting my first shows to air, I accepted these Peter Myers stories without question, much as I accepted his unexplained presence on the fringe, contributing nothing except whispered diagnoses, and disappearing into the shadowy realms of ATN's film vaults where he ran old musicals and – legend has it – slyly clipped out all the big production numbers for his own private collection. After a couple of months, he disappeared completely. Despite their alleged illnesses, Arlene Dorgan went to England and married a comedian, and Gwen Friend was still around forty years later.

This, then, was the wildly disparate platter of people and performers I was presented with to launch *Mavis* into 1966. I was also presented with an office – a tiny cramped space overlooking the car park from its one small window, a garret I would occupy with my right arm, Ken Shadie. Ken is the most un-show business person I know, but one of the best comedy writers ever. He occupied a desk in the corner by the window. He got the view of the car park. My miniscule desk was shoved against the wall near the door. There was no room for anything or anyone else. Just us, our typewriters and our ideas. We sat in that shoebox week after week for a year and a half and wracked our brains to come up with a fresh show, an hour of original material, every seven days. Rod Kirk was our inventive 'film' man who created the hilarious montages that opened and sometimes closed the show, bits and pieces he raided from old movies, or specially filmed with cast members. Ray Wilson, our wardrobe master and his hard-working assistants produced glamorous gowns, as well as coping with the demands of special costumes and character outfits. And there was Hugh Taylor, my quiet and patient camera director whose unruffled demeanour was soothing in the most stressful situations, and he efficiently turned out a good-looking show under tremendous pressure week after week.

Having suffered Thody and Dorgan, I played safe and recruited a capable performer/writer from my Melbourne revue days, Barbara Angell, as third girl.

Assembling enough material for each new show became the major hurdle. Every day, the studio mailbag brought a pile of submissions. New writers surfaced. Eleanor Whitcombe, Lynn Foster.... and a Catholic schoolboy called Bill Salmon who wrote risqué, untidy, sometimes out-of-control sketches under his desk during lessons. They needed editing, shaping and cleaning up, but they were brilliantly quirky.

I started my stint as Executive Producer with many disadvantages, other than my own shortcomings. The show had lost its figurehead, 'Mavis Bramston' and had totally reversed its original policy, a stand against the importation of overseas performers. Two of the popular original cast were gone. We had new faces, some yet to prove their value, some of no value at all. But the show had won a Logie as best comedy show the previous year, and the viewing public was waiting for more.

I determined that my shows must have a different look, a different feel, but with the same irreverence. And relevance. If the viewers had relaxed in their armchairs, we were going to make them sit up and take notice again. We were going to raise issues and choose subjects and people begging for a serve. Harold Holt was the new Prime minister and pledging to go all the way with LBJ, the American President, in a dazzling display of arse-licking that was to be repeated even more fervently years later by John Howard. Decimal currency was about to be introduced. Utzon had resigned as architect of the Sydney Opera House and everyone was wondering how it would turn out without him. The first National Service recruits left for Vietnam. New South Wales was under the rule of a corrupt government. It was a time more than ever ripe for satire. It was my time.

I climaxed my opening show with something that hadn't been done before, but has been copied many times since. I took a filmed press conference with the ex-PM Sir Robert Menzies and cut-in our cast as journalists asking fake questions that made Sir Robert's real-life answers appear asinine, ribald or downright offensive.

It worked. Apart from the fact that our ratings equalled any of the previous year, the complaints flooded in. This was great. People had been getting upset ever since *Mavis* began, and when they stopped getting upset, it would be time to throw in the towel.

The finale of the show was always the hardest item to think up. None of the hopeful contributors sent in finale material. It required some big song or sketch involving the cast of six in a riotous climax, so it was usually up to Ken or myself to come up with something. We took alternate weeks. One week he would write a big sketch, the next I would write a big musical number. The three most dreaded words in our little office were: "It's your turn!"

One of most memorable finales came from Ken's agile mind and involved a member of the Royal Family. We restaged a popular panel show of the time *Beauty and the Beast*, solving the problems of a very important guest – the Queen Mother. Ronnie Stevens, in a brilliant impersonation of the beloved 'Queen Mum' entered Studio 'A' to a fanfare of trumpets. The entire studio audience rose to its feet as in the presence of royalty. The floor crew was lined up and the 'royal guest' progressed regally down the line, saying a gracious word to some, nodding, smiling and waving all the way. Afterwards, we heard that some viewers actually thought this was all on the level – for a minute or two, anyway. The cast were excellent in their cruel facsimiles of the real-life panelists, and it was a triumph for all concerned.

Something else was happening in the show. I started to build up a collection of regular characters that the audience would immediately recognize. One recurring sketch – "Under the Driers" had two society ladies at the hairdressers, their conversation depicting the shallowness of Sydney's constantly partying social set.

Ron Frazer's gallery of characters included a zany (read 'gay') gushing type inundating Johnny Lockwood with stories about his 'second-best-friend'; and 'Ocker', the archetypal Aussie working man swilling beer in the pub with his dumb mate and philosophizing on current events, years before Paul Hogan adopted the same image.

It was felt that Ronnie Stevens, for all his needle-sharp comedic abilities, lacked a little warmth in performance. We corrected this by bringing in the notable actress Neva Carr Glynn as a little old lady whom Ronnie met on a park bench every couple of weeks. Their chat allowed us a gentle insight into the problems of pensioners as well as giving Ronnie the requisite human touch.

Lots of people claim they wrote for *Mavis.* Some have approached me over the years and told me they sent in material that was used, and I have to tell them I have no recollection. Others even go into print asserting they made masses of contributions over which they slaved night and day. Whatever, it was always a source of pride for me that the end credits had a long list of writers. Some would appear only once, others from time to time, a few regularly. Ken and I would grasp any fun idea, any interesting perspective and – if it failed to measure up – we would work on it to bring it up to our standard. And the writer involved would be paid in full and credited in the end titles, in the hope that they'd not only send in more stuff but would improve in the process.

I was so dedicated – and desperate! – to encourage new writers, that every Friday afternoon after rehearsals, I would drive into the city to Anzac House where a conference room had been reserved for me to talk to any writers who might be interested in writing for the show. The roll-up varied. Sometimes there were only three, other times six, but I could never work out why more budding writers didn't jump at the opportunity to make contact and learn about what was required of them. One of the regulars was the aforementioned schoolboy Bill Salmon, whom I'd only known previously for his hilariously quirky postal contributions. He turned out to be as precociously funny as his writing and we became life-long friends. Later he changed his name, and as Bill Harding was prominent in the manifestation of such media oddities as 'Auntie Jack' and 'Norman Gunston.'

Roger and I moved from Woollahra to Cremorne Point into an apartment that had a glassed-in verandah that overlooked the Harbour. And it was from there that I worked late into each night and ventured out each morning to face the baptism of fire that was my helming of *Mavis.*

As a job, it occupied eighteen hours a day, seven days a week. We taped the show every Tuesday evening before a live audience. The show went to air the next night. From Wednesday morning, it would be all about the following week's show. My first stop, Wednesday morning would be Tommy Tycho's home in nearby Seaforth, where I would hum the tunes of the numbers I'd written and go over any other musical items with him. It was always a pleasure to work with The Maestro.

Then it was on to the studio, where for the rest of Wednesday morning, Ken and I would assemble the available content for the next show and decide what to do about the inevitable blank spaces. Wednesday afternoon was taken up with the production meeting with everyone involved in staging the show, all of the people a lot more experienced than I in creating the magic of television, and all of them willing and eager to help me.

Thursday morning meant the first read-though and rehearsal

for the next show. Driving to Epping each morning, I had to psych myself into a rage. I'd pick on some real or imagined hurt and use it to generate anger. I didn't necessarily express this anger, but it bolstered up my fragile insecurity about the job, and toughened me up enough to assume the persona I attempted to present to everyone except Ken Shadie – the confident, self-possessed Executive Producer. Maybe June Salter saw through my façade that first time, hence the derisive look I caught, but I had to plough on and actually *sell* each show to the cast at the Thursday morning read-through. If they suspected I wasn't confident in its potential, they would lose heart. We only had three days to rehearse, Thursday, Friday and Monday, before camera rehearsals and taping on Tuesday evening, so every minute counted.

Every evening after dinner with Roger, I'd go through the daily mountain of mailed contributions that I'd taken home with me. If any item had possibilities I'd put it to one side. On the other stuff, I wrote what I hoped were helpful suggestions to the writers, as to where they went wrong and how they could improve. A positive suggestion was always better than a rejection slip. All this would take me into the early hours of the morning. I would usually go to bed around 3 am and be up again at seven. This was my nightly ritual. There was no socializing, except perhaps over the week-end.

Every Friday afternoon, immediately after lunch, an odd thing would happen. A chauffeur-driven black Rolls Royce would glide through the Eastwood shopping centre. In that suburban setting it was as incongruous as a prowling grey nurse shark in a paddling pool. It would park outside the shops over which our rehearsal room occupied the first floor. Out would trot a little old man who would join us for a very rough run-through of the current show. The cast had scarcely had time to familiarize themselves with script, songs and dance routines but would soldier on for Rupert Henderson's approval.

He would sit beside me and I would explain in as much detail as possible how a number or sketch would be staged and explain – if necessary - the subject matter. He would nod and smile, hardly ever saying a word, just taking it all in. At the end, with his usual impeccable behaviour he would shake hands with all us guys, kiss each of the ladies on the cheek, wave a cheery good-bye and leave, as happy as if he'd made another million dollars. That happened every Friday, without fail. One Friday, I was ill with a virus and rather than risk passing it on to the cast, I stayed home, leaving Hugh and Ken to preside. That evening, I got a call from a worried Jim Oswin. "I think you should know, Mr Henderson's very concerned about this week's show. He says it doesn't seem as good as usual."

I understood the situation immediately. "No-one probably explained it to him," I said. "That's what I do every week. No wonder he's concerned – he didn't understand what was going on." And needless to say, his fears were unfounded.

Tuesday. The big day. Taping day. The morning was spent ironing out any last-minute production problems. Last minute? *Everything* was last minute in this clambake! The cast came in at lunchtime. Camera rehearsals took us through the afternoon, and we would tape the show before a studio audience in the evening. This, of course, would take much longer than the official one-hour timing of the show, because there were stops at what would be the commercial breaks to allow the cast to change costumes and sometimes make-up, and sets removed and replaced.

It was scary and it was wonderful, scary because in such an off-the-cuff, under-rehearsed show, anything could go wrong. The wonderful part came with the audience reaction – gales of laughter in all the right places, and some unexpected ones, too. Unlike some alleged 'live before a studio audience' shows, we never used canned laughter to bolster the studio reaction. We never needed to. The hard work of the cast and crew was also wondrous, making it all happen, coping with lack of preparation, dealing with any last-minute inclusions that we might shove in to preserve our reputation for topicality. An hour of original material every week. This was something only attempted up until that time by British TV – but on a budget that far exceeded our miserly allowance and with a production staff three times as large. It didn't matter if our standard varied because of the weekly content. I regarded every show as a major achievement by everyone concerned.

Every Tuesday night, up there in the viewing room, watching it all going on through the huge plate glass window that overlooked the interior of Studio 'A', was our biggest fan, Rupert Henderson. After the performance, we would all be expected to join him for drinks.... his children, his family. To leave the studio without attending this after-show wind-down session was unthinkable.

Occasionally, Rupert would, almost shyly, make a suggestion to me for a future send-up. One of his ideas actually worked itself up into a sketch. I sent him a 'Suggestion Fee' of ten dollars, and he never stopped laughing at that. Make no mistake, this was a man who was notoriously ruthless in his business dealings, never less than respected, most often feared. I was cheeky with him and made him laugh and I think he found that a refreshing change to the usual kow-towing he was accustomed to. Of course, had I not been delivering the standard of show he wanted, it might have been a different story.

As it was, he appeared delighted, week after week.

And so was the viewing audience. The critics, however, were constantly asserting that *Mavis* had lost her punch. Strangely, we were being more outspoken and politically incorrect than in the show's early days, but what none of the so-called critics appreciated was that we'd all grown up a little and had become more accustomed to satire. And although no-one could call *Mavis Bramston* a *Fair Lady,* they'd grown accustomed to her pace. Except in Melbourne, it seemed, where our ratings began to slide.

And then we discovered why. In Victoria, we were being censored.

I went into print immediately, to let Victorians know that their purity was being safeguarded by local channels which cut out items that might harm their morals. "So, if the program suddenly jumps, or blacks out, or ends abruptly, you can settle back secure in the knowledge you're being protected by some anonymous godfather with a large pair of scissors," I was quoted in the press. I was very angry but there was nothing we could do about it. I was angry too at the constant knocking from a few scribes when, other than Victoria, our ratings remained high. I tagged onto my barrage in the press: "At a time when it's become rather 'in' to knock *Mavis,* the old girl goes merrily on her way, still an easy target for any jaded TV critic with space on his page to fill, still thumbing her nose at pomposity, inefficiency, intolerance, injustice and sex….in fact, still going strong!"

As the weeks went by my mail increased dramatically. Submissions were pouring in from all over Australia, three hundred a week written by would-be satirists, footballers, teachers, housewives, clerks and even an Anglican bishop, who sent two items that made it into the show. There were also the cranks, anonymous and otherwise, who put more filth on paper than would ever appear on our show. And on a couple of occasions, outpourings of filth ended in death threats to me personally. Although I made light of them, I was unnerved. I had my home phone number made ex-directory, and took pains to keep my home address secret. The five most dreaded words when you're in that situation are: "I know where you live."

Every so often, Rupert Henderson would nudge me and murmur: "They treating you alright? Anyone tries anything, you come to me." On the two occasions I put this to the test, Rupert kept his word. The in-studio objection or obstacle suddenly disappeared, and I was allowed to proceed as I wished. Naturally, this didn't make me the flavour of the month with some of the executives, but there was nothing they could do about it.

On one such occasion, I decided to air the growing resentment against Australia's involvement in Vietnam. It was the only serious finale in *Mavis's* history. In a jungle setting, I had the cast dressed in combat gear holding military weapons, singing a number I'd written, which began:

"When we get back, we'll march on Canberra

And tell them where to stuff their bloody war..."

At the end of the number, there was a burst of gunfire and they all fell to the ground, dead. Our end titles followed in complete silence, except for the noises of the jungle.

It caused quite a stir. Not only then, but twenty years later when that particular episode was shown at a late-night session of the Sydney Film Festival. The following day, the newspapers reported how shocked the Festival audience was by this number and its outspoken sentiments, and marveled that twenty years earlier, it had been shown on television.

At the time of the show, there were certain quarters that didn't like it, but nobody accused me of being a terrorist or a traitor. I wasn't regarded as a criminal or charged with sedition. The song presented a point of view, and I was allowed to present it.

Try doing that now.

As mid-year approached, I realized the constant pressure was affecting me. I felt constantly exhausted, meeting the never-ending deadline of the next show. I kept thinking of Michael Plant and what happened to him. I told Jim Oswin everybody was tired, not just me, and if I could be allowed to put together three or four *Best of Mavis* specials from previous shows, it would give us all a few weeks off. Oswin rightly pointed out that topical material didn't age well, and the viewers wanted freshness in our time slot every week. He also pointed out the difficulties in paying out extra royalties, and the fact that everybody in the cast was under contract for a certain number of shows and that didn't allow for holidays. I told him in that case, I'd be leaving mid-year. He came back to me with another suggestion, after discussing the situation with Mr Henderson. If I agreed to stay on, they would fly me anywhere I chose in Australia for a week's holiday at their expense, and not only that, they'd double my salary.

I chose to go to Cairns because it seemed the furthest away from all the pressures of my work. Of course, in agreeing to their terms, it meant I really had to pre-prepare most of the show that would be done while I was away, so that involved two weeks work in one. There was no way I'd think of leaving Ken Shadie and Hugh Taylor to cope unless they had at least the bones of a show. And this, naturally, is what management counted upon.

I scarcely spoke to anyone during my week in Cairns, in contrast to my existence as a motor-mouth in Sydney. I lay in the sun, and my only utterances was to order food and drink.

I returned to the grindstone refreshed. The break hadn't been long enough, but it helped. Ronnie Stevens was nearing the end of his six months contract as star of the show, and I worked especially hard to give him material that stretched him. The more tongue-twisting the lyrics, the more complicated the routine, the better he liked it and the harder he worked.

The only ripple came when Barry Creyton was offered a junket to a movie premiere in Hollywood. I gave him a week off and replaced him with my old friend Stuart Wagstaff, writing him a single called "Jack of All Trades" that amusingly illustrated what he seemed to be doing regularly in those days, stepping into people's shoes as a replacement. I had also written Ronnie's solo, one based on a current incident in which a sailor had smuggled his girlfriend aboard ship for sex.

Actors can be very sensitive about the amount of attention they get, some more than others. For Ronnie, read 'more.' I think he feared Stuart might steal his spotlight. His 'sailor' routine grew to the stage where he was now doing the hornpipe and anything else he could throw in, to take attention away from Stuart and make it the hit of the show. The only thing he left out was a tidal wave. Stuart's "Jack of all Trades", delivered with his usual urbane charm, brought the house down. Ronnie worked even fifty times harder than he usually did, which is certainly saying something, and jigged all over the set in a display of physical and verbal brilliance that was more exhausting than entertaining. His competitiveness really wasn't necessary. In their own special ways, both performers were great. However, I should have learned more from this incident. It would have prepared me for a nasty experience the following year.

But even before that, there was a disaster for which I certainly wasn't prepared.

It happened in August, when Ronnie Stevens left the show to return to England. And the frisky poodle was replaced by a pit-bull.

5

I didn't dislike John Bluthal, at least not at the start. It wasn't exactly love at first sight, either.

Born in Poland but raised in Australia, Bluthal was on one of his infrequent visits 'home' after working solidly in England for several years. He'd got his start through Spike Milligan, and made his name by supporting another 'Goon', Michael Bentine, in Bentine's successful TV series.

During his first few weeks as replacement for Ronnie Stevens, he appeared restless and uneasy. He didn't just have a chip on his shoulder, he had epaulettes. He did everything that was asked of him and used his talent for portraying a diverse array of characters to good effect. However, possibly because of the early influence of Milligan and Bentine, he was constantly at me to inject some Goon-type humour into the show. Now, there's nothing wrong with Goon-type or absurdist humour. It just didn't belong in *The Mavis Bramston Show*, and I was certainly disinclined to start experimenting at a time when our regular viewing audience seemed happy with what they were being served.

Matters came to a head during a taping, as usual, before a live audience, a few weeks before Christmas and the end of his contract.

A disagreement arose about the interpretation of sketch, and as a result Bluthal walked off the set.

I followed him to his dressing room, which was off to one side and shielded by the scenery 'flats'. When I got there, he was facing his mirror, using a hairbrush aggressively to swipe at the sides of his head, needlessly as his hair was so short.

I stayed in the doorway. "Okay, John," I said quietly and amiably. "There's an audience waiting. Let's do it, huh?"

He snapped around, advancing, and I could see he was absolutely seething with rage. "You're nothing!" he snarled, and unexpectedly threw a punch at me. It missed my face, but connected forcefully with my shoulder, sending me off-balance and staggering back. I hit the edge of one of the scenery flats and sent it and others crashing down in a domino effect. Luckily, no actors, floor crew or equipment were hurt or damaged. I went down with it, but I wasn't hurt.

I picked myself up from the chaotic mess that was once a set, marched up to the control room, told Hugh to go on with the show if and when Mr Bluthal was ready, got my things and left the studio. I heard later that eventually taping continued.

I stayed incommunicado at home the following day and did not respond to attempts by Mr Henderson's secretary to get in touch with me. On the second day, I relented and went to his office. The old man was in a frantic state. In his eyes, if news of 'the brawl' got into the press in those relatively scandal-free days, it could ruinously affect the popularity of his beloved show.

"Chalk and cheese," he ranted shrilly, waving his thin arms. I thought this was a mild summing up of two people who were now as chummy as Von Helsing and Dracula. "We knew it'd never work out between the two of you," Mr Henderson railed on, "but we never expected things to blow up in front of an audience." He leaned across his desk intensely, his voice lowered. "He's got four weeks before his contract's up. I want you to go away. Anywhere in the world. You name it, we'll pay!" So that's how important it was to keep it out of the papers, I thought. Not just

Cairns, this time…anywhere in the world.

Visions of the Bahamas faded quickly. I realized they couldn't get rid of Bluthal because of his contract. I didn't have a contract, so I was the one expected to leave town…. except I had no intention of running away. My loyalty was to the show.

"I'm not leaving," I said. "I'll continue on as Executive Producer, just as long as I never have to speak to that man again."

And that's how we finished the year. I continued to assemble each of the remaining shows from my office, but didn't go to rehearsals. Hugh Taylor presided at those, equipped with my suggestions. I coached the rest of the cast in private, either over the phone or in dark corners. Interestingly, along with my absence from rehearsals, Mr Henderson also called a halt to his regular Friday visits, which must have pained him considerably.

I continued to write for Bluthal, and he continued to turn in a professional performance every week. In one solo turn, ironically as a punch-drunk boxer – he was particularly effective. Possibly because he'd practiced on me!

We all got through those last difficult weeks somehow. Bluthal was going to make a final grand gesture by throwing the Christmas break-up party himself. The cast, knowing that I would never attend this less-than-convivial knees-up, went to the management and urged them to give the party instead. So, it was held in the studio canteen after the final show, and the management hosted. Bluthal returned to England and was soon supporting Spike Milligan in a much-lauded TV series that reflected Milligan's fragmented mind. It sported deliberately half-finished sets and costumes and supporting players who sometimes exited chanting: "What do we do next?" Bluthal must have been in Goon heaven.

One advantage of not having to turn up at rehearsals those last few weeks was that I had time to consider my future. As I had done six months earlier, I decided I'd had enough. I told both Oswin and Mr Henderson that I wouldn't be coming back in 1967, so they promptly doubled my salary again. I honestly wanted to leave, but that kind of money, after years of struggling, was too hard to resist.

I also had time to think about the future of the show. June had told me she would be leaving at the end of the year. The two second string girls, Andonia Katsaras and Barbara Angell were fine in what they were doing, but I felt neither had the star quality needed to replace June Salter. And now the show desperately needed the kind of boost that only a star could give.

I had to find a dazzling new replacement. As Christmas and our final show loomed, and Jangled Nerves threatened to replace Jingle Bells, I decided to end the year with a bang that had nothing to do with my knocking down the scenery. I planned to have lots of well-known people pop in as surprise guests. If they couldn't make it on the night, we pre-recorded them, as we did with the *Mavis* theme song "Togetherness" sung verse by verse by the stars of other Channel 7 shows with appropriate lyrics.

I ran all this by Rupert, casually mentioning that I wanted to invite Carol Raye back as one of the surprise guests. As always, he listened with interest. "I fact," I said, "I'm planning to ask Carol back as star in the New Year."

"Do as you like," he replied airily, which sufficed as a cool nod of approval.

Considering the tension behind the scenes was as rife as it would be at an Arab-Israeli Tupperware party, the last *Mavis Bramston Show* of 1966 came over as light and bright, thanks to the lift given to it by surprise guest stars. Carole Raye and June Salter, to great effect, reprised a duet "You're so London, You're so Aussie" that they'd done right at the start of the series. Carol agreed to do a return season on the show in the New Year, the deal sweetened by the Channel's offer to her of her own situation comedy later in 1967.

I was so wrung out, I needed to get away. My parents came up from Melbourne for week's holiday and Roger and I squired them around in style, sightseeing, restaurants and shows. Then I flew to Bangkok for two weeks. I went alone. Roger had his work commitments, and he was also saving for a trip back to England to see his family.

My last six months with *Mavis* were the happiest and most relaxed I'd had on the show, as well as the most lucrative. Again, the management had doubled my already doubled salary to keep me on.

The break had refreshed me and by now I was so used to the punishing pace of the show, I could take it in my stride. Carol Raye re-energised not only the show, but the entire team with her sparkle and enthusiasm.

In some quarters, Carole had been rumoured as difficult. I found none of that. She once confided to me: "I can be extremely difficult, but only when I feel insecure. And I'm only insecure when I feel I'm at the mercy of incompetents." Her presence was a blessing.

Again, the management of Channel 7 had gone against the original concept of *Mavis* and imported another overseas performer to star opposite Carol. This time it was Peter Reeves, who nobody in Australia had ever heard of. He was a pleasant guy, conscientious and dedicated to the show. He also had talent as a writer and contributed some facile and clever lyrics. He worked hard, but he didn't work magic.

Ron Frazer, meanwhile, had steadily eased himself up into the major league with his continuing characters. As well as his 'Ocker' and his 'Second Best Friend', his wildly funny impersonations varied from honky-tonk black pianist Winifred Atwill ("Come and hear Winnie murder the pianola!") to Prime Minister Harold Holt. Finally, he was able to go on and star in several stage productions tailored especially for his talents.

As for Johnny Lockwood, the ever-reliable Johnny always eager to drag you to one side and tell you his latest joke, he was like a rock; never a problem as long as he had his own moments to shine, he gave strong support to Ron and Carol in their continuing characters. One of Carol's staples quickly became a favourite – the whinging Lancashire migrant, Mrs Chomley, who hated being in "this miserable rotten country." Carol had difficulty grasping the North Country accent, so for the final few moments before she taped the sketch I would be there, talking to her in my resurrected Lancashire accent, and then she'd go on and do it.

I remember, too, a tiny incident which demonstrated her confidence in my judgement. During a taping, she appeared on the set to do a simple straight-to-camera announcement wearing the 'little black dress' that was standard gear when not in character costume. This time she had added a pair of dangly earrings which, when viewed on the monitor were distracting. I went onto the set where she was waiting for her cue. "Carol? The earrings." I pulled a face and shook my head. Whereas other actresses of my acquaintance might have demurred and tried to debate the matter, Carol just pulled them off and handed them over. "See that they're put in my dressing room, would you, darling?"

With more stable conditions at the studio, I was able to pay a little more attention to my private life. The first surprise of 1967 came with a letter from my parents saying they'd so enjoyed their holiday in Sydney, they were selling up in Melbourne and coming there to live. And sure enough, a few weeks later, they arrived with just their suitcases and a TV set. I couldn't believe that after uprooting themselves in England, they had done it again and would be more or less starting from scratch. But they had tremendous optimism and an adventurous spirit. Must be something they put in the Lancashire hotpot! They quickly bought a unit in Cremorne, but found they didn't like living in an apartment, so moved to a house in Awaba Road, Mosman.

Fortified by my pay increases, I too began looking for a place to buy and eventually found an apartment in a new block of twelve in Neutral Bay. Roger was about to return to London for a few months to be with his family after six years in Australia. The evening before he left, we went around to my new but empty apartment and sat on the floor in the dark looking out at the commanding view of the Bridge, the Harbour and the city skyline. For a little while, we felt closer than we had been since I began producing *Mavis.* I had lived and breathed the show 24 hours a day for more than a year with little time for anything else, including Roger. I knew he felt shut out by this. It was the old but proven cliché of career versus relationship, and was just as damaging to us as it would be to a straight couple. We sat there quietly in the dark, looking at the immense vista of twinkling lights, at last regaining some of the intimacy we had been missing.

The next day, he left for England. By the end of the week, I had moved into the apartment.

Suddenly, I was on my own. I could work hard all day at the studio and bring home the usual pile of submissions, and not feel guilty about neglecting my partner. The more relaxed conditions in doing the show and my comfort at being in my own home with my own fantastic view of Sydney made an incredible difference to my sense of well-being. I realized how out of condition I had become and began exercising at a small Health Studio in North Sydney on my way home in the evening. A couple of times a week, I'd then call in at my parents for dinner and, like we had done in Melbourne, we began chatting again like friends.

About this time, I began to get material in my studio mail from a young guy who had recently returned to Australia from Europe, where he and his new wife had been hitchhiking their way around. His writing intrigued me. The subject matter was strange and his technique even stranger. There was certainly nothing that could be used in our show, but after a number of (sympathetic) rejections, he came in to see me. He looked pale and undernourished and pleaded with me to use my influence in getting him a job at the studio. "I'll do anything," he said desperately.

I went to the studio's Employment officer, Alan Mewton, but he stated firmly there were no vacancies anywhere. I persisted, telling him how desperately this young guy needed work, and that he had a talent that could develop into something useful. I must have done quite a job of convincing him, because Alan finally relented.

After that, I'd encounter the young man, his thin frame now clad in white overalls, sweeping the studio floor in Studio 'A', probably the lowest job at the Channel apart from cleaning the staff toilets. I'd smile and wave, and call: "Better than nothing, huh?" And he'd nod back.

After I'd left the show and Channel 7, he began doing crazy little film clips and eventually, they were used. And that was how distinguished film director Peter Weir got his chance. I later attended a preview screening of his first feature movie *The Cars That Ate Paris* and afterwards, he walked right past me without acknowledgement. I put it down as accidental. After it happened on a couple more occasions, I was forced to accept that he had passed onto loftier realms in which I didn't even exist.

I had made it clear that I would be leaving *Mavis* mid-year and as the time for departure approached, I began to wonder who would replace me as Executive Producer. The management had once again asked me to reconsider, saying they were having difficulties finding someone to replace me. But after eighteen months, I'd had enough.

A few weeks before I was due to leave, Johnny Whyte flew in from London. Johnny was an experienced writer of revue who had also contributed to BBC dramas like *Coronation Street.* He originally hailed from the North of England, as I did. He loved *Mavis* from the first show he saw. We discovered we had the same sense of humour, and we clicked. We became colleagues and best friends in a working/social relationship that had its highs and lows, tempestuous and funny, nasty and explosive, that would last for years until it finally blew up.

He immediately realized that his hardest job would be meeting the weekly demand for original material, and made me promise I'd continue to contribute numbers and sketches after I'd passed the show onto him. Of course, I agreed. Channel 7 still had me on salary, even though I had no contract. Despite this, Johnny always paid me the standard fee for my weekly contributions. Somebody in the Channel's accounts department wasn't paying attention!

I wanted to help him all I could. I was getting out while the going was good. I could see signs that *Mavis* had had her day. The regular weekly format of topical songs and sketches was getting stale. New local shows were diverting the attention of viewers. The drama series *You Can't See 'Round Corners* caused outrage when the hero's hand went a little too far up his girlfriend's skirt. The sitcom *My Name's McGooley, What's Yours,* with *Mavis* alumni Gordon Chater and Noelene Brown was becoming a huge comedy hit.

Mavis trudged on like an amiable old dowager, but when Johnny began recruiting the likes of Dawn Lake and Bryan Davies, she lost what was left of her cutting edge. He even signed Phillip Street revue favourite Barbara Wyndon, but her eccentric personality failed to register on television.

Meanwhile, Channel 7 had come up with a new assignment for me.

Respected current affairs commentator and *Beauty and the Beast* panelist Anne Deveson had created a funny idea for a sitcom to star Carol Raye, and I was asked to co-write it with her. At the outset, we seemed very much the odd couple, but in reality Anne and I got on splendidly and we were soon churning out scripts together. The 1960s were all about James Bond-type spies, and Anne's concept was a spoof that had Carol as a daffy ASIO operative sent out on quirky assignments.

While Anne and I were happily busy on our project, we became aware that we had a 'twin'. Former *Mavis* leading man and Rupert

Henderson favourite, Ronnie Stevens, had been brought back to Australia to star in another sitcom, a 'work in progress' presided over by fellow Brit director, John Walters.

Anne and I had completed five or six scripts to our mutual satisfaction when we received shattering news. The Ronnie Stevens project hadn't worked out. So, with the magnificent stupidity that I was becoming to expect of television executives, the Channel 7 bunch decided that as our Carol Raye sitcom was going so well, any success it promised could be doubled by the addition of Ronnie Stevens as co-star and John Walters as director.

Much against our instincts, Anne and I found ourselves trying to incorporate another lead character, to be played by Ronnie Stevens, into our tightly-written scripts. All the jokes and situations had to be more or less split in half to encompass not one, but two leading players. *The Delightfully Daring and Dangerous Doings of Daphne Davenport* became *The Delightfully Daring and Dangerous Doings of Daphne Davenport and Dudley.* We abbreviated this, for our own reference, to 7-D. We should have added another D – for Disaster!

When you have a rich and delicious sauce, you don't make it better by diluting it.

We went into production in the enormous new studio space that Channel 7 had added to its facilities. Ronnie and Carol laughed a lot when they found their dressing rooms, in a typical architectural stuff-up, were like broom cupboards and Ronnie could not reach his without marching through Carol's. The shared hilarity dissipated once we moved onto the set and faced the real reason why we were all there.

We taped three episodes which, in terms of intrigue, rivaled anything written by John Le Carre....and I'm referring to what went on *behind* the cameras. As I had learned in *Mavis,* Ronnie Stevens guarded his perceived status assiduously. Unfortunately for him, merely by appearing in a scene, Carol captured focus of attention. Ronnie, for all of his technical skills, couldn't compete with the natural charm and effervescence Carol brought to her work. Carol complained to me in private that due to John Walters' direction – possibly as compensation? – she found herself doing important scenes with her back to the camera. Stevens, on the other hand, asserted that the scripts rewritten by Anne and I still favoured our original star.

It was a war zone. There were more "Darlings" than explosions.... more "Of course I'll do it that way," than casualties. But we completed three episodes as if we were working on the Gaza Strip.

Early one morning, we gathered in our rehearsal room for a read-through of our fourth episode, Carol, Anne and I, and the supporting cast. The only absentee was Ronnie Stevens. We waited. We sat there in the cold for three hours. This was the time before mobile phones. It's difficult to believe, but people then could actually be out of touch. And we remained out of touch until somebody from the studio finally arrived to tell us all to go home, the bomb had dropped, the series was cancelled.

Ronnie Stevens had had a meeting with Rupert Henderson. Obviously, no-one knows what passed between them, but one can assume Ronnie's dissatisfaction with the situation featured predominantly. Without further ado, he flew back to England. The rest of us – Anne, Carol and I – and, of course the series, were dumped.

Television manifests its cruelties in many ways. It brings out the ugliness in people. The clever ones keep it hidden. They do their damage subtly and continue on, much loved, much admired. The industry conspires to keep their secrets. And so it was back then, this uncivilized cruelty that left our little group sitting in the cold for hours, waiting to rehearse a show that was already cancelled. Three hours of increasing anxiety, followed by a devastating shock. No concern for feelings. We could have been spared the pain. We were not.

It was a tremendous disappointment to all of us who had worked long, hard and enthusiastically on a project we believed in. But I was learning to roll with the punches. Suddenly, I had more time on my hands and I used it to scour the newspapers to find subjects I could lampoon and help Johnny's weekly problem of material for *Mavis.*

One of the last numbers I wrote was prompted by a news item that announced the Federal Government was planning to attract more Americans to migrate to Australia...'including American negroes.'

Imagine that! It was those last three gratuitously racist words that inspired me to write the following lyrics that were performed in a full cast opening number the following week:

Hey, Mr Negro
You'll be welcome here
We know how to treat our coloured people, never fear
We'll teach you how to throw a boomerang
And how to live in squalor
And how to bum a hand-out
When you're really in need of a dollar
Hey, Mr Negro
We'll see you're okay
Throw away that suit you bought back in the USA
You'll be more happy when you're naked
More comfortable in rags
Hey, Mr Negro
Come on - pack your bags.
Hey, Mr Negro
Brains you can discard
We'll try to educate you, but we won't try very hard
We'll provide you with a humpy
An isolated shack
Hey, Mr Negro
Who cares if you're black?

As I re-read these lyrics now, I see that sadly, little has changed… except the freedom to perform a number like that on television.

As the end of 1967 approached, I was getting decidedly twitchy about collecting my formidable salary from Channel 7 for staying home and doing nothing except writing *Bramston* numbers, for which I got paid extra. It didn't sit well with my North Country work ethic. Finally, I put the question: "Do you have anything for me coming up in the New Year?" The reply was negative. "Then take me off the payroll," I told them. It was farcical, really. I didn't have a contract, they could have dropped me any time. Maybe they didn't realize I was still *on* the payroll. People in television have such short memories.

After two hectic and demanding years at the top of the television tree, I faced 1968 like an author with writer's block. Everything henceforward was a blank page. I remembered it was exactly the same feeling I'd had when my parents and I first arrived in Australia…

6

We docked at Port Melbourne one blisteringly hot morning with northerly winds blowing, it seemed, directly from a furnace. It had cost my parents twenty-five English pounds to get there, ten pounds each for them, five pounds for me. And they had just over double that amount in their pockets to get them started.

We were met by some distant relatives of dad's, Cissy and Eddie and their two sons, who had migrated a couple of years previously. Quite a lot of passengers were disembarking. We were going on to Sydney, but had the day free to explore Melbourne, and Cissy and Eddie had offered to show us around. They lived 'a bit out of town' they told us, so we'd just keep to the city. We all crowded into an ancient, rusting ruin of a car and chugged away from the dockside. Already, our clothing was wet with perspiration. We drove through several bayside suburbs and into the central city area. I noticed the wide, orderly streets and the trees lining the pavements.

"They call this the Paris end of Collins Street" Cissy announced importantly, like a tour guide. It could have been the Moscow end of Tobacco Road for all I knew or cared.

However, despite my misgivings, I became impressed by the geometric spaciousness and cleanliness of the city. I noticed a great number of cinemas, and that raised my spirits.

We left the smart part of the city and had lunch in a dingy, back-street café. At fifteen years of age, I had the first steak I'd ever eaten in my life. I enjoyed it so much, I wanted to bury the bone for later!

It was quite a day, but despite the kindness of the distant relatives in meeting us and showing us around, I didn't take to them. So when they dropped us back at the ship and we said good-bye, I was glad to see the back of them. Very small doses, I thought. Little did I know!

We were headed for Leura, in the Blue Mountains of New South Wales. This had been arranged by another English migrant family, also living in Leura. I began to realise how much my father had been net-working – and this was fifty years before the computer, so God knows how he did it. Despite his gloomy silences at home, he could obviously ingratiate himself with strangers when he chose. We moved in with the English family, a couple with one little boy, in a spacious weatherboard house nestled amongst a lush backdrop of trees and bushes.

Coming from the drab greys and blacks of a cloud-dominated Manchester, I felt as if I had surfaced in a technicolor wonderland after a long, murky swim underwater. The mountain scenery was magnificent, the air was clear, the sunshine brilliant and the native flora was overwhelming in its variety and profusion. Leura, in the early fifties was a sleepy little place. The neighbouring Katoomba, just down the road, was a more bustling centre, its main thoroughfare lined with shops.

For the first time, we felt as if the move from England had been worthwhile. We strolled along the mountain paths taking in the majestic beauty of the Three Sisters, dallied at the lookouts, and descended into the cool mystery of the Jenolan Caves. The tourist industry really hadn't caught hold then, so sightseeing was peaceful and uncluttered by crowds.

The idyll lasted for about a month, and we were so relaxed, it took that long for us to realise it had to end sometime.

The only industry in Leura was a pen-nib factory. People were still using fountain pens, but these were soon to be outmoded by ballpoints, so even that little factory was puckering up for the kiss of death. There was no employment for an aircraft fitter. They didn't build aeroplanes in Leura and Katoomba. Not even models that dad could pass off as mine. There was, in fact, little employment for anybody. We had only rented our house in Newton Heath, so there was no money from a sale. Dad had no savings. Being an aircraft fitter was extremely patriotic in wartime, but it didn't pay much and when the war ended, there wasn't even overtime to boost his weekly wage. The furniture had gone for a little over one hundred pounds. ($200). Now, we had less than sixty pounds left. Something had to be done.

My father rang Cissie and Eddie in Melbourne at the phone number they had given him and explained our situation. They immediately suggested that we go down to them. There were plenty of jobs to be had in Melbourne, they told him. I suppose we could have just gone down the mountains to Sydney, which was much, much closer, but we didn't know anybody there and being newcomers in a strange country there was this need to be with people we knew.

They were all there to meet us again, Cissy with her wispy faded red hair, Eddie with his wispy fair hair and the two boys with their blazing carrot-tops. I wondered if they ever went to school. I wondered whether Cissy and Eddie had ever *been* to school. In a repeat of the first time, we all piled in the car, but this time our luggage was strapped precariously on top. This time, we were here to stay.

It was a little cooler now, and we passed through neat suburbs. 'A little bit out of town', they'd said on our first visit. So far, not bad.

My spirits dropped with every kilometer as the car jerked and grunted through suburbs with names like Collingwood, and Northcote, and Preston. The houses were thinning out, and the two lane road seemed to be running parallel with a rail track. We clunked over a level crossing and I saw the name Reservoir on a signpost. It seemed to consist only of a couple of shops and the level crossing. Then I saw a funny little hall with a cinema sign *Plaza* out front. All was not lost.

Or was it? All we could see now from the main road were expanses of coarse, dry grass and threateningly huge clumps of thistle that looked as if, under cover of darkness, they would wrench up their roots and walk by night, like Triffids.

At least we're on a main road, I thought.

As if to contradict me, Eddie made an abrupt turn cornered by the only large building in sight, an impressive factory-size complex adorned by a sign with the words *Fowlers Pottery*. Now, we were travelling down a narrow dirt road, cut through the paddocks and stretching as far as the eye could see, not a tree in sight, totally unshaded.

I came to know this primitive thoroughfare as Settlement Road. And the district was called Thomastown.

After about fifteen minutes, this long, long track ended with a turn to the right. Then a turn to the left. And there, on each side of the road we could see what appeared to be two ramshackle structures.

Farms, I supposed you'd call them, but only if you were in a benevolent mood or under the influence of illegal substances.

"We're in that one," said Cissy pointing, "the one on the right."

We turned into a gate and the car lurched to a stop amidst clouds of red dust. Chickens scratched at the dry earth behind a picket fence that leaned crazily, as if swooning from the heat. We were looking at some kind of rambling farmhouse structure. The weatherboards were warped by the heat, the paint was peeling. The corrugated iron roof was fighting a losing battle with rust. Rotting wire screens hung from the windows like tortured slaves on a rack. The entire structure looked as if it would have fallen down had it not been for several lean-to supporting sheds.

The smell was like an invisible fog. A stench like nothing I'd experienced before. I had never been close to rotting flesh, but this was what I imagined it stank like, cooked by the sun, suffocating.

A guy in his thirties, with a lined, weather-beaten face, was approaching us. Cissy said: "This is Brian. He inherited this place from his mother. She'd let it run down, but you're getting there, aren't you love?" Brian nodded, smiling. He wore a wide-brimmed hat (sensible!), shirt and jeans.

Cissy introduced us. "Brian's renting us the back part, and he's agreed to us putting you three up until you get on your feet."

My only contribution to the introductions was a faltering: "What's that smell?"

Brian said: "It's the bloke across the road. He's got two thousand chooks and he feeds 'em chopped rabbit meat. It goes off quick in this heat, even quicker than the rats can eat it."

"Rats?" my mother asked, falteringly.

"Yair," Brian replied amiably. "The rabbit meat attracts 'em. I give my chooks regular grain feed, but there's nothing I can do about what he feeds his on."

The McGraths took us around the side of the homestead to a side door leading off a veranda. Inside was a big kitchen, the wooden framework unlined and rough. "This is where you'll be," Cissy said, opening a door off the kitchen and ushering us into yet another unlined room, hardly big enough to accommodate the one double bed that was in there. She nodded in my direction. "You'll have to make your own arrangements about junior."

That night, I slept on the suitcases and continued to do so until we got a camp stretcher. Space was so tight, my parents had to crawl over me to get in and out of their bed. The close proximity was something I had to get used to. Even when we moved, we slept in the same bedroom for the next two years.

Brian and his wife Alison, who came from Liverpool, occupied the front of the farmhouse and worked feeding their chickens, and collecting the eggs, which were sorted, packed and sold. They also had to cope with the hordes of rats foraging from over the road. There were so many of them that the stinking rabbit meat served in the chicken farm opposite wasn't enough - they were also after the regular feed that Brian used, and not only that, they were after our food, too. We were under constant siege. Everything edible that wasn't canned or perishable enough to be kept on ice, had to be stored in airtight tins. In normal circumstances, this might have been enough. However, our benefactors were not exactly the most hygienic or house-proud of people, but then again how could anyone be proud of the near pigsty we were living in? This made our little hovel in Newton Heath look like something out of *Vogue Living*. Now I was in a Ma and Pa Kettle movie, I thought to myself, not only the ramshackle farm, but with our own version of Ma and Pa, thrown in for good measure. Crumbs and bits of food were dropped on the floor and left there like canapés for the rats, unless one of us swept up. But it was well nigh impossible to sweep up after every meal, with Cissy stationed by the sink, on her imaginary soap box, waving a ladle and complaining incessantly about how tough it was to get a foothold in Australia, and Eddie and the boys sprawled around looking as though a foothold was the last thing they wanted.

My parents and I became obsessive about what we ate. One day, I threw out a whole loaf of bread because I thought it was covered in insect eggs. It turned out they were poppy seeds, something I'd never seen before. My father began to live almost entirely on bananas. He said if he peeled them himself, he knew they were clean.

And always, night and day, was the overpowering stench of the rotting rabbit meat.

We ate our evening meal early, before Cissy and Eddie came home from wherever they worked. At least with my mother preparing it, we could be reasonably sure it wouldn't give us ptomaine poisoning. Later, we had to sit there while they ate. And afterwards, there was nowhere for us to go, nothing for us to do. There was a small bakelite radio, but it was no competition for Cissy. Waving a ladle, she'd launch off on the same spiel night after night.

"Eee, if they could see us now, the folk back home. They'd think we were ravin' mad, living like this….." was the usual introduction. We thought so, too, but there was no point in reiterating it over and over again. Then would come a run-down on all the migrants living in the area, their ups and downs, mostly ups because they all seemed to be buying blocks of land and making plans to build their own homes.

"They're lucky, they are," Cissy would say enviously, as if hard work and sensible strategies had nothing to do with it.

Within days of settling in, my parents both got work at a factory in North Fitzroy. They had to walk to catch the train. Most of the trains from the city terminated at Reservoir. Every eighth or tenth train ventured further into the hinterland on a single line to Keon Park, then Thomastown and on to Epping and Lalor. Given the flat, desolate terrain, a covered wagon would have been more appropriate. Keon Park was the nearest station to where we were and that's where my parents had to walk, rain or shine, with no shade or shelter.

Left on my own all day, there was nothing for me to do. The only sounds were the clucking of the hens, the occasional mad laughter of a kookaburra and the rusty-gate gurgles of magpies as they circled in a blank sky. I began to develop a guilt complex. I felt I should be contributing to the joint income. The rats appeared to have no fear. In broad daylight, I saw two of them feeding from the same tray of grain as several hens. We heard that the owner of the farm across the road would pay sixpence a head for every rat killed, so one Sunday I went over with the younger of Cissy's boys, Leon, who was a wiry ten-year-old. We were both armed with pieces of wood, as thick and heavy as baseball bats, and accompanied by an enthusiastic dog. As we entered the evil-smelling chicken pens, the floor would cave in under our feet. It was hollow, riddled with passages clawed out by the rats. As they crumbled, the dog would begin scratching, and the rats would pour out. The ones the dog didn't get, we would bash with our heavy sticks, and the air was thick with dust, dog-growls and death squeals. One rat jumped between my legs, and I held it there, caught, while Leon bashed its head in from behind, as well as inflicting damage to my calves.

We progressed from pen to pen. Finally, we dragged all the rat corpses together for counting. We had killed a grand total of fifty-nine. The owner handed over thirty shillings, fifteen shillings each for Leon and I, which I then handed over to my parents feeling as though I'd earned my keep for that week. It was the first money I had ever earned. I was disheveled, dirty and bruised. And I was a killer, if only of vermin. My life was certainly changing.

As the weather turned cooler, Brian and Alison, would invite us up front into their living room, where they had a fire. The walls were lined with a depressingly brown plasterboard, and I noticed midway to the ceiling, a small round hole from which trailed a long stain of dried blood.

I asked Brian about it. He told me that a possum had taken up residence in the cavity between the lining and the outside wall. It constantly chewed noisily at the support jambs and its shuffling back and forth added to the disruptiveness it was causing. Something had to be done. Brian got his shotgun. He placed the palm of his hand flat on the wall and moved it around until he could feel the warmth of the possum's body. He aimed for that area of warmth and shot at it. No more possum. At least, not alive. If its carcass was rotting in there, it wasn't noticeable. There was too much competition from the rabbit meat in the stink department.

And while we're in the stink department, let's dwell for a moment on yet another downturn in our lives that was transforming our memories of Newton Heath into something akin to the pleasure palaces of the French Riviera.

Thomastown was not sewered. This meant that the outside toilet, something I was accustomed to, turned out to be something new, but definitely not fresh in the true meaning of the word. A dunny. A seat over a large metal container that held everything, and I mean everything, until someone called 'The Night-Soil Man' came to collect it in a truck and replace it with an empty one. If Stephen King had been writing novels then, imagine what he could have done with a character called 'The Night-Soil Man'.

His visits were regular - let's face it, they *had* to be if everybody else was! An overflow situation was something to be avoided. His pick-ups became a landmark of our week. So I was well and truly ready for him on his third weekly visit.

I was all spruced up, ready to hitch a lift with him up to the top of Settlement Road. This might seem strange, getting all spruced up, to jump on board a truck loaded with twenty canisters of shit but there was a method in my madness. Or a madness in my method. I couldn't see myself ever getting a start in journalism, a kid whose education had finished at fifteen, now living on an unsewered chicken farm, infested with rats, miles away from anywhere and only the 'wanted' ads to scan when someone occasionally brought a newspaper home.

Without discussing it with my parents, I had made up my mind.

When 'The Night-Soil Man' dropped me at the junction of Settlement Road and went on his merry way, I marched into the Fowlers Pottery complex and found the offices.

I said: "Look, I'm a migrant, living down the road, and I need a job."

"How old are you?" asked the hiring and firing guy.

"Sixteen," I said bravely, starting a trend for upping my age.

I started the next day as a Junior Clerk, which was just a bullshit name for office boy. I didn't care. The wage was thirty shillings a week - the equivalent of killing fifty-nine rats, without the squeals.

My father was furious. I really couldn't work him out, other than he wanted me to be somehow, a more successful reflection of himself - like with the models I'd had to pass off as my own work. If I wanted to be a journalist, then that fitted in with his plans, but starting out as an office boy in a factory that specialized in toilet bowls was not on his agenda. Did he really expect me to launch out at the top instead of accommodating other people's bottoms?

Fortunately for me, but unfortunately for my mother, there was a distraction. She developed a swollen foot. The skin began to peel from her toes. It was horrible. Obviously, she had to give up her job and stay home because she couldn't walk on it. The doctor said it was some kind of bite that had become infected, possibly a spider bite.

We all shivered. Spiders. Spiders and snakes. We hadn't seen any, but we were assured by the locals that they were around. Lucy stayed home until the infection cleared up, lying on the bed in our small bedroom, with the door to the kitchen wide open, and occupied herself by throwing shoes at the rats that ventured into the kitchen when they thought nobody was home.

As for me, I joined half a dozen guys in white short-sleeved shirts, thin ties and flapping trousers and was given the daily invoices to file as basins, sinks and bathtubs were shipped out to the retailers.

They found my Lancashire accent amusing and tried to imitate and make jokes about it. As often as I could, I retreated to my own special place, a little cubby hole between stacked toilet bowls which served to remind me that somewhere, people were civilized enough to pull a chain.

One good thing those other guys did, they brought in the morning papers, including *The Age*, which had a most comprehensive ad section, including *Positions Vacant*. So I'd sneak away with the papers after they'd been discarded, sometimes going through the trash bins to find them.

It paid off.

After two weeks, I spotted an ad. I cannot pretend to remember the exact wording of this ad, importantly contained in a panel of its own, but what it amounted to was that the Australian Broadcasting Commission, the A.B.C., was seeking a young man for the position of 1st year cadet journalist with its radio news department. Age 18 with educational qualifications and preferably, some professional experience in writing.

I was about as qualified to answer that ad as I would have been had it been for a urologist, but it was the chance I'd been waiting for. I rang and made an appointment for the following day.

The next morning, I rang Fowlers Pottery and reported sick. As I had done for my onslaught on that factory, I spruced myself up in my best (and only) suit, but unfortunately for me, it wasn't a 'Night-Soil' visiting day. I resigned myself to having to walk to Keon Park Station. However, Brian told me the night before that by crossing the paddocks, I could cut out the long trek up Settlement Road. If I struck out through the parched, grassy fields behind the chicken farm and kept angling to the right, I'd eventually see the little shaded platform that was Keon Park Station and reach it in half the time. Then I could catch one of the few trains that ventured beyond Reservoir, on its return journey to the city.

I'd like to be smart and write that I edged myself elegantly into my future career. In actual fact, I staggered into it, pursued by a bull, with bleeding palms, bruised knees, and with considerably less sartorial elegance than your average derelict.

To be fair, it *had* been mentioned that a bull called Trevor roamed the paddocks aggressively, but he hadn't been seen for several weeks, and certainly not since we had arrived.

My appointment wasn't until the afternoon, but I set off in the morning figuring that as this would be my first trip to the city of Melbourne on my own, I would be able to fill in time by looking around.

The sun was already high in a cloudless sky, and knowing it would get hotter as the day progressed, I was glad of the early start. I strode through the paddocks, through the dry, waving grass, and as instructed, I angled my progress in a diagonal line to the right. I'd worked out my strategy for presenting myself as a candidate for the job on offer, in other words a string of lies, and I was feeling good.

It was then that Trevor made an appearance.

I heard this thudding noise, or maybe felt it as the parched earth beneath my feet started to vibrate. I looked behind me and was horrified to see an enormous bull, not running at me, but making short spurts in one direction, then another, tail swishing, head tossing. I'd seen this sort of demonstration in movies, but they'd been set in Spain, like in *Blood and Sand*, with Tyrone Power as the matador, twirling his cape to show off for Rita Hayworth, the bull half dead anyway, with all those pointy-things stuck in its bleeding back.

This was different. There were no barriers between me and this raging bull. No cameras, no Rita. And where was Tyrone Power when I needed him? Trevor was now scraping the ground with his hooves. Another sign of anger that I recalled with a fresh spurt of fear.

So far, he wasn't looking in my direction. Maybe he was so caught up in his own performance, he hadn't seen me. Or maybe he was ignoring me on purpose so that an eventual attack would have a dramatic resonance in accord with the rest of his operatic posturing.

My confident strides quickened into a run. I couldn't see any fence that I could duck under and put between me and Trevor, but I just kept scurrying. I shot a glance over my shoulder. For the first time, he was standing there actually faced in my direction.

I scurried on. Another glance back and I let out a yell. Trevor had started to walk - not run - but walk, very firmly towards me, at - it seemed to me - the same pace as I was running.

I stared ahead in vain for a fence. Nothing. Nothing, except the thin white rim of what was called an aqueduct. I'd heard about it, how it was used to channel rain water, but because of summer's drought had dried up completely. I veered towards it.

Trevor had started to trot. I could now actually hear, not only the thud of his hooves but his snorting. Suddenly, I was in a one-man Pamplona run! I put on a spurt and got to the aqueduct. It was like an empty canal, stretching it seemed to the horizon both to the left and the right, its smooth cemented sides forming a V-shape. Now, without any water, the narrow end of the V at the bottom was just filled with rubble. I stood on the rim and looked back. Trevor's trot had accelerated into a run. His head was down. I saw the horns pointed in my direction. I remembered Tyrone Power being gored in the last reel.

I lowered myself into a sitting position on the rim, then slid down the steeply-angled wall to the bottom. My feet hit all the dried-up detritus and I struggled to keep my balance, standing there, listening.

The thudding of hooves stopped. The snorting continued. I fully expected Trevor to look over the side to investigate where I'd gone, but he didn't. I suppose in his bull brain, which was naturally filled with bull shit, it must have seemed to him that I'd just vanished. Brains full of bullshit don't extend to such luxuries as logic, as I found later in life when I entered the strange world of TV executives.

I waited. The snorting subsided. Silence. I didn't even hear Trevor leave, but I presumed he had. A bull is not a stalking animal. It is a wham, bam, thank you ma'am-type quadruped. Ask any cow.

Just to be on the safe side, I stayed still for several more minutes

Then I started to stumble along the base of the aqueduct to the right, which was always the direction that would (hopefully) lead me to Keon Park Station. It was tough going. Underfoot were dried out twigs, leaves and pebbles. It occurred to me that if someone at some far distant control center decided to open the sluice gates, a flood of water along the aqueduct could sweep me away and I would be drowned with even more certainty than if I'd been a steerage passenger on the Titanic.

I decided I'd progressed far enough away from Trevor's territory. But then, and only then did it hit me.

I couldn't get out.

The walls were steeply angled and concrete-smooth. And – in the days before metric – about 10 feet high. I was about 5 foot six (I grew another couple of inches or so as I progressed through my teens) and there was no way I could scrabble my way up to grasp the topmost rim even by stretching my arms to their limit. I tried gathering stuff from the bottom together to form a platform that I could stand on. This didn't work. It wobbled. I wobbled. And I collapsed full frontal against the sloping wall.

By now, I was desperate. Getting into town for the job interview was now less important than just escaping from this open-air prison into which I'd landed myself.

I stumbled on. The aqueduct stretched before me into infinity. Above were blue skies, a merciless sun, and the mournful squawking of circling birds, hopefully not vultures.

I felt utterly defeated. I was sweating. My clothes were a mess. I didn't know what to do, other than to keep on walking, blinking back tears.

Eventually, up ahead, I saw what I thought was a smudge on the sloping wall. When I got to it, I saw that it was –or had been - a burst bubble in the concrete surface which had left an indentation. It was chest high. I put the heel of my right hand into it, braced my feet, and used it to heave myself up. It was a long process. A couple of times I fell back. I tried again, and this time I held myself flat against the sloping surface while my left hand groped up above for the rim of the aqueduct. It connected. And I managed to pull myself out.

I arrived up top breathless, sweaty and heaving with the nausea of fear. But I'd progressed so far along the aqueduct that I could now see the toy-box platform of Keon Park Station and its corrugated iron roof.

Obviously, I had missed the train I'd been aiming for. Fortunately, I'd set out early, so I still had plenty of time to make the interview. I sat on the one bench on the platform and assessed the damages. My hands were grazed and bleeding. My knees were tender with bruises. There were various sharp spasms in muscles I never knew existed, and my one good suit was dusty and crumpled. And the pants were actually frayed at both knees from the friction of climbing up the cement walls.

Keon Park Station didn't even have a toilet, let alone a washroom. I cannot recollect my thoughts at that time, but I'd hazard a guess they were somewhere in the region of suicide.

When I finally made it to Princes Bridge Station in the heart of Melbourne, I headed straight for the Men's Toilets. Fortunately, there were sinks. No paper towels, no hot-air-dryers – this was the fifties, remember? I tried to clean myself up. I washed the dried blood from my hands. I tamped down my hair. I brushed as much dust off my suit as I could with the palms of my hands, and I cleaned my shoes with wet toilet paper.

I was still less than presentable. But it was the best I could do.

With my plan for a leisurely trawl around the city ruined, I headed straight for the interview.

Jack Taylor, the News Editor of ABC Radio at the time, was – thank God – a nice man in the best sense of the word, but I was intimidated, of course. Betty, his secretary, had ushered me in. She would soon become Jack's second wife. And what a wonderfully warm couple they made. I had no CV – they didn't exist in those days - and if they had, my attainments would not have covered one side of a corn flake. I just told him of my desire to write, to make it my career. To my discredit, again I upped my age. A fifteen-year-old, whose only work experience was hiding behind toilet bowls, wasn't exactly the best candidate for a journalistic cadetship with ABC Radio News.

There is a desperation born of being a migrant-stranger in a new country that brings out resources of survival never envisaged. And I was desperate. Not for money, not for glory, but for the chance to do something – the only thing I could do, which was to write – and use it to prise myself out of the future that threatened to trap me at Fowlers Pottery, just as I had been trapped in the aqueduct. I don't know how much of that desperation, that yearning to better myself, showed in that initial interview with Jack Taylor. I don't know how much of my distress remained after my earlier encounter with the bull, nor what he thought of my dishevilled appearance. I don't even know whether he believed this fifteen year old passing himself off as eighteen.

What I would like to know, and I never did find out, is whether there were any other applicants. I didn't see any, but, without any false modesty, surely there must have been other young guys, better educated, more intelligently equipped for a start in journalism? Where were all the budding movers and shakers in Melbourne that day? Maybe they'd all moved to Sydney!

I got the job. And for that, I will be eternally grateful.

Soon afterwards, Jack Taylor and Betty married, and she stepped away from her job as his secretary. But she always arrived on Jack's arm at staff parties, and would inevitably recall my first appearance at the ABC. Inaccurately, though perhaps with great perception as to the real me, she'd incorrectly remember me turning up for the interview in short pants… "and I said to Jack: 'That. Kid's. Got. Guts!'" It was embarrassing, and it got to be a running gag, but it was, in its way, a complement.

Jack's young son by his first marriage appeared on school holidays to courier news bulletins between the news department and the ABC and Radio Australia studios. He grew up to be Lynton Taylor, a powerful and positive influence on television at Channel 9 in Sydney.

Being accepted as a first-year cadet journalist, I should have felt grateful that my feet were on the first step of the ladder. Instead, all the inbred insecurities kicked in. I didn't know that at the top of that ladder, like a fairy atop a Christmas tree, a wild lady called Mavis was perched precariously, waiting to embrace me.

7

Sandwiched between other buildings at the then-unfashionable end of Collins Street, the Olderfleet Building had (and still does have) an elaborate Gothic entrance and façade more suited to a cathedral than a place of business. This was the unlikely home of the ABC radio newsroom.

A long, wide hallway with a polished floor and lined with the doors of many anonymous offices, led from the entrance foyer to the very back of the building where the newsroom was located. I was rostered on the afternoon and evening shift, and at night when the rest of the building was empty, things got very spooky indeed. *The Shining*, anyone?

The newsroom consisted of a main area with desks that remained empty for most of the time. After being assigned their jobs for the day, the reporters usually left the office and worked from the various press rooms around town, phoning in their stories to be taken down by typists wearing headsets. There were always three or four typists on duty at any time of the day or evening, an interesting array of ladies ranging from young and giddy to smart and sophisticated and all varieties in between. The other sections, for the chief of staff and the sub-editors, were all separated by flimsy glass partitions so there was no privacy at all. Only Mr Taylor, the aforementioned News Editor, had a private office.

I was assigned a small desk in a corner, which suited me fine. I was shy and inarticulate, embarrassed by my Lancashire accent which few could understand. I kept mostly to myself. Unlike the other reporters, I was strictly office-bound, doing all my work on the end of a phone. This work consisted mainly of 'rounds' – lists of telephone numbers which were rung daily or nightly to check for stories. There was the 'hospital round' for checking if there had been any major accidents, or if any important people had been admitted for treatment. And there was the 'undertaker's round', similarly to check if anyone important had died.

My accent was a problem. Almost every time I rang someone, I'd get: "What did you say?" "Sorry, would you mind repeating that?" I'd repeat what I'd said, and still get: "Sorry, can't understand what you're saying."

I knew the accent had to go, so I began to work on it right away. I was also becoming acquainted with everyday Australian sayings. At first, if someone said: "See you later", I'd reply: "Oh no you won't, I'll be going home soon", not realizing they meant 'later in life'. And if asked: "How're you goin'?" I might reply: "By train, and then I'll walk the last bit."

Why the ABC had located its newsroom blocks away from the studio headquarters at Broadcast House in Lonsdale Street was another of life's mysteries I never solved. It was so inconvenient, newsgathering being such an urgent, minute-by-minute operation. The bulletins had to be prepared, then rushed across town to the studios. When young Lynton wasn't doing the courier bit in his school holidays, there was a succession of kids who earned spending money by doing the same, like the pizza delivery boys of a future generation. One of them, who had just left when I joined the organization was a youth of tender age called Graham Kennedy. He swapped running bulletins at the ABC in favour of a move to commercial radio station 3UZ, where the seeds of a fabulous career were planted. Another who moved on from the ABC newsroom to greater fame was a bright young journalist a few notches above me called Tony Eggleton, who was quickly promoted to Chief of Staff, and in later years became Press Secretary to Australia's 17th Prime Minister, Harold Holt. It was Tony Eggleton who had the unenviable task of fronting to the media when Holt went missing while swimming in the seas off Portsea.

I was anchored on the 2pm - 11pm shift for two years. I had no social life and no means of meeting people of my own age. The result was that at the end of those two years I knew nobody but the people I worked with. If I went out - and that usually meant to the movies - it would be alone or with my parents to the local at Reservoir. Some mornings, I'd get into town early for the first session at the movies, and lose myself in the totally comforting Technicolor world of MGM. Then, I'd lunch at Coles' cafeteria. Oh, that food, after years of dull wartime fare! I'd devour huge chunks of lemon meringue pie, and servings of trifle topped by turrets of whipped cream. The lack of social life meant total concentration on work, but at least this got me moving along in my cadetship. In those two years, I graduated from 1st to 3rd year cadet in record time.

Not, I might add, without some hiccups.

One Sunday evening, I was given my first outside job to check on a concert called *Symphony Under the Stars* being performed by the ABC Symphony Orchestra in the Botanic Gardens. "Just check to see it's going well, then phone in a couple of paragraphs from Princes Bridge Station before you catch your train home," I was told.

I followed instructions, and checked in on the concert. All was going well. It was a beautiful, balmy evening, and the orchestra was performing before a big crowd. To me, a big crowd was five hundred people, so that is what I put as the attendance in my story, blithely throwing accuracy to the winds. My little story went to air that night on the eleven o'clock news, and then again the following morning.

When I arrived at work, Monday afternoon, I was immediately called into Jack Taylor's office. His face was ashen, his demeanour apoplectic.

"You've made the ABC look ridiculous!" he shouted at me. I had never heard him raise his voice before, and I was petrified. "Five hundred people? When Hector Crawford conducts *his* orchestra, he attracts crowds of at least five *thousand*! According to your story, the ABC Symphony Orchestra is a failure! The concerts department is at panic stations, management is after your blood, and it'll be all I can do to stop you from being fired immediately!"

I crept to my desk in the corner, cringing with embarrassment, going to the bathroom for some quiet weeping, and awaiting the axe to fall.

It didn't. I don't know for sure, but I think Jack Taylor saved me. He wrote a thundering memo to all staff, quoting my mistake in all its horror, and forbidding anyone to repeat it by making stupid, ill-advised estimates of crowds.

Mind you, I wasn't the only one at the ABC making mistakes. A distinguished announcer, John Chance, became forever known as John 'Funnel-Finger' Chance after he misread a news item, proclaiming to the listening public that a woman had been 'bitten on the funnel by a finger-web spider.' One of our typists mistyped the letters of the word 'showers' in a weather report, and it landed on the newsreader's desk as '…and there will be scattered whores along the coast.'

It was a time of innocence. Certainly, there was political manipulation. The 'White Australia' policy, and the fear of communism had us fearing 'Reds under the Bed.' So what else is new? Certainly not politicians using scare tactics to keep the voting public occupied. Now, it's 'Terrorists under the Table.'

Someone described the nineteen fifties as ten years of foreplay. Me? I didn't even know what foreplay was. I was a poster boy for that decade, bland and innocent. The early fifties were pre-rock'n'roll, pre-Elvis. My music was the songs from MGM's musicals.

I'd sing them all as I made my way home at dead of night. I'd leave the newsroom promptly at my finishing time, 11 pm. I'd literally run down to Princes Bridge Station to catch the 11-15 train to Reservoir. (If I missed that, perish the thought, I had to wait until the very last train which left at midnight). Arriving at Reservoir, I'd get on the bike I'd left there (nobody seemed to steal anything, then) and cycle off towards Thomastown, then down Settlement Road which was pitch black because street lights hadn't been thought of yet out there in the backblocks, and after 45 minutes, I'd be back at the chicken farm. The bike had been an essential acquisition, the only alternative to walking for hours in total darkness.

Around half-past midnight, I'd go around the side of the farm building to the back verandah, and then I'd stamp a lot, because when I opened the door and turned on the light, literally scores of rats would scatter to their hidey holes all over the kitchen. So ended my day.

Fortunately, this routine didn't continue for too long.

Her foot healed, my mother had resumed work, and in a matter of months, with our combined wages, we had enough to buy a block of land up beyond the top of Settlement Road and along towards the Thomastown Rail Station. It was just a pegged-out section in the midst of uninhabited paddocks, but to us it meant an escape from the rat-infested, suffocating rabbit-meat stench of the chicken farm.

I began to marvel at my parents. They coped without a grumble. They trudged back and forth to work, bringing in money as if the challenge of this new life had reinforced the urge to survive that had brought them to Australia in the first place. I recognized it as something that had happened within me, too. With the callowness of youth, I just didn't expect them to react in the same way. And wonder of wonders, they had stopped quarrelling. And miracle of miracles, my father was becoming more friendly.

In his spare time – which meant weekends – he built a two-room bungalow on our plot of land. It was weatherboard, with a sloping corrugated iron roof. Inside, it was unlined, but partitioned into two rooms. One room was our bedroom, the other was kitchen/living.

We acquired two beds, a double for them, a single for me. There was a wood-fired stove for cooking, an ice chest for refrigeration, a kitchen table and four chairs. Oh, and a couple of kerosene lamps.

Our block of land had no amenities. No running water, no electricity, and no sewerage. It was back to pioneering days for us. Dad had built the inevitable dunny and installed a can. Welcome, to our new home, Mr Night Soil Man! And welcome Mr Ice Block Man who delivered a huge block of ice twice a week for the upper compartment of the ice chest. As for water, we had to carry it in buckets from a tap, two paddocks away. I had my weekly scrub at the City Baths when I could fit it in with my shifts, an echo of my childhood.

When we moved in, we bonded together as never before. The future suddenly appeared to promise so much. Out there in the middle of nowhere, the summer nights were like warm milk, and there were so many stars in the sky, it made us dizzy to look up at them.

Almost immediately, my father began building a house in front of our bungalow. He had the plans drawn up, and then followed them, with the advice of locals from whom he bought the timber. I helped dig the post-holes, and then we sank the uprights and cemented them in firmly. The framework began to take shape. My father even tiled the roof over the framework. Just as he'd finished, it started to rain, and the three of us ran into the framework and looked up to see if there were any leaks. There weren't. Not a drop came through that roof.

My feelings towards my father were now very confused. I admired his hard work, this new friendliness, but for all his aptitude at doing jobs, he had never taken the time even to teach me how to drive in a nail. Sadly, I realized it was too late. I was in my mid-teens. The damage had been done. It's the early years that count. My basic attitude towards him had been set in concrete like the uprights of our house, and we never really had an emotional connection.

We acquired a dog. This was to make up for the loss of Glen. We called him Toby and he was a mongrel, a loveable mutt. But I wasn't having much luck with pets. He was poisoned, by a bait, and died in convulsions.

Time passed. The skeletons of other houses began to rise, as others bought blocks of land and moved nearby. There was a German couple, Gerda and Jordan, with whom my parents became especially friendly. The antagonisms of war were not forgotten, they were sensibly discussed. And they came to the conclusion, the four of them, that wars were not caused nor perpetrated by ordinary people like them, but by governments and power brokers who cowered safely in bunkers and sent young men out to fight their battles and die on their behalf.

There were two families from Liverpool, a local Australian family and some people from Holland, all in make-shift temporary dwellings assembled from the cheapest materials.

We all banded together with a cheerful, indomitable camaraderie, in the midst of those parched paddocks, sharing tips on house-building, lending each other a hand when necessary, recommending the best tradesmen and suppliers, all of us stuck together with the glue of survival. And of course, such a new and striving community had its bizarre moments. There was a British lady called Mrs Trumper who seemed permanently in a state of disarray. Everybody called her 'Trouble' and sure enough, she lived up to her name, particularly in one instance.

Mrs Trumper had an extremely buxom daughter of about fifteen years of age. One morning, after the daughter had gone to work, Mrs Trumper went in to make her bed, threw back the sheets and found a new-born baby kicking its legs under the bedclothes.

The daughter was so overweight, her pregnancy had progressed undetected. And she kept her little secret until it happened or, maybe was too dumb to recognize her condition, and apparently coped instinctively with the delivery, then in a post-natal daze, got up and went to work. Needless to say, just as Mrs Trumper's jaw was dropping at the unexpected reality of becoming a grandmother, daughter had collapsed at her place of work and was taken to hospital. She was fine. The baby was fine. Daughter hadn't gone through any pre-natal care, no vitamins, no calcium pills, no pelvic exercises. Not even a husband to attend the birth, holding her hand.

What remains with me from this story is a suspicion that the whole baby-birthing industry might have become just a little over-extended. So hasn't everything? All I know is, mother and child were both healthy and thriving, years after this strange incident.

It took two years for dad to finish our house, two years of living in the tiny bungalow in the midst of nowhere and coping with inconveniences that would have had some migrants heading back to where they came from. However, by the time we moved into the house, we had electricity and water on tap, and even indoor plumbing, with a bath and a shower for the first time in all of our lives. It was a small but comfortable three-bedroom place, the likes of which we would never have dreamed of, had we stayed in Manchester. The kitchen was equipped with a refrigerator and a washing machine. Most of the furniture was second-hand (like most of our clothes), but at last we had a home.

I admired what my father had achieved, but I was happiest for my mother because she would no longer have to live in constant drudgery. Neither Lucy nor Ernest had been educated beyond their early teens, and had been factory workers ever since. But with dogged determination, they had achieved the dream they were seeking, a positive alternative to the dead-end life they faced in England. In doing so, they found a decent, comfortable, low-key lifestyle that made them happier than at any earlier time in their married life.

It all had a lasting effect on me, too. Forever more, I never once took anything for granted and have always appreciated the creature comforts of life, no matter how big or how small.

Apart from Thomastown, things were also changing at the ABC. Someone eventually realized how inconvenient it was to have the newsroom billeted several city blocks away from the studios, and we were all moved back to Broadcast House in Lonsdale Street. Well, not exactly into Broadcast House, but into premises just as peculiar as the Olderfleet Building – a large, terrace-type house which had obviously been enclosed and trapped when Broadcast House was built, joined to the main building by a bewildering rabbit-warren of corridors and passages.

The newsroom now took up the entire first floor of this erstwhile terrace house, a maze of rooms being divided up amongst reporters, sub-editors and typists. One of the advantages of the place, and there weren't many, was that there were gas fires in every room, for which we were all thankful during Melbourne's bleak winters.

I had become much more at ease amongst my fellow workers.

However, away from these familiar surroundings, I was still shy about meeting people. Therefore it was with mixed feelings that I greeted the news of what amounted to a promotion. I was to be released from the confines of the newsroom. As the ABC's reporter on what was known as the Town Hall Round, I'd also be working during the day, have the weekends off, and for the first time since I arrived in Australia, I would have the opportunity to lead a regular life – whatever that was! Added to these plusses, I was upped to being a fourth-year cadet with a rise in salary. The big downer was that now I'd have to start meeting people, and for an inexperienced, unsophisticated lad from Lancashire with all the charisma of a bedsock, it was a daunting prospect.

Nucleus of the Melbourne Town Hall press corps was the press room on the first floor. There were five reporters, representing the various newspapers, always bustling in and out, chasing up leads to stories on the civic scene. I just sat there, to begin with. Fortunately, it wasn't long before the others took me under their wing. In particular, the *Sun* reporter, Patrick Tennison became a mentor, guiding me through the intricacies of the Town Hall milieu, introducing me to city councillors, and advising me on the protocol in the hallowed halls of the second floor where, midst burnished panels and expensive carpeting, resided the Lord Mayor of Melbourne, like a Queen Bee in one of the inner caverns of the Hive. From that beginning, Patrick and I became lifelong mates.

Every afternoon around five, we would troop to the second floor for a session with the Lord Mayor, in his palatial office. As it was the cocktail hour, drinks would be served as we gently grilled him for news. It was my first experience of alcohol. I tried to limit it to one beer, and did so for a time, but that didn't last long. What the hell – if you're going to drink, you might as well start at the top!

I loved being the ABC's Town Hall roundsman. It had an exclusivity about it, particularly as we reporters had an entrée to all the civic receptions for visiting big-wigs; suddenly, I was mixing with a lot of interesting people and learning how to hold my own in conversation.

A new recruit to the ABC Newsroom staff, the cadet reporter hired to replace me, was a terribly funny person called John Howson. Later, he inserted 'Michael' between the John and the Howson. He seemed to be laughing all the time, and sending the whole thing up. Everything and everybody was 'camp'. I had never heard the word before, but John applied it to people and situations like salt and pepper to a meal. "I love Queen Elizabeth – she's so camp!" "Oh, that thunderstorm last night – it was so camp!" and "Did you ever see *Mourning Becomes Electra?* – it was so camp!" He didn't last long at the ABC. He knew, as everyone else did, that he was too much of an individual to fit into any rigid mould. Cleverly, he parlayed his 'camp' persona into a varied career that continues to this day.

Even though we laughed a lot, it still surprised me just recently that, talking about those early days in a TV interview, John Michael described me as the happiest person he had ever met. I guess I must have been on a permanent high. For the first time in my life, I loved being who I was, and where I was. And I reckon I still do.

With my week-ends free, I'd spend some of them with John and his mother Mary at their beach-side apartment in Sandringham. I was also discovering the joys of dining out, although really interesting restaurants in Melbourne were still thin on the ground. The burgeoning migrant population was introducing Australians to their various cuisines but it hadn't yet taken hold. The 'dish de decade' was still something called *Chicken Maryland* – a haunch of deep-fried chook accompanied by battered, deep-fried banana and a pineapple ring, decorated with – you'd better believe it – a glace cherry! These days, if I forget my appetite depressant pills, I only have to recall Chicken Maryland.

The label 'teenager' had been coined, but pre-Rock'n'Roll it really meant nothing. Teenagers still behaved themselves. They dressed conservatively and hormones, if they began to rage, were firmly suppressed. Everybody's genitals were still under warranty. The only rebelliousness was the ponytail and the mid-calf jeans (girls) and 'desert boots' of soft suede (guys). Oh, did I get snide comments for daring to wear these so-called 'brothel sneakers!' It was a risky business for a young man, this slight departure from the norm, because everything else was strictly on the straight and narrow. If you took a girl to a dance or a ball you arrived to pick her up clutching a corsage, usually an outsized orchid tizzed up with fern, the whole monstrosity encased in a celluloid box tied with ribbon. No matter what dress she was wearing, the girl would pin it to her bosom or shoulder, where it sat as if she had suddenly started to sprout foliage. A slice of garlic sausage was a gastronomic adventure. Jingles on commercial radio told us we'd be "happier in a Hoyts Suburban Theatre" and if the movie was preceded or followed by a creamy milk shake at Herbert Adams', that made a real night of it.

It was all to change, and soon.

Garlic was finding its way out of the salami-like sausage and into other foods. Cappuchino bars started to open, with machines that erupted with sounds like mass vomiting. Suddenly, everyone had froth-topped coffee to drink with their new, luxury-length, filter-tipped cigarettes. The young were becoming a little more assertive, aggressive. And I began to get a little assertive and aggressive, myself.

She was a secretary in the Lord Mayor's office, a little older than me and certainly more sophisticated. Her name was Moira and she was extremely attractive. I had become aware that a good-looking girl on your arm was part of the natural progression of things. I'd learned that from the movies, not from any sex education classes or information from my parents. I was so inexperienced in matters of intimacy, I was hardly capable of sharing a confidence, let alone a bed.

My platonic friendship with Moira, charming as she was, would not have rated even a mention in this book, if it were not for an innocent suggestion she made one evening over dinner.

And she changed my life forever.

Kew Repertory Players was one of many amateur dramatic groups that proliferated in Melbourne's suburbs in the mid-fifties. Mostly, they did plays that nobody ever heard of for people who wouldn't be going to see them if friends and/or relatives hadn't been appearing in them. However, in the days before television, these groups provided many enthusiasts with a stimulating hobby and – in my case – turned a life upside down.

Moira was a member of Kew Rep. "We're so short of men," she said. "Why don't you come along?"

"Who – me?" I replied, aghast.

Actually it sounded more like "*Oooo* – me?" When caught off-guard my Lancashire accent popped up as if it had never been away, and actually it hadn't. Now, I used that as an excuse to rebut Moira's suggestion.

"Nobody would be able to understand a word I was saying," I told her. "And anyway, I'm much too shy to get up and start acting the fool in front of people."

"It's fun," Moira replied.

Fun? I scarcely knew the meaning of the word. I hadn't had much fun in my life up until then, unless you included all the hours I sat by myself in the dark watching movies.

I allowed myself to be persuaded….and when we turned up at the casting read-through, I landed a part. I was to play opposite Moira, as her romantic interest. It was quite a stretch for me, any which way you looked at it!

By the end of the first rehearsal, I was hooked. I couldn't wait to start learning my lines, and in fact had them down very quickly, a practice I followed with every stage appearance after that.

I did three other plays in quick succession with Kew Rep, and from that time onwards, journalism gradually receded in importance. I had found the world I really wanted to be in, the world of Show Business. I knew, deep down, that I was never going to be a threat to James Dean, but I was on such a heady roll of enjoyment it didn't seem to matter.

Moira, by this time, had sailed for England, on the kind of requisite trip 'home' that every young Australian was expected to make as part of a rite of passage. I quickly chummed up with another girl at Kew Rep, a vivacious, personality-plus combination of reigning MGM ingénues, Debbie Reynolds and Jane Powell, who fitted perfectly into my fantasies of life as dictated by Hollywood. Suddenly, we were inseparable. We went everywhere together, restaurants, the movies, parties. Our friends at Kew Rep began to anticipate an early engagement. What they – and certainly I – did not realize at the time, was that my attraction to her was based more on film than flesh.

I suppose it was in line with the innocence – or rather the suppressed emotions of the era – but we continued on with this brother-sister relationship for the next three years. The experience of assuming other characters in plays and saying lines out loud in public, was doing wonders in reversing my shyness. Going around with a stunning girl on my arm did wonders for my ego.

Furthermore, I got to meet two genuine Hollywood stars. Well, I actually got to meet and talk to one, Katherine Hepburn. But prior to that, who should materialize in the staid mahogany corridors of the Melbourne Town Hall like a starburst; glossy, perfectly groomed and bright as Technicolor, MGM's Queen of Tap, Miss Ann Miller. Chaperoned by her mother, who looked startlingly like a slightly older but just as beautiful version of her daughter, Ann had been sent by the studio to publicise a new movie called *Interrupted Melody* based on the life of Australian opera singer Marjorie Lawrence, who made a comeback in a wheel-chair after being crippled by polio. It seemed a strange vehicle for such a frenetically-lively dancer as Ann Miller to be promoting, and by vehicle I mean both the film *and* the wheelchair. She wasn't in it, a fact that both she and everybody else seemed extremely relieved about, particularly given Hollywood's reputation for bizarre miscasting. Ann was given a civic reception, and typically, delivered a peppy, good-natured speech in which she laughingly echoed her bemusement at being sent to promote a movie, not only that she wasn't in, but one that was right out of her field. But she was quick to assure us all that the film was extremely faithful to its Australian subject, and when we saw it, we would be proud of it. She was right. The film later won an Academy Award for its screenplay.

Later I heard stories that illustrated how dumb she was. Like, when she was in *Sugar Babies* on Broadway, with a Jewish holiday coming up, one cast member asked if she was going to be busy on Passover. "Not at all," Ann is alleged to have said. "I don't do game shows!" But this doesn't fit in with the poised lady I saw – or maybe it was just her sense of humor, misinterpreted for the sake of a good put-down. Believe me, that is not uncommon.

Miss Hepburn was another matter entirely. I was assigned to cover a press party in the upstairs foyer of Her Majesty's Theatre for Robert Helpmann and Katherine Hepburn. Helpmann had persuaded his close friend to do a season of Shakespeare in Australia – *The Merchant of Venice* and *The Taming of the Shrew*. As to the latter play, there had been a lot of ribald speculation as to which of them would play the Shrew. This 'official launch' came after both stars had spent time in Queensland on a relaxing holiday.

When I got there, the press party was in full swing, if one can apply that expression to an event that resembled a social gathering in an ant-hill where all the workers were gathering around the queens. I had no interest in Mister – as he was then – Helpmann. My sights were set on Miss Hepburn, who was immediately recognizable because she was wearing a loose, extremely unattractive man's suit. She was surrounded by Melbourne's social page ladies, a formidable corps of relentlessly hard-faced society jotters, dressed in the best that Collins Street's boutiques had to offer.

I sidled in and insinuated myself just behind Hepburn's left shoulder. They were grilling her about domesticity – which was about as bizarre as asking King Kong who does his nails. But nails, since I mention them, were to become a talking point, and not one that Katherine Hepburn enjoyed, any more than King Kong would've.

"Where's your home?" asked one of the viragos sweetly.

'Well, the family home is in Connecticut" And I heard that

distinctive, flat delivery I'd heard in movies for the first time in reality.

There were astonished "ooo's" and "ahhh's" from the circle. It was as if she'd revealed that her family had pitched a tent in the Hanging Gardens of Babylon.

"Connecticut," someone repeated. "That's where Peggy Sage has her headquarters". There were affirmative murmurs from the rest of the group.

"Peggy Sage?" Hepburn inquired.

"Peggy Sage – the high priestess of nail varnish and hand cream!"

From behind, I saw Hepburn's shoulders visibly wilt. She tucked her hands to the rear, where I could see them. They were red and horny, like claws. She started to step away. "I'm sorry. I'm not into all that kind of thing."

I was so close, she nudged into me. I blurted out: "Hartford, isn't it?"

She turned to me. "What did you say?"

"Hartford…in Connecticut?".

Her face looked like grilled beetroot. She was a redhead, she had been up in Queensland, and she had fried herself. I had never seen so many wrinkles. She had more lines on her face than she'd ever learned from a script. Compared with her screen appearances, it came as a shock. But then she smiled, and the smile illuminated her face, negating all the unattractive features. Her lips were generous and the teeth were whiter than anything I'd seen this side of a glacier.

She turned fully, her back to the social column ladies. "How did you know that?" she asked in a tone that fitted with the amiability of her smile.

She moved closer. I moved back. I realized immediately that she was using me to get away from the society page ladies. I didn't mind.

"I did my homework," I said. "On you. When I knew I was coming here."

We were now an intimate twosome. "Well, that's most commendable, young man. But how did you end up in Australia? You must be English of some sort." (I remember to this day that 'of some sawt' delivered in that flat accent.)

So we talked. I told her briefly about myself, and she appeared intensely interested, but for an actress that would have been easy. And yet I could sense she was far more comfortable one-on-one than being the central focus of a group, and she had the kind of inquiring mind that made her curious about practically everything. Then, she launched into an account of her Queensland holiday, and how she put on her 'cossie' and claimed her 'possie' on the beach, all related with much guffawing about how quickly she had mastered the Aussie abbreviations.

And, not daring to interrupt us, the social ladies glared, as captured in the front page photograph of Katherine and I in the following day's *Argus.*

About eighteen years later, I was in London and had attended a Saturday matinee of an Alan Ayckborn play at the Globe Theatre in Shaftsbury Avenue. When I left the theatre, it had grown dark, even though it was only around five o'clock. Rain was pelting down. I pressed myself against the wall at the side of the entrance, hoping it wouldn't last long.

I became aware of a little old lady sheltering next to me. I recognized her, even though she had diminished with age, was underdressed in a black coat, with a black chiffon scarf tied tightly over her head. Dilemma. Should I say hello to Katherine Hepburn and attempt to remind her of our encounter? Or should I not? Out of the corner of my eye, I could see she was ill at ease, darting looks this way and that, and I remembered that she hated crowds. And Shaftsbury Avenue at that time on a Saturday evening, was full of people, scurrying by under umbrellas. I stood there, my back pressed against the wall of The Globe, and decided against an intrusion. A limousine drew up opposite to where we were standing, and she ran across the pavement and jumped in. Farewell, Katherine.

Meanwhile, back to 1955. My annual holidays came up and I went to New Zealand for two weeks to meet Auntie Florrie, Uncle David, and my cousins Ernest and Muriel, who by that time were married and had children of their own. It was all lovely, but dull, and it left me glad that some glitch in the immigration laws had caused us to switch from New Zealand to Australia.

My father, who had been bouncing from job to job because of his hands-on adaptability, was now working on converting the Melbourne Cricket Ground into the main venue for the 1956 Olympic Games. It paid good money. And when the Stadium was complete, he and my mother followed in my footsteps and went to New Zealand for a holiday – their first since we'd arrived in Australia.

When they flew back home, I was there to meet them. They were practically glowing. I had never witnessed them in such an over-the-top happy state.

There were no hugs, embraces or kisses when they reached me. There was never any physical show of affection when you hailed from the North of England in their generation. But my parent's joy certainly made up for any overt physical contact. They were brimming over with how much they had enjoyed their holiday and how much they loved New Zealand.

"You'd like to go and live there, wouldn't you". It was a statement more than a question.

They both launched into accounts of the advantages, how much cheaper everything was, the wonderful, peaceful scenery, and how nice it had been to connect with their relatives.

"Well, why don't you move there?" I suggested. "I couldn't because of my work, but New Zealand isn't all that far away, and I could come and visit you."

My father suddenly reverted to the dour persona we hadn't seen since we left England. "We 'aven't come twelve thousand miles to be separated," he declared gruffly.

And that was that.

I honestly couldn't see myself swapping all I was enjoying in Australia for the rural and, frankly, dated and confining atmosphere of New Zealand, as it was in the fifties.. And what's more, television was on the way. The plan was to introduce it in time for the 1956 Olympic Games in Melbourne. And already, I knew I was one of the chosen few to make the transition from radio to television news. I'd gotten to be very comfortable at the ABC, and, having overcome the mistakes I had made in ignorance at the start, I'd settled in and was obviously doing a satisfactory job. Now, Tony Eggleton and I were sent up to Sydney to attend an introductory course in TV news procedure. Tony and I were the chosen ones and Jack Taylor came up to Sydney with us for the first couple of days, just to look after us and make sure we were settled in.

What Tony and I were taught about translating news into visual terms would be deemed laughably basic these days. Available film clips and graphics to illustrate stories; and really, that was it. Tony made a great show of writing everything down into a notebook. He was the most ambitious guy I'd encountered, and he knew how to play it for effect. I didn't take notes. It all seemed so simplistic, I found it easy to remember. If a story warranted a picture or a graphic, you'd better use it.

Then in the midst of the course, I went to the theatre. And nothing was ever the same again

The theatre in question, *The Phillip Street* was more like a church hall, which it had been until fairly recently. Located in the city's central business district, it was now a unique part of Sydney's entertainment scene, Australia's first permanent home for intimate revue and satirical comedy. As I quickly learned, it was wildly fashionable amongst the social set, many of whom it lampooned mercilessly. It didn't seem to bother them, in fact just the reverse. It had become rather chic to be 'sent up' by the Phillip Street mob.

I had seen a couple of student revues at the Melbourne University's Union Theatre and enjoyed them, but they were nowhere near as smart as the show I saw that night at the Phillip Street. Nowhere near as witty, nowhere near as accurately performed, and nowhere near as devastatingly on target. I was totally knocked out.

The show, as I recall was *Mr and Mrs*, and featured amongst others, a young Barry Humphries who'd already reduced me to fits of laughter in the Melbourne University revues in which I'd seen him. In fact, he might have been the main reason why I went to see *Mr and Mrs.*

In those days, Edna Everage was a rather shabby, gray mouse of a housewife, who gave no indication that she would erupt volcano-like in an explosion of sequins and blue rinse into the rainbow-hued Dame she eventually became. No chartreuse wigs for the Moonee Ponds domestic in those early days. She shared her limp, lank dull brown hair with her creator.

I left the theatre in a blissful daze. Bugger journalism. This was what I wanted to do – write clever lyrics and funny scripts and (in an overblown fantasy) perform them, too.

My dreams faded a little the next day, as it was back to the course in compiling news for television. Even so, they influenced me in taking another bold step, when I got back to Melbourne. I auditioned for the Melbourne Little Theatre, an auspicious establishment in South Yarra, a small, newly-built theatre run for amateur actors, but professionally administered by the father and son team, Brett and Peter Randall, with Irene Mitchell, and George Fairfax.

To any aspiring amateur from the suburbs, The Little was Mecca. Contemporary and modern, it had a perfectly raked auditorium, a large stage, excellent dressing rooms for performers, and a facility for set design and construction presided over by the overwhelmingly talented John Truscott. Not surprisingly, The Little had an overall reputation for excellence.

It is some indication of my increasing self confidence, that I would even consider a step-up from Kew Rep to the Melbourne Little Theatre. Obviously, their standards were far higher than Kew Rep because I only managed a couple of small parts. It didn't matter. I loved acting, and I was meeting a whole new crowd of creative people.

This was how I progressed into 1956. At the Melbourne Little Theatre, I was mixing with people who were theatrically-inclined, and if you deduce that meant that some of them were gay, you would not be wrong. At this point, I had started to observe, but not to participate.

Meanwhile, the ABC Television studios were under construction in the grounds of a grand suburban mansion called Ripponlea. A skeleton staff from radio news, including me, moved there while the place was still a disaster zone. Concrete shells of offices were reached only by staggering over mountains of excavated soil, negotiating hills of sand used to mix the concrete, avoiding mounds of bricks and other building materials, and scurrying around construction machinery. And, of course, being Melbourne, it rained. Regularly. And the rain turned the construction site into a quagmire. And of course, being the ABC, the news department was a long way from the studio from which the news was to be televised – across the quagmire!

My life in Thomastown had prepared me for this kind of pioneering stuff and I coped rather better than the rest of the staff who slipped and slid all over the place as we rehearsed 'dry runs' of news bulletins, to prepare us for the day when the cameras would really be switched on..

And when they finally were, the selection of a suitable reporter to be sent out on assignments depended, not on ability but on who was appropriately dressed that day. I happened to be the only one in the office who was wearing a tie, when a call came through that the visiting

Royal Ballet company, headed by Dame Margot Fonteyn was having a press reception in the upstairs foyer of Her Majesty's Theatre.

The logical thing for me to have done would have been to pass my tie onto someone else, perhaps a little more experienced in the art of television interviewing. Except that nobody else had any experience, either. Mine was nil, which matched my knowledge of ballet. I headed for Her Majesty's Theatre with one of our two TV News cameramen, Harry Lehrer, hoping for an experience at least as pleasant as my encounter there with Katherine Hepburn.

It wasn't.

Television was so new and intriguing, that anything to do with it, had people agog. They stood for hours in the cold outside electrical appliance shops, watching programs on the screens of TV sets displayed in the windows. They went into debt in order to be the first on their street to buy a set. And now, as Harry set up his lights and angled his camera, before an assembly of Melbourne's socialites, theatrical elite, and ballet enthusiasts, the following portentious announcement boomed out:

"Please gather around and be absolutely silent! Dame Margot is about to be interviewed for television!"

Talk about the Odd Couple. There we were, Dame Margot and I, faced not only by Harry Lehrer's camera, but a hushed and formidable half-moon of breathless spectators.

I'd hardly had time to introduce myself to her. I was certainly not equipped with the kind of background information I had gathered on Miss Hepburn. This assignment had happened too quickly. And unlike Miss Hepburn, Dame Margot's considerable talents in the world of the dance appeared to be unadulterated by any warmth whatsoever. Mind you, she had probably been interviewed by the best. And here she was – slumming it!

Harry turned on the lights and gave me a nod. I was petrified. All my newly-found confidence drained away. This was not amateur theatricals. I started by uttering all the usual platitudes of welcoming her to Australia, and extracting from her, like pulling wisdom teeth, a few condescending words about how delighted she was to be here.

Then I stepped into the danger zone.

"Will you be seeing any of our local ballet, while you're here?" I inquired, thinking this would at least squeeze some enthusiasm from her.

I might as well have tried juicing a brick.

She turned to me, her face uplifted (she was really tiny), her perfectly-arched eyebrows raised.

"What local ballet is there?" she asked.

I was stumped. My theatre-going was restricted to amateur theatricals, Sydney's Phillip Street revues, and big, brassy musicals. Frantically, I searched my mind.

"Well..." I floundered..."there's the Borovansky company....and – and the School of Modern Dance."

"Modern Dance?" Her face creased as if she'd heard a fart, and then her nose twitched as if she was smelling the result. "They dance without shoes, don't they?"

My mind goes blank about the rest of that interview. I scurried back to the studio in a melt-down of embarrassment. The film had to go to the labs for developing, so there was always a waiting period and in this case it was akin to waiting for the results of a pathology test on a very painful lump.

It was used, of course. In those early days, it had to be. If there'd been a story about the spread of paspalum over lawns, they'd have shown five minutes of it growing.

As with the Hepburn story, there is an epilogue even to this tragic saga. A couple of years later, Dame Margot was arrested and spent 24 hours in a Panamanian jail. My God, just imagining this lady-like creature being shut up in a cell was far more riveting than half a dozen episodes of *Prisoner*. She was incarcerated while police hunted for her husband, Dr Roberto Arias, a former Panamanian ambassador in London, who was suspected of planning a coup against the government of President Ernesto de la Guardia.

When the story hit the news sources and came to us at the ABC, the immediate reaction was how to illustrate it for the TV News. And of course the only footage we had on Dame Margot was the interview by me. So they ran it, silent, as the news story about her arrest and the search for her husband was read, voice-over. This was a couple of years on. I curled up in embarrassment at the visuals. There was I, like the proverbial deer caught in the headlights, eyes popping in panic, mouthing stupid questions that mercifully, couldn't be heard.

I was returned to sanity and laughter later that night when John (still-not-Michael) Howson rang me. "I caught one of your old movies on television tonight. I wouldn't have known it was one of your old movies, except that it was silent, you wore a cloche hat, and you were doing the Charleston!"

There wasn't much time any more for amateur theatre, but I guess the occasional on-camera interviews and also the short subject films we were assigned, not only to write but direct for weekly magazine-type programs, satisfied my creative impulses for a while.

By this time, I'd completed my cadetship in what seemed like record time, and was a 'D' grade journalist. On two or three days a week, I was even given the responsibility of being line-up editor which meant I had to supervise the assembly of international and local news, which was transmitted to us on clattering teleprinters, decide on the inclusion of stories, view all film and offer guidance to the film editors on how it was to be cut.

On these days, of course, I didn't get any outside assignments. My entire day was centered on supervising what would become the fifteen minute nightly news bulletin. It was always enjoyably tense and a relief when it was over, but provided there were no disasters, it all seemed excitingly well worth while.

The girl-friend/pal relationship was in hiatus. I believe she saw the reality of the situation before I did. There was certainly no future in it for her and she had every right to back off. I wasn't just stitched up. Sexually, I was hermetically sealed! Gradually, it had been dawning on me that I was attracted to males. I hadn't done anything about it. It wasn't that I didn't want to. Difficult as it is to believe, I didn't know how!

That situation was about to change.

8

I wasn't mentally retarded, merely a victim of arrested development. Consider the circumstances. No sex education at school, and precious little dirty schoolboy talk, either...well, not enough to be specific. And there was certainly no helpful enlightenment from my parents. Two years of more or less isolation in my mid-teens, with no peers and no friends. Add to this the fact that it was all taking place in the 1950s where sex wasn't really supposed to exist. Sure, I had urges, but they had no focus. I was desperate for intimacy, but didn't know how to get it. As I've said before, I was a poster boy for the fifties.

The electric light bulb above my head was slowly illuminated. I found no reason for guilt, shame or disgust. I didn't try to analyse, to delve into alleged causes such as heredity, early environment, absence of hormones or mutations of glands, simply because none of these things ever occurred to me. I never felt a misfit. Given this gradual understanding of myself, I felt comfortable in my own skin, in my surroundings, and with my peers. I've since heard horror stories about the agonies of self-loathing some young men have suffered, even to the point of suicide. I felt none of that. I was old enough and sensible enough to realize that my feelings were perfectly natural. I hadn't been molested as a child. I hadn't been seduced in puberty. Nobody had forced me to be the way I was. I'd tried so-called normal relationships and they hadn't worked. And I'd been on the fringes of the entertainment business long enough to know that there were plenty of others like me. This wasn't a case of frivolous choice. There was no choice to be made, no alternative. I was determined to be neither a victim nor a rebel. If this was the way it was going to be, then I would try to cope with it as decently as possible and, obviously, given the attitudes of the time, with discretion.

Needless to say, I did not run out into the world proclaiming that I was gay. For one thing, 'gay' was not a word that had been universally coined then – although it had been used to denote homosexuality in the 1930s amongst sophisticated New Yorkers like Cole Porter, who actually used the word in this context in the lyrics of a patter song he wrote called *Down on the Farm*. 'Queer' wasn't used much either. Around that time in Australia, 'camp' was used a lot, and if a person was said to be 'camp' (particularly 'as a row of tents'), it usually meant he (or she, come to that) was homosexual.

I continued on with my life feeling a lot more settled in my mind, holding my secret close. Now I knew for sure, I was ready, but still in no desperate hurry.

There was a party at the ABC studios one evening, for some reason that I have forgotten. Everybody was there, not only from the newsroom, but film editors, production people, administrative staff, the lot. And I found myself chatting to one of the directors who was regularly assigned to the news bulletin. Besides being efficient at his job, we shared the same sense of humour and he seemed the gentle, thoughtful type of person I liked.

We stayed together, chatting, for most of the party. I knew something was happening, but that was fine. It couldn't be happening with a nicer guy.

He invited me to his place for dinner the following week and I accepted. And then began The Game. When we were both working on the news, me as line up, he as director, we'd behave amiably as coworkers. At the end of the news, we would say "'Bye" to each other and to the rest of the staff and leave separately. Fifteen minutes later, we would be together at his flat, having pre-dinner drinks.

He was an excellent cook, and our evenings were the perfect antidote to a Melbourne winter, full of good food, warmth and the kind of intimacy I had been longing for. Thank God, for someone as kind and considerate as he was. I had never been happier.

Neither of us was the flamboyant type. Our affair was conducted with a discretion that suited us both. We mostly spent evenings at his place, and rarely went anywhere public. We didn't need to.

I was still living in Thomastown with my parents. I longed to move out into a place of my own, but even the thought of doing so brought on feelings of guilt. We had been through so many struggles together, my parents and I, I felt it would be deserting them to move out. "We haven't come twelve thousand miles to be separated," my father had once said, and it still rang in my ears.

A reason to move out – an excuse, to be truthful – presented itself later in the year.....along with an opportunity I'd only ever dreamed of.

I was still mixing with the group of young acting hopefuls that hung out at the Melbourne Little Theatre even when they weren't in the current play. There were always opening nights and the parties that followed, and closing nights, and the parties that followed.

At one party, I was raving on to Irene Mitchell about the Phillip Street Theatre revues, and how there was enough talent at The Little for us to do a similar kind of show. She looked at me with her kindly but piercing eyes. She was the motherly-type, but obviously a whole lot more because as a producer/director her steely skills were renowned.

"We've never done a revue," she mused thoughtfully. There was a pause, and I waited. I knew I wasn't one of her favourites, but maybe.... just maybe...

"Tell you what," she said, suddenly businesslike. "Round up the people you want and present me with a half-hour audition one Sunday afternoon."

That was all I needed. I rounded up the people I wanted – Joy Griswold, Don Battye, Myles Grindal, Su Israel and others, and we had a meeting. Everybody was willing, but there was one drawback. We had no material. They all looked at me. I was the only writer on board.

I'd never written revue material before, but I knew that if I didn't give it a try then the chance would fall through. Suddenly, it was *Babes in Arms* with Mickey Rooney and Judy Garland saying: "Let's put on a show!" I soon discovered I wasn't too hot at the kind of smart dialogue needed for sketches, but I did have a facility for writing funny lyrics that rhymed, and Don Battye was a good pianist/composer, so he got the tunes down and we were on our way. We all rehearsed the requisite half-hour over and over again and then performed it for Irene Mitchell one Sunday afternoon in the empty theatre.

She laughed her head off. And then she jumped up and cried out: "Stay right where you are. I'm bringing in Peter (Randall) and George (Fairfax), and I want you to do it all over again for them!"

She did and we did. And the result was the first Melbourne Little Theatre Revue. *Little by Little* opened pre-Christmas, 1957, played for a month, and was hit with critics and audiences.

I worked hard writing satirical lyrics such as *The Juvenile Delinquents of Toorak*. My material was augmented by older, tried and tested stuff from London revues, but it was the local references that really got people in. The show was designed by future Academy Award winner, John Truscott. As the lady with the big voice sang in *I've got Rhythm* "Who could ask for anything more?"

I couldn't. I was in seventh heaven. In fact, all the success had gone a little to my head. With local celebrities coming in every night and flocking backstage afterwards with effusive congratulations, my material making people laugh as well as performing in it myself, who could blame me for getting carried away? But there's always the voice of reason to cut you down to size.

As I sat before the dressing room mirror smearing five and nine greasepaint on my face, I asked airily: "Anyone important out front tonight?"

"The audience", the cast member next to me declared flatly.

It was a lesson I never forgot.

When the prospect of the revue became a reality, I confronted my parents and told them that with all the night-time rehearsals, following on a full day's work at the ABC, it would be better for me to find somewhere closer to live, rather than drive back and forth to Thomastown. It was an excuse, but it was viable, too, and they saw the sense of it. So now I had my own place, first a small flat in St Kilda, then another, even smaller, in South Melbourne, basically one room with a pull-down Murphy bed and tiny kitchen, and a shared bathroom down the hall, but I didn't mind. I had established my independence, my sexual orientation, and my future career path all within a matter of months.

All through 1958, I did my work on ABC's television news, maintained my cosy relationship with the director and when asked repeatedly: "Are you going to do another Christmas revue?" I always answered: "I hope so."

It happened. And the 1958-59 revue *A Little More*, opening number written by new arrival in Australia, British actor Stuart Wagstaff, was an even greater success. I'd gone all out on my contributions, and I worried it was interfering with my work at the ABC. *The Juvenile Deliquents of Toorak* became *The Mothers of the Juvenile Delinquents of Toorak* – performed by we same three guys in tuxedos but this time with little fur wraps and 'fascinators'. I lampooned Melbourne's Moomba celebrations, and wrote a potted musical version of Ray Lawler's hit play *Summer of the Seventeenth Doll*. We had three suburban housewives ready to accommodate Gregory Peck, Ava Gardner and Fred Astaire, who were shortly due in town to make the movie *On the Beach*; and John Batman 'discovering' Melbourne.

Writing and performing in the revues convinced me that my future was in show business and not in journalism. So I had to rethink my ties with the ABC.

The weeks of evening rehearsals leading up to the revue, and then the season itself, meant that instead of the cosy dinners at the director's place, I would race off immediately after the news bulletin ended, either to rehearse or to perform. I'm sure he felt neglected, and I am sure I was being selfish. Either way, the relationship suffered. There were no rows, no recriminations. It faded as gently as it had begun.

And there had been a complication in that regard, though one not brought on by me.

As rehearsals for the second revue got under way, I became conscious that our designer, John Truscott, also had designs on me. Measuring me for my costumes, he whispered: "I'm going to make you look fabulous in this show." And when it came to the fittings, I realized that wherever possible, this future Academy Award winner (for *Camelot)* had dressed me in attention-getting gear. Then, when the show opened, I arrived in the dressing room each night to find an 'anonymous' gift had been left in my place at the long dressing table. While we were actually performing the show on stage, John would stand in the wings, in all his dark, brooding magnificence, just watching me. I was extremely uncomfortable about all of this. John was in a committed relationship and I wasn't doing a thing to encourage him, even though with his black, floppy hair, and his dark, intense eyes, he was as handsome as any matinee idol. Yet, others in the cast were looking at me as if I was some sort of home wrecker.

I finally burst out and whispered I had to talk to him in private. He suggested his apartment, one night after the show when his partner was away. In desperation, I agreed. We had drinks and I told him I didn't want any more gifts, and the smouldering looks had to stop, too.

I told him I liked his partner too much ever to come between them even though John kept assuring me the relationship wasn't what it was. "But you're still living together, and he adores you, so I don't want any part of it," I said, as firmly as I could. At that moment the doorbell rang.

It was none other than Robert Helpmann. That ended any more discussion between John and I. Bobby, as usual, took centre stage, demanding a drink. He was in a fury, those protruding eyes threatening to pop right out. Apparently, Welsh playwright/actor Emlyn Williams had gone into print saying nasty things about actress Vivien Leigh, whom Bobby adored. "We all know she's as mad as a hatter," he stormed, "but it should never be made public. The poor darling should never have married Larry Olivier. She's a raving nymphomaniac, but she told me Larry couldn't perform unless she stuck her finger up his bottom. No wonder she's out of her mind!"

This, and more like it put an end to any further intimate conversation between John and me. But he'd got the message. John and his partner remained close and devoted to one another all of their lives, and I've always been grateful that this situation never went further than I have described.

But my life had certainly turned topsy turvey. The one good thing had been moving out to my own place. Now, when I went back home to Thomastown for a meal, my parents and I sat around the table and actually talked like real people, discussing current events, new television shows they'd seen, and asking, then answering, each other's questions. I had never felt more relaxed and comfortable with them. They had been to see me in the Kew Rep plays, and had come to both the Little Theatre revues and I could tell they were proud of me. This was pure guesswork. Lancashire folk don't over-enthuse. They were so happy in their new home with money to spend, and we often thanked God for guiding us to Australia. There were 'whingeing Poms' around, of course, but we could never understand anyone regretting coming Down Under. It had provided us with a life we would never have had if we'd stayed in Manchester.

And yet, I was already moving away from this new life I had fashioned for myself. My boyhood dreams of becoming a journalist had paled. I had been bitten by the show business bug, for which there is no antidote except death. A significant symptom of my unrest was that I cheated on my responsibility to the ABC by applying to be an extra in the film *On the Beach*, the Neville Shute novel about the end of the world, set mostly in Melbourne. Earlier in the fifties, it would have been shot on the studio backlot in Hollywood, but with the increasing popularity of television, more authenticity of backgrounds was necessary. Movies were venturing further afield for their locations, and early in 1959 the Hollywood bandwagon descended on Melbourne and deposited Gregory Peck, Ava Gardner, Fred Astaire and Anthony Perkins, as well as esteemed director, Stanley Kramer.

Now, I got a call from the casting people. Two day's 'extra' work at the Melbourne Showgrounds where livestock pavilions had been converted into studios. Not exactly MGM. Unless the initials MGM suddenly stood for 'Melbourne's Greatest Moment.' A lot of the kids I knew had been co-opted into standing all day in long queues, supposedly in line to receive poison pills to be taken when the nuclear cloud finally reached Melbourne from the rest of the world. This was exterior work and – by all accounts, pretty boring.

I struck lucky. My call was as one of the guests at a party, supposedly being held in a beach house which had been built in one of the Melbourne Showgrounds pavilions. I phoned in sick to the ABC, and just doing that implanted a guilt complex that remains to this day. But at the time, I didn't care – particularly when I arrived and found that all of the stars would be working in the 'party' sequence.

I was in seventh heaven. There was Fred, ever the pixie, doing a time-step, each time he fumbled a line. And Ava, looking fabulous and laughing and joking as if she were at a real party. Mr Peck, handsome and dignified. And Anthony Perkins, who had a reptilian quality with those nervous eyes darting everywhere, even then pre-empting the character he was to play in Hitchcock's *Psycho*, two years later.

We 'guests' stood around and were shepherded around the fake living room as various shots were taken of Fred Astaire (surprisingly cast as a nuclear physicist with a penchant for racing cars) giving a speech designed to ruin the party atmosphere as he pronounced we were all doomed! This lengthy diatribe demanded many retakes, not all of them due to Fred's inability to really get a grasp of this serious character. Once, a plane flew over, and in the non-soundproofed Showground set, it sounded like it was going to land right there in the living room. Eventually, with Fred – and everyone else – exhausted under the hot lights, a break was called.

The other extras headed for the canteen that had been set up to provide free coffee and snacks. I just went outside and sat on the fake veranda outside the fake living room, because I didn't want to break the spell of actually being on a movie set.

The veranda was furnished with a set of wicker furniture. I sat down, prepared for a long wait. I felt decidedly uncomfortable when Ava Gardner materialized and flopped onto the two-seater next to me, followed by her hairdresser, who proceeded to tend the dark Gardner locks. Should I get up and go? Scurry away? Or should I just sit there? Before I could make up my mind, Anthony Perkins came through the French windows from the living room and stretched out in a chair. I was fascinated. What would these two big stars have to say to one another. What inside gossip would I hear?

I sank down, trying to blend into the wicker like I was just a few of the strands. Finally, Anthony spoke.

"Ava, when you make a Caesar salad, do you rub the bowl with garlic first, then throw it away, or do you use garlic in the dressing?"

I couldn't believe what I was hearing. It was my first experience of realizing that even the biggest stars were human beings, not the magnified giants that they appeared up there on the screen.

Ava told him she liked the garlic in the dressing, which prompted further discussion on salads. Perkins was called away. Ava sat there silently, while the hairdresser fiddled endlessly. Had I actually become part of the wicker chair and was therefore invisible? It was if I was not there, because then Ava began to confide in her hairdresser that she didn't get letters from any of her friends.

"I had one letter from Lena", she complained. "But no more. Nobody writes me...." Her voice trailed off, complainingly.

"But Ava," the hairdresser replied, fussing around with her comb, "in order to get letters, you have to reply – and you don't write to anybody."

"I can't write," she replied with a big shrug. And then, with a playful dig at me, as if I was one of her pals, she turned and confided: "I can't even spell."

"Why don't you use a dictionary?" I blurted out.

She nudged me again and winked. "The words *I* wanna use aren't in a dictionary!"

It made me laugh. She laughed too. The hairdresser complained: "Oh, be STILL, Ava!" And then everybody was called back into the living room set, where Fred was about to attempt his "We're all doomed" speech again. These were close-ups, and the extras were not needed. I just stood in the French windows and watched as Ava entered from the kitchen and reacted to Fred's doleful predictions. It was a study in performance. Every time, during multiple retakes, she reacted freshly, and I saw what movie acting (*and* reacting) was all about. Around about the fourteenth retake, a heavy arm descended on my shoulders. I looked up at Gregory Peck. He looked down at me, grinning "I gather we're all doomed, wouldn't you say so?" Little did I know then that I would become great friends with the man who discovered him, *and* the wife he had recently ditched.

We were all re-called for the following morning. By that time, yet another snide article had been printed about Ava, accusing 'the alleged Love Goddess' of turning up late for filming the previous day. This was rubbish. According to the roster we'd all been given, she'd been called for midday, and that's when she showed up. The press seemed to have it in for her, more than the other stars. There were stories of the 'wild parties' she was throwing at the house she had rented in South Yarra, just a few doors along the street from John Truscott's place. Since the nearest Melbourne got to an orgy in those days was a keg of beer, a handful of snags on the barbie and a Patti Page album on the record player, even a Tupperware party was viewed with suspicion. I fully believe the remark attributed to Ava was her attempt at retribution, the one about the movie depicting the end of the world – "and Melbourne's the best place to make it." It has been denied in some quarters that she ever said it, but I think she did. When ex-husband Sinatra married the androgynous waif that was Mia Farrow, Ava said: "I always knew Frank would end up with a boy." And her 'dictionary' remark to me showed that Ava knew her way around a good quip. Oh yes, that Melbourne crack was her revenge for unfair treatment.

The two days of my call were over, and I went back to my job at the ABC feeling even more disinterested. I wasn't the same person any more. My emotional inclinations had finally been defined. My career path was no longer the one I wanted. I was a different person, but in the same place. I felt that I didn't fit any more.

Something drastic had to be done.

I decided to go back to England.

9

I sailed away from Australia on the *SS Fairsky* in April of 1959. I had done a lot of growing up from the innocent, naïve boy who had roughed it catching rats on a chicken farm and lived for two years in the middle of a paddock without benefit of power, water or sewerage. My ambitions had shifted from journalism to show business. My sexuality had defined itself. But uppermost in my mind in returning to England was to turn professional actor in a place where no-one would laugh at me if I failed.

On arrival in England, I immediately went up north to see members of the family we had left behind, but I made the reunions brief and quickly returned to London, where I booked into the Overseas Visitors Club in Earls Court – a haven for impoverished Aussies on their first trip 'home'. The accommodation wasn't much more than a single bed in a cubicle, but to someone who'd slept on suitcases in the back room of a rat-infested chicken farm, it was the Ritz.

I gave myself a week to get an acting job. If I didn't have a job by the week-end, I would take off for the Continent, do some touring around, then return to Australia. This decision, in a country in which around ninety percent of the acting population is permanently out of work, now seems like utter madness. Put it down to the sheer optimism of youth, coupled with vestiges of the naivety I thought I'd left behind in Australia. The five-week sea voyage had left me fit, tanned and raring to go. But first, I headed for Australia House in the Strand. That was where you went, in those days before credit cards, to transfer your bank account and set up a line of finance. There, I was shocked, but pleasantly surprised to bump into Patrick Tennison, my mentor from the Town Hall Round in Melbourne

Patrick had been appointed the *Sun-Herald's* London Correspondent, and he and his wife Olga, and their infant son Max were living in Chiswick Gardens. By chance, a neighbour of theirs was "an old guy called Doug Murray, who's some sort of theatrical agent." I told Patrick of my ambition to break into show business before that week was ended, and asked him to put me in touch with his neighbour. "But it has to be today!" I was filled with an urgency I couldn't explain.

Douglas Murray, it transpired, was a partner in the prestigious firm of Herbert de Leon Ltd., theatrical representatives who were not just agents, but personal managers. Commensurate with this status, their offices were in South Audley Street, Mayfair.

As I started up the thickly-carpeted staircase to their suite of offices, I passed Margaret Lockwood, who had been the reigning queen of British films since the forties and was still pretty big. If Herbert de Leon Ltd represented her, I was really starting at the top.

Doug Murray, a formal, elderly man, would not have looked out of place managing a bank, which he probably was, given the money they were raking in from stars of the magnitude of Margaret Lockwood. Seated across from him, I felt the force of his scrutiny. I had nothing to lose, so I reiterated what Pat had probably told him, that I was an amateur from Australia.

His assessment was brutally honest. "You're ugly. But you have personality, and I suspect you can channel it very effectively into character parts."

He continued talking, but it was lost on me. It's not every day you're told that you're ugly. It was a cruel assessment, and one that I wasn't willing to accept. Who would? I was no matinee idol, but I certainly didn't qualify to be swinging from the bell ropes in Notre Dame, either.

"First, you must join Actors Equity." He started to scribble an address down on a pad. "Their office is really quite close, and while you're at it you can register with a much more acceptable name than Ernest Swindells." He looked across at me. "There is no way that name is ever going to look good in a program." He tore off the sheet and handed it to me. "You can think up a new name on your way over there."

And I did. I was only two tube stations away. Had it been six, I probably would have ended up with something like 'Godfrey de Havilland'. As it was, I didn't have time. My last stop up North had been to see friends in Sale, Cheshire. It was spring in London, and every department store window had 'Sale' signs plastered across them. It was short. It was easy. Sale. 'David' was a good, solid first name that I liked.

David Sale. I repeated it over and over and liked it more and more as I entered the offices of Actors Equity and filled in my membership application.

The sting of Doug Murray's 'ugly' assessment stayed overnight, and actually projected me into an "I'll show you!" mood. The next morning, I pored over a copy of *The Stage*, and made a list of agents. I called about ten of them. Six of them granted me appointments the following day.

At each interview, I breezed in, telling myself I couldn't care less, and repeated what I'd told Doug Murray: "This'll kill you! I'm an amateur from Australia." And laughed a lot. But strangely, the reaction was positive. Apparently, a lot of Aussie actors had arrived in England and fabricated wonderfully fictitious CV's of their careers, like they'd played *Hamlet,* and then been unable to fulfill expectations when sent to auditions. Now, here was I, breezily confessing the opposite. And the agents laughed with me. A couple of them actually admitted they found me refreshingly honest.

One of them called back the next day. "Can you do a Scots accent?"

Desperately, I searched for a reply. "Well, I come from Manchester. How much closer to Scotland can you get? Of course I can."

The agent was not overly impressed. "They need a Carnoustie Bligh for *Sailor Beware* at the Roof Garden Theatre, Bognor Regis. I'm taking a chance on you, because they need someone right away and you look the type. In fact, they need a juve (juvenile lead) for the rest of the summer season. If you're no good, you'll just get the week's rehearsal and then the week's performance. If they like you, they'll ask you to stay on for the entire summer season."

And that's how I gave myself a week to get a job in theatre, and landed one in four days. I took great pleasure in telephoning Doug Murray and telling him airily not to bother looking for work for me just yet, as I was off to appear in weekly rep. This was greeted with stunned silence. I packed, took the train to Bognor Regis and went straight into rehearsals with the Pendragon Repertory Company for *Sailor Beware.* A week later, after the dress rehearsal, the producer, Roy Adams came and asked me if I'd like to stay on for the rest of the summer season. *Would* I?

And suddenly, I was no longer an enthusiastic amateur but a professional actor, actually earning a (meager) living from the stage. The rest of the Pendragon company was friendly and helpful. I was billeted with a nice family and was provided with my meals. They got half my pay, which was only seven pounds a week.

That summer was glorious with warm sunshine every day and a bracing saltiness in the air. Not that I ever saw much of it. Weekly Rep is a never-ending grind, but an excellent training ground for young actors. Our schedule involved performing the current play each evening, with matinees on Wednesdays and Saturdays, and rehearsing the following week's offering during the daytime. Lines had to be learned as we went along. An entire play was memorized in a few days, and that meant burning the midnight oil because there was no other free time. It was hard work but tremendous fun. And I was working as a professional actor for the first time in my life. Fortunately, I was a quick study but it was all surface learning. The minute the curtain came down on the final performance of a play, every line went out of my head to make room for the next lot. I couldn't quote lines from any of the plays we did, even just a short time afterwards. Now, I scarcely remember even the titles of the plays. But there were a lot of them, eight or nine, in fact.

I returned to London a seasoned professional…well, lightly salted, anyway. I rang the Herbert de Leon office to let Doug Murray know I was back. I found a new address – No. 10 Penywern Road, Earl's Court. I had the dormer (attic) room at the top of a very tall house – one of many in what seemed an endless row. In bygone years, my room had probably been inhabited by a 'tweenie' or serving maid of the lowest order, and was reached by climbing three steep and narrow staircases. It had a gas ring and a single bed. The bathroom was down the hall, and the telephone was on the ground floor near the front door. If a call came for me, I was summoned by a buzzer outside my door. If I had a visitor, I leaned out the window and threw down the keys. With all those stairs, one adopted as many short cuts as possible.

Then a strange thing happened. I got a call from one of the actresses with whom I'd worked in Bognor. Her name was Beryl Beare, and she had written a play called *We Dress for Dinner* which was being done at a place called the Hovenden Theatre Club, off St Martins Lane in the West End. After its first week, which had just ended, the actor playing the leading part had walked out, and Beryl wanted to know if I'd take over. There was no money involved, I'd only have two days to memorize the part, and I'd have to go on without a rehearsal.

Did any of this turn me off? No way!

She sent over the script immediately, and I spent the week-end learning it. My part was that of a fast-talking Cockney burglar, Theobald

Salticow. As the curtain goes up, I'm climbing in through a window, and I never leave the stage until the play is over. The occupants are at home, and they adopt me rather like a pet. Obviously, it was intended to be a comedy.

The Hovenden Theatre Club was up a narrow flight of stairs, in the Garrick Yard, off St Martins Lane. It seated about fifty people and had a small bar in one corner. It was a licensed club, which meant it was open only to members, and it could serve drinks before and after the pubs closed. The 'stage' was a curtained-off area on the same level, and backstage was practically non-existent. Valerie Hovenden, the founder of the Club was there to welcome me on that first Monday evening. She was a short, plump, formidable lady who obviously ran a very tight ship. She had to – it was her enterprise and know-how that kept the club open as a 'shop window' for new acting and writing talent, and she appeared to know everybody who mattered in both theatre and films. I sensed from the start that taking on the part at a moment's notice, was a good decision. It had put me right where things might happen.

The first thing happened immediately. As I walked in, I encountered a tall young man fronting up at the tiny bar. "Are you in the cast?' I asked. "Not likely," he replied, with a laugh. "I'm just a member." He had a nice smile and was very attractive. Then Valerie came out from behind the bar and I introduced myself, and she shepherded me backstage. She left me to familiarize myself with the set, which was so basic there was hardly any furniture to bump into. And I have to admit, my first priority was peering out through a slit in the curtain to have another look at the tall young man. Now, when I think of myself doing that, just before I was to go on in a play I hadn't rehearsed with a cast I hadn't met, I cannot believe it. Didn't I have any nerves? Didn't I have any common sense? I guess lust conquers all.

I have to admit I breezed through that first performance without fluffing a single line. Everyone else in the cast did. They were the nervous ones – they didn't know what I was going to do next. I didn't move around much. I stayed put and let them move around me, and move they did – or buzzed - with all the subdued but frenzied panic of bees that find a stranger in their hive. Thanks to the script, I had no exits to worry about. Once onstage, that's where I stayed.

There were about twenty people in the audience (including the Tall One), and they seemed to enjoy it. Afterwards, Valerie poured me a glass of wine at the bar and was very complementary. And, of course, I ended up chatting with the tall young man. He told me his name was Roger and he worked in stock-broking.

Little did I know I was talking to my partner for the next seven years. And little did I know that Valerie Hovenden was so impressed with my efforts that night, that she was about to throw a great opportunity my way.

I did my Cockney burglar act for the rest of the week, hoping against hope that a powerful agent or movie casting director would pop in and catch my performance. No such luck. But on the last night of the play, Valerie asked if I would come and read for her the following week. 'Asked' is rather a weak description. A Royal Command would better describe it. When I showed up, there were a lot of other actors waiting around. Valerie took me into a corner and handed me a script to read. After a couple of pages, she stopped me. "Go over to that table and sign your contract."

Not only was I stunned at getting the gig, but also surprised that the Hovenden actually used contracts. Contracts meant money. My surprise must have shown. "Oh this isn't for the club. It's for Malta," I was told.

"Malta?" Now my surprise detonated into shock.

"Yes. I've been asked by the education authorities in Malta to assemble a company to take a repertoire of six plays over there. We'll be in rehearsal for the next two months, and we'll fly there for four weeks, just before Christmas."

I turned the script back to its cover page. *The Moustrap* by Agatha Christie.

The next morning, I was on the phone to Doug Murray. This was becoming a running gag! "I'm going to Malta with Valerie Hovenden!" I announced. "I'm playing the lead in *The Mousetrap* and I have parts in five other plays!"

It was now mid-October, and London was shivering with the approach of winter. We rehearsed in the evenings, because most of the other actors chosen for the Malta company had day jobs. We were not paid for rehearsals, and would only start to be paid when we reached Malta. This meant I had to drastically curtail my spending. During the day, I stayed in my dormer room, huddled over the gas fire, learning my lines. I never went out. For food, I existed on toasted slices of Hovis bread spread with Marmite – the nearest to Vegemite I could get. I had become more Australian than I realized..

Each Saturday, Roger would come up to London from Chingford, where he lived with his family. Saturday night, we'd splurge on a visit to the theatre. Then he would stay overnight, and it says a lot for our compatibility that, even with his build, we had no problem sharing the single bed. Sundays, before he went home, we'd go and have a curry – my one cooked meal of the week. Needless to say, this diet regime had more effect than if Jenny Craig, Gloria Marshall, Weight Watchers and Pritikin had all joined forces to make me shrink. The pounds dropped off at such an alarming rate that when I saw some photographs Roger had taken of me in Hyde Park to mail to my parents, I was so shocked at my skeletal appearance, I couldn't possibly send them. "They'll think I'm terminally ill," I wailed.

Nowadays, that sort of shrinkage isn't just the norm, it's regarded as the essential emblem of being famous.

I was having my first experience of bitterly cold weather in years, and I didn't like it one bit. Apart from not having much flesh on my bones, my clothes had been bought for the Australian climate and offered no protection against the harshness of an English winter. I allowed myself one glass of red wine just to warm myself up each night when our little company gathered at the Hovenden. Rehearsals kept the buzz going. Valerie Hovenden was an excellent, if unorthodox director, and had assembled an enthusiastic but wildly assorted group of actors to go to Malta.

The Mousetrap at that time, had been playing in London for ten years and was already a legend. This would be the first time it had ever been done outside the West End. And I had the lead! We soon found the plot was full of holes. It really didn't make a lot of sense, but the magic of it was that when performed for an audience, the people loved it. And it's STILL going strong after all these years! A bit like me, I suppose.

The weeks passed and I existed only for the nightly rehearsals of *The Mousetrap* and the other five plays in our repertoire, and the weekends with Roger. We saw some terrific shows together, including the big annual charity event, *Night of a Hundred Stars*, at the London Palladium, and who should we bump into as we entered the theatre but Australian entertainerToni Lamond and her husband, Frank Sheldon. I knew them from Melbourne just to say 'hello' to in those days, but our paths would cross far more significantly later in our lives.

It was snowing the night our company flew out of London for Malta, and the weather over Europe worsened so much that we had to make an unscheduled landing in Geneva and wait for it to clear. In contrast, Malta, the largest of three densely populated islands in the Maltese archipelago in the Mediterranean, looked like a sunlit, glowing paradise. The islands, Malta, Gozo and Comino, are formed of soft limestone, the golden building material used in all of the baroque architecture. Our hotel was in Valletta, the city of the Knights of the Order of St John, and a place steeped in history. Our theatre, the De Porres Hall, was in the fashionable area of Sliema, located to the north on the other side of the Grand Harbour.

There was a great deal of antagonism in Malta against Britain at the time, and in going to and from the theatre for last-minute rehearsals, our coach had to negotiate several angry-looking demonstrations. Before we left London, Valerie had told us not to worry. We had not been foisted on the Maltese by the British Council, we had been invited by Malta's own educational hierarchy, and were therefore most welcome. And, like most of what Valerie said, this proved to be the case.

Besides *The Mousetrap*, I was also to play Malcolm in *Macbeth* and required to wear a blonde pageboy wig that made me look like MGM's girl-next-door, June Allyson. After I went into a rendition of her hit number *Thou Swell*, nobody could keep a straight face. Valerie told me very sternly to desist!

But *The Mousetrap* was to be our premiere, attended by the Governor and other ruling dignitaries. All of Malta's social elite turned out in their finery to make it a glittering occasion.

The performance went without a hitch. As has been proved over the years, nobody notices the obvious flaws in the plot, something with more holes in it than the ozone layer, they just involve themselves in the classic clichés of the 'whodunnit.' I will never forget the audible gasp from the audience when I revealed myself as the murderer. And when I was led off, suddenly and inexplicably as mad as a hatter, there was a big round of applause. Talk about my finest hour! Or maybe they were just glad to see the back of me! Less than an hour later, I was facing another bizarre situation that had nothing to do with Agatha Christie.

After taking our bows, the cast was required to attend a celebratory drinks party onstage for the VIPs. I mingled, was introduced to a lot of people including the Governor, and a top Government Official and his charming wife, and many others who all seemed happily satisfied with the evening's offering. After a while, the crowd began to disperse and I went back to the dressing room to pick up my bag. As I emerged from the stage door into the street, I looked for the bus which ferried our company back and forth between the hotel and the theatre. An attendant appeared and pointed to a black limousine parked a little way along the street. "There is your transport, sir," he said.

My God, I thought, they're doing us proud on our opening night! I hurried over and slid into the passenger seat.

Then I saw the driver was the top Government Official. I started to get out. "Oh, I'm sorry. My mistake. I thought this was -----"

"No, no, no. There is no mistake. I will take you back to your hotel," he assured me, and drove off.

I glanced around the otherwise unoccupied limo. "Where's your wife?" I asked.

"Oh, she is not my wife, she is just a good friend."

Something clicked in my mind. Yeah. A good friend, a *beard*, to be dumped when something better offered. This whole set-up was getting decidedly creepy. I sneaked a side look at him. He bore a more than passing resemblance to horror movie star Bela Lugosi. Even his voice had the menacing, velvet purr of Lugosi's *Dracula* as he guided the car at crawling pace and pointed out various buildings of interest.

My only interest was getting out of the car. "I'm so grateful for the lift," I told him diplomatically, " but we should really hurry it along. Our company is having a celebratory supper back at the hotel, and I really must be there."

This didn't faze him in the least. He rolled the car leisurely around the waterfront. "Surely you cannot deny me the pleasure of showing you Malta by moonlight?" he purred.

At that point, I'd rather have seen Glasgow on a wet Wednesday. "I'm afraid I must," I replied, faking a congeniality I didn't feel. "As I told you, all the company will be waiting for me at the hotel."

Maybe because he was distracted, he turned into a narrow street, and immediately a policeman stepped out of the shadows and waved us to stop.

I gathered from the exchange that my high-ranking chauffeur had turned the wrong way into a one-way street. I also gathered, by his commanding tone to the policeman, that I was in the presence of a rather powerful man, because the cop backed off practically touching his forelock and we continued the wrong way down the one-way street.

When we parked in front of the hotel, I practically fell out, muttering feverish thanks and good-nights. I raced into the hotel and up to the dining room, where all our company was already seated around a banquet table. Our Maltese manager and host, Captain Bugeja, grinned at me. "Ah – you escaped from our distinguished friend!"

I glared at him. "You *knew*?"

"He's notorious!" our manager roared, and collapsed into boistrous laughter.

That inflamed my anger even more, and I treated him and the others to a great show of outraged heterosexuality. "Well, just you listen to me. If you allow that man anywhere near me again, I walk out of this company!" Obviously, I was being a total hypocrite. If my exalted admirer had looked less like Bela Lugosi and more like Dirk Bogarde, I'd probably have still been in that limo, enjoying Malta by moonlight.

The next night's play was *Macbeth.* "Is *he* coming? You-know-who?" I asked our manager anxiously. "Because in this one I'm in tights, and once he gets a gander of me in tights, you'll have to tie him down!"

The following night, I made sure I left the theatre escorted by my colleagues to the bus. Our manager later told me that 'you-know-who' had attended the performance, alone, and that he was still sitting in his limousine down the street from the stage door when we left in a bunch. He was observed doing this on several other nights during our season, obviously waiting for the chance to catch me alone.

I loved our time in Malta, but I constantly had the eerie feeling that Bela was going to swoop out of the shadows and bury his fangs in my neck. At least I was bulking up on the unexceptional but hearty pasta-based cuisine of the island, and no longer looked like a forerunner of the later-to-come anorexia brigade.

We returned to London's freezing winter. Our trip had been tremendously successful. The company had blended into a family and it was hard to split up, but some of us would later reunite to repeat a couple of the plays in London.

My homecoming was made even better when Roger announced he wanted to move out of his parents' home in Chingford, to live in London with me. I knew our relationship was getting very serious, and I felt I had to be honest with him.

"I think I should tell you that I don't intend to stay over here permanently," I told him. "I love Australia, and I want to go back there, eventually."

"Of course you do," Roger replied. "And I'll be coming with you."

I was totally overwhelmed by his commitment. We began to look around for somewhere a little more salubrious than an attic in Earls Court, and as luck would have it, an actor I'd worked with at the Melbourne Little Theatre, Ian McDermott, was looking for two other people to share a basement flat in Montagu Square, near Marble Arch.

Montagu Square was – and is – one of those elegantly beautiful London squares arranged around a private, fenced-in central garden, reserved strictly for residents. Our basement flat, reached by steps from the pavement, was terribly smart. The rent was very reasonable, even though I knew I'd have to do something to supplement my miserable actor's income.

Thus began a wonderful, crazy year. And good old Doug Murray at Herbert de Leon Ltd, probably still reeling at this upstart from the colonies who kept getting work without his help, finally came up with a job for me.

The movie was definitely a 'B'-grade, called *Just Joe*, but I had no less than six scenes – most of them with Jon Pertwee, who would go on to become the second or third *Dr Who*.

Jon Pertwee turned out to be the most helpful, selfless actor I had ever worked with. He coached me on my lines, and subtly and unselfishly placed me in our scenes so that I wouldn't be upstaged. It was a wild experience, talking intimately to someone, barely above a whisper, with a camera lens glaring from about twelve inches away, and a whole crew crouched around it. Intense concentration was necessary, but because Jon and I had evolved an ad lib quality with the lines, it felt comfortable.

I refused to go to see the rushes at the end of the day. Douglas Murray's 'ugly' comment had hit hard. The tall Jon Pertwee reported: "All they'll see of me is the top of my head. I'm constantly bending down to talk to you." But he said it without rancour. A nice man.

I had a chance to repay him for his kindness. In my final scene, Jon had to be totally immersed in a vat of soapsuds (the comedy took place in a soap powder factory, with Jon as a research scientist and me as his assistant). It was the climax of a big fight in the laboratory. Jon ended up in the vat, and I had to deliver an entire speech before he emerged from the suds. "Please, please, try to do it in one take," he implored, "otherwise, I'll drown!"

It was a tongue-twister of a speech. Something like: "*Now* I get it! It's the black spreckles in Squizz that make every Monday morning a white washday." Try saying that on a movie set with the lights on you, the camera rolling, twenty crew-members poised with bated breath, and the star almost drowning in soapsuds behind you.

I don't know how, but I did it. In one take.

After *Just Joe* there was a hiatus, so I joined a temporary typist agency. Typing was something I could do really well, because of my time as a journalist. I was sent to offices on a one or two-day basis, and got a taste of the dull and dreary lives of the inmates. As soon as I appeared, they homed in on me, relating all their health/marital/family problems. I was a fresh face, and having bored each other to death with their whinges, they saw me as a new wailing wall and gave me every painful detail of their tortuous little lives. My God, the stories I heard! It was all too depressing, but the wages helped pay my share of the rent.

Then Valerïe asked me to do a couple of weeks at the Hovenden in her *Widow in the Bye Street* adaptation of the John Masefield narrative poem that we had earlier done as part of our Malta season. Again, I was appearing opposite an intriguing lady called Lorenza Colville, a Rumanian-born cross between Marlene Dietrich and Morticia Addams. She was terribly gentle and elegant, with long jet-black hair, and I was told she used Marlene's trick of meticulously filling every crease in her face with a paste of cornflour and water, before applying her make-up. I must say, it worked. Her face, under the lights, looked luminous. And she was praised for her 'superbly confident' portrayal as a village femme fatale. I got my plaudits for having "vigour, freshness and the enthusiasm needed to sustain a difficult portrayal of a lad torn between mother and mistress." But plaudits don't pay the rent and I was feeling the pinch, particularly as I wasn't being paid. During the day, I was still being a temporary typist.

The agency had sent me to Fortnum and Masons, the elegant department store just off Piccadilly. To shop there, was akin to being invited to a stately home, administered by bulky men in top hats and uniforms that looked straight out of Gilbert and Sullivan. The lady assistants were something else. Under a cloud of misty, blue-rinsed hair, their faces were peach-dewy masks. They all wore little black dresses and pearls and – on the floor – exuded upper class civility as if they were all from the aristocracy.

In reality, at that time, they were mostly disagreeable, illiterate harpies.

I was assigned to bring the correspondence department up to date. I found chaos. There were towering piles of letters from customers, with queries and complaints that had languished unanswered for months. Each letter was scrawled over with a rude, sometimes indecipherable answer from the sales assistant. I settled in and began to write charming apologies, inventing excuses for the non-availability of produce or merchandise.

The piles of letters diminished. Sometimes, one of the blue-rinsed, pearl-decked ladies in the regulation little black dress appeared at my desk, throwing a customer's letter down. "I don't give a fuck how you put it, but tell 'er we ain't got any," was the usual instruction.

I found myself writing apologetic letters to the Prime Minister's wife – the melons delivered for a luncheon at Number 10 Downing Street were unripe; and to Judy Garland, at the Dorchester, gently reminding her that a consignment of twenty pairs of pantyhose had not yet been paid for.

By the time I left, the mail department was right up to scratch, but I knew it wouldn't remain that way for long. They actually asked for me to return for the two weeks before Christmas, and it was as chaotic as ever.

I scored another B-grade movie. This little number was called *Crossroads to Crime*. It was set mainly in a roadside café frequented by transport drivers. Dressed in black leather, I was supposed to be a 'wide boy' who was forever playing loud music on the juke box.

The inimitable Miriam Karlin played the lady serving food behind the counter. "Fancy some chips on toast, dear?" she asked me jokingly when I first walked on the set. I felt at home with her immediately. She was appearing nightly in Lionel Bart's hit musical *Fings Ain't What They Used to Be*, and would later go on to have a tremendous hit in *The Rag Trade* on television.

I only did two days work on this film. Towards the end of the second day, I became aware that Miriam was waving at me to come over to where she was sitting. I'd had no actual conversation with her, so I wondered what she wanted. "Listen dear. You know I'm in *Fings*, don't you?" I nodded. "Well, Joan Littlewood's having a lot of trouble with the lads playing the wide boys in the show. They turn up late, or don't show up at all. Anyway, give me your phone number. If Joan has any more trouble, I'll pass it on to her, because I think you've done well in this gig." I was overwhelmed at this kindness from a woman I'd hardly met. Nothing came of it, but I always remembered her gesture, and happily enough was able to repay her kindness in years to come.

I repeated my role of Malcolm in *Macbeth* with the Hovenden cast, for a one-off performance in an outdoor Festival of Shakespeare. It just required a couple of rehearsals to refresh our memories, and then we did the performance. No money, of course, but I did get a mention in *The Times*. "Mr David Sale was a princely Malcolm." Better than nothing, I suppose.

The agent who had got me the season in Bognor Regis, contacted me with an offer to do six months with a repertory company in Staffordshire. I didn't want to do it. Summer was drawing to a close and by all accounts, Staffordshire was cold and grim in winter, like many of England's industrial regions.

I was still agonizing over a decision, when Valerie got in touch. She wanted me to do two weeks in a play at the Hovenden. Unpaid, but it meant work in London, and there was always the chance of being 'noticed'. I told her I'd do it, and knocked back Staffordshire.

The play was called *The Sudden Whisper*, a muddled study of – as *The Stage* put it "several types of failure, expressed in degrees of sadism in which the protagonists relieve their own sense of limitation by playing upon that of others." Sounds like *Big Brother*! It was a turgid drama, to say the least, during which I had to be chained to a fake rock, half naked while an artist painted my portrait. I remember the title of the portrait: *Adonis Unchained*. What a laugh. I'd bulked up a little since my starvation days, but I was still more fruitcake than beefcake.

The actor playing the artist was a thundering mountain of a man, Paul Stockman, who'd just finished playing a monster in one of

Hammer's horror films, and apparently hadn't got over it. Each time he lashed me to the fake rock, he really pulled the chains tight with a sadistic show of force more suited to a creature from hell primed for mortal combat than a fragile, sensitive artist on the verge of creating his masterpiece. Adding to my discomfort was the cold snap that descended on London in that early autumn. I was bare from the waist up, in a very uncomfortable pose, restricted even more by the chains, for most of one act – nearly forty-five minutes. I was hoping to get discovered. What I got was the 'flu! Oh – and a great notice in "The Stage": "There were beautifully integrated and moving performances from Susan Saunders and David Sale as ill-starred young lovers."

Doug Murray got me two or three bit parts in TV comedy series, but if it hadn't been for my typing, I couldn't have managed, financially. Early in the New Year, (1961), I had a chat with him about my prospects. He told me they wanted to promote me as the next George Cole, which strangely enough didn't thrill me to bits. Cole, who had to wait until late middle age for his biggest success in the TV series *Minder*, currently specialized in playing repellent young losers such as Uriah Heep. Murray saw the look on my face. "He's never out of work," he told me. "Stars don't go from job to job, character actors do."

Even so, the thought of being groomed as the next George Cole finished me off. Roger and I began making plans to go on the Continent in the coming summer, then fly back to Australia before the English winter set in. But to do that, we needed more money than we were making in our day jobs.

That's how we became charladies. Much to the amusement of our friends, we'd set off from our exclusive address every morning at 4am do four hours wielding the mop and bucket, return home to clean ourselves up, and then go off to our day jobs. It was tough going, but it gave us extra money to put away. It wasn't the untidy offices that got us down, it was having to clean toilets. That was really gross. At one point, too, I had to mop and polish the huge black marble concourse of the EMI building. Just as I'd finish, the first employees would arrive and one or two of them would inevitably spit a revolting glob of phlegm where I'd cleaned. I also had to polish glass doors, which they'd also ruin by pushing them open with the flat of their hands. To this day, I am always considerate enough to use handles.

One Saturday night we gave ourselves a much-needed treat and went to the opening night of a new show at the London Coliseum. As we left, we bumped into John Michael Howson, who had just arrived in London. "Can you come to supper?" he asked, "or do you have to stay behind and scrub the theatre?"

I was still doing my typing, odd bits on TV, and occasionally seeing casting directors in the hope of landing a well-paid part so that I could give up being an early morning cleaner. The casting people at Granada seemed very interested when I resurrected my Lancashire accent for them, and said they definitely saw me as a future possibility for *Coronation Street.*

With the start of summer, Roger and I took off for the Continent.

The weather was wonderful in Europe and we had a great time doing France and Spain on the cheap, but I never had any misgivings about returning to Australia. I somehow knew I'd have a better future there than existing in cold, miserable London and being the next George Cole.

When we got back to London, Ian McDermott told us that Granada had telephoned the flat several times for me. I decided not to return their calls.. We were due to fly to Australia, and I didn't want to delay our departure. In addition, *Coronation Street* was filmed in Granada's Manchester studios. I could have been stuck in Manchester for weeks, months, even years, depending on what they had for me. No thanks. I'd had my fill of Manchester. That place belonged in my past. I knew now more than ever that Australia was where I wanted to be.

10

Our first stop was New York, and our first stop in New York was Broadway. Cutting down on expenses by staying at the YMCA enabled us to buy tickets to all the current hits.

We also glimpsed life as it could be lived on Manhattan's plush East Side, provided one was prepared to make sacrifices of a certain kind. We had an introduction to a designer of stage costumes who had come to New York from London to work. This guy - let's call him "Terry" – immediately invited us to dinner.

His apartment was in a high rise (what else in New York?) right behind Radio City Music Hall, with a fantastic view of the city. Terry proved to be charming and down-to-earth. He, too, had originated in the North of England, and proved it by serving us a home-made steak and kidney pie for dinner. We enthused about New York and how much we'd like to stay longer than the week we could afford.

"There are ways of doing that," Terry told us. "It all depends who you know."

We marveled at his sumptuous apartment. I remarked that stage design must pay very well, but Terry winked. "It's actually my boy-friend's place, but he travels a lot in his business so I'm on my own for a lot of the time." A few drinks further on, and Terry was telling us what he did in his partner's absence. Our provincial jaws all but dropped, as he elaborated.

"Not to put too fine a point on it, I'm an Escort. Oh, nothing sordid, I don't solicit business, and it's all done with absolute finesse. My gentleman guest of the evening arrives, we have a couple of civilized martinis, and then he takes me to dinner – but only to one of the best restaurants in town. Then, if the subject comes up, we have sex. Simple as that. I enjoy a lovely evening, and collect a hefty fee into the bargain."

Terry saw our dubious expressions. "These are very wealthy, successful, sophisticated men," he assured us. "No creeps, kooks, or out-of-towners." He grinned disarmingly. "It makes for a very interesting social life, as well as a very sturdy bank balance."

Later in the evening, Terry took us on a pub crawl of several bars in Greenwich Village. At the last one, he excused himself to make a phone call. When he came back, he said: "Finish your drinks, we're moving on to see a good friend of mine."

We took the lift up to the top of an apartment building in Manhattan. The lift doors slid open and we stepped out right into the foyer of this luxurious penthouse that looked as if it had been designed by Vincente Minelli. I was beginning to feel even more like a yokel.

A small swarthy guy, a Danny de Vito type dressed only in a short, white terry-towelling robe, bustled up to meet us. We were introduced, he poured us drinks, then he regarded Roger and I analytically. "Terry, here, tells me you boys would like to extend your stay in New York."

"Well…it would be nice," I murmured hesitantly. I glanced at Roger. He was becoming as suspicious as I was.

"It can be arranged, you know," our host went on, waving his cigarillo like he was conducting an orchestra. "No problem at all. You'd have a nice place to live, and you'd be introduced to some of the most influential men in the Big Apple, and basically have a wonderful time." He winked. "And there'd be no problem with visas. All that boring stuff can be taken care of."

A few nights later, we went to Terry's again for cocktails. There were other guests, two very elderly guys who had apparently been in a relationship for something like forty years. We thought that was sweet... until they began fawning over Roger and me. I caught up with Terry in the kitchen, where he was refilling the ice bucket.

"Are these the sort of clients you have?" I inquired. "Well…yes," he replied. "Some not quite as old as they are, but they're all very wealthy and ----"

I grabbed the ice bucket from him. "Let me take that in," I said. "We need to hurry things along because Roger and I have theatre tickets."

We made our exit as quickly as possible. Old men's darlings? No thanks. I suppose it's ageist and shallow - but I wonder, after the success of *Pretty Woman* - how many girls pondered on the advantages of being a hooker, if someone like Richard Gere was waiting at the end of the rainbow? And how soon they'd be disillusioned?

Perhaps, underneath his fun-loving façade, Terry felt something of this. A year later, we received the sad news that he had committed suicide.

We continued on across America, catching Carol Channing's night-club act in Chicago, and another theatrical legend, Ethel Merman, in *Gypsy*, in San Francisco. We landed in Sydney in September. Sydney in the spring. For Roger it was a great introduction to Australia. Vivien Leigh was starring in *The Lady of the Camellias* at the Theatre Royal. At the Phillip St Theatre's new venue, later called the Richbrooke Theatre in Elizabeth Street, we saw the latest revue, *Yes, Please* in which the ebullient Gordon Chater performed his masochistic but hysterical turn, smashing and smothering himself with flour, eggs and custard pies.

I also scored a session with leading agent Gloria Peyton of International Casting. I laughingly told her of my amateur-into-professional career in England, and she said that if ever I came back to Sydney permanently, I was to get in touch. At that time, this seemed an unlikely prospect. Roger and I were headed for Melbourne.

I presume my parents got the drift of our relationship, even though it was never mentioned, never discussed, like everything else of a personal nature had never been discussed. But their total, immediate acceptance of Roger said more than a million words. In the two years I'd been away, they had sold the house in Thomastown, moved to another one closer to town, renovated it, sold it, and were now living in Thanet St, Malvern. This would be the pattern of their lives for years to come. I joked that they were the reason I had to throw out so many address books – their page was always full of new locations.

Almost immediately Roger became like a second son to them. My father, by this time, had become a different person. He was friendly, obliging, and – if I'd let him – would have crawled over broken glass to do anything for me. And continued to be this way for the rest of his life. The sad thing was that the way he was during my formative years could never be erased. Nowadays, when I read advisory articles to young parents, I long to underline the basic fact that the way you behave to your kids during the first years of their lives, makes an indelible impression that lasts forever.

Roger started work with stock-broking firm, J.B. Were, almost immediately. I paid the obligatory visit to my old stamping ground, the ABC TV Newsroom, to catch up with my former colleagues there. I felt totally out of place and although Jack Taylor offered me a job at 'C' grade level, I knew I could never go back to journalism. The following week I received a telephone call that kick-started my career in Australia.

"Hello darling," came the perky voice, "this is Toni Lamond. I've just been given my own *In Melbourne Tonight* show on Monday nights, and I want you to write it!"

I'd been spellbound by the talents of Toni Lamond since catching her as a young soubrette at the Tivoli, and subsequently as the first local leading lady in an imported Broadway show, *The Pajama Game*, as well as in numerous television appearances. I remembered the brief encounter I'd had with her and husband Frank Sheldon in London. On their return to Australia Frank, a former dancer, had been appointed as a TV director at Channel 9, while she'd gone back to working on the incredibly popular Graham Kennedy's nightly *In Melbourne Tonight* with predictable success. Graham Kennedy absolutely ruled Melbourne television. Already he was 'The King', even though it would take him several years before his reign extended to the rest of Australia. The Channel had now decided that to lessen Kennedy's punishing schedule of five shows a week, the Monday night show would be given to Toni, with Frank directing.

With typical hutzpah, she had decided to depart from the usual format of hosting a *Tonight* show from behind a desk, and do 'storyline' shows. And she wanted me to write them!

I was thrilled, not only with the offer of work, but also by Toni's faith in me as a writer. Television in Australia was then only five years old, a new branch of show business wide open for original ideas and fresh talent. Toni's Monday night 'themed' shows were well-received, and she, Frank and I moved quickly into a compatible working relationship. My scripts had to include regular IMT favourites like Rosie Sturgess and Buster Fiddes, and also one-off guest stars and interview subjects. One show had a wild west theme, with the Allan Brothers, Peter and Chris as the Dalton gang and Toni as Calamity Jane. Another was a murder mystery with Toni as Agatha Twistie, a Miss Marple-type detective. They sound corny now, and were probably a mishmash of styles but they were an entertaining mishmash for an audience that sat in their living rooms every night and lapped up enthusiastically everything this new medium had to offer.

After three or four of these shows, I arrived at Frank's office in Channel 9 to deliver my script for the following week, to find him looking grim. "We've been cancelled," he told me. "I just found out. I don't know how I'm going to tell Toni."

I couldn't believe it. "Why? I thought we were a success, I thought they liked us." My words tumbled out. "What possible reason could they have?" Frank replied: "Graham. We were too good. He didn't like the competition." Frank turned his thumb down.

I never discussed this with Toni, even though we have worked together many times since and are close friends. It was only recently I found out Frank had never told her the real reason for our cancellation. "But it comes as no surprise," she said.

My disappointment at the time was intense, but there were compensations. With Christmas approaching, and after a two-year hiatus while I was away, Irene Mitchell was ready to do a third Little Theatre Revue in December.

It made me very happy to be back at the Melbourne Little, even though it was more of a step backward than progress. *Truth*, Melbourne's notorious scandal sheet said: "The first night sizzled along at an electrifying pace." But to me, it was the least satisfying of my three Little Theatre revues. The chemistry of the cast wasn't quite as magical this time, and I didn't think the material reached previous high standards – and that included my own contributions, even though *Australian Theatregoer* claimed: "...most of the show's best material was written by David Sale, who in his own right is no mean performer." We had a new musical arranger and pianist, Alan Barker, but unaccountably, Irene Mitchell insisted on pairing him with a violinist. This 'fiddling', besides being squeakingly intrusive in all the musical numbers, added a peculiarly cornball flavour to what should have been a sophisticated revue.

I bummed along, writing material for Toni Lamond and others to perform on television, and did another revue, *Outrageous Fortune* for three nights a week at the Arrow Theatre. This was tremendously popular, and much more clever than the Little Theatre effort but unfortunately three nights a week on minimum pay didn't exactly fill the coffers. I auditioned for the Melbourne Theatre Company, and was almost immediately cast in a tour of Alan Hopgood's play about Australian Rules Football *And the Big Men Fly*. Of course, I accepted the job, but it meant three months away from home doing one-night stands all over Victoria and South Australia. We played in the most incredible assortment of ill-equipped halls, and our accommodation was similarly uncomfortable in broken-down country pubs rather than the more expensive motels. It was what the Americans call "a bus and truck tour". We travelled in a huge van along with the scenery and when we arrived at the next date, we had to unpack the scenery and help set it up before we even saw the pub, hotel, or whatever was that night's resting place. After the performance, we'd have to dismantle the set, load it into the van, then drag our weary bodies off to bed. The following morning, we'd drive off and the whole ghastly routine would be repeated. I played Harry Head, a football commentator. At one point in the second act, I had to sit at a table with 'co-commentator' Brian Young, as if in a box overlooking the playing field, and call the state of play of an entire football game, facing the audience. This was quite a stretch, considering I'd never attended a real Australian Rules footy match in my entire life. But I learned the lines and used my imagination, and a soundtrack of an excited crowd punctuated my commentary, giving it a quite amazing illusion of reality. One night I got so carried away, I jumped around in my seat and sent the table and myself tumbling over the edge of the stage. Fortunately, the audience thought it was part of the act and its laughter and applause covered the vital moments in which I picked myself up, decided I hadn't broken anything, and scrambled back up onto the stage to continue yelling excitedly, minus desk and on my feet, until the conclusion of the game.

This amusing debacle was actually topped when we did a performance at the Woomera Rocket Range in the barren wilds of South Australia. Woomera, as an experimental missile-launching facility, was always very much in the news in those days. Only a couple of days before our performance there, the Blue Streak missile had been launched successfully. So the scientists, staff and their families were on a high because after a long period of seemingly nothing happening, they had finally justified their existence by this bravura thrust into outer space. The brand-new theatre, as part of this high-tech complex, was the best we had performed in, but on top of that, the vibes from the audience crackled with expectation. They were in the mood to celebrate. So, when I artfully included in my frenzied football commentary, a reference to our hero scoring the winning try: "And there he goes….blazing along like a Blue Streak!", the people went wild. I got a standing ovation. The stage manager had to stop the background tape of cheering, and I had to sit there at my desk onstage, for literally minutes. So much for interpolating the right comment at the right time.

Back in Melbourne, I resumed my hand-to-mouth existence of supplying material to TV personalities. I wrote the scripted links between song numbers for musical comedy star Evie Hayes in her own series on the ABC without ever meeting the woman. I also did the same chore for Vikki Hammond in her ABC series. Every week, I supplied a duet of up-to-the-minute topical lyrics, based on the old vaudeville number 'Mr Gallagher and Mr Sheen' for American comedian Jonathan Daly, who had his own *Tonight* show on Channel 7, and actor Frank Thring, an unlikely duo to say the least. And as both of them were tone deaf without any sense of music, rhythm or tempo, the mess they usually got themselves into trying to do the number raised many more laughs than my sweated-over, carefully crafted lyrics. What the hell, it was money!

At this point in my life, writing was a lucrative appendage to what I saw as my real calling as an actor. Consequently, when I heard Garnet H. Carroll was planning a production of Rodgers and Hammerstein's *The King and I*, I saw it as an opportunity to enter the mainstream of Australian theatre. I auditioned, and was offered what amounted to a chorus part, one of a team of six 'boys' who would play priests, guards, slaves etc. in the court of the Siamese King. I took it, reasoning that with a show to do every night, I could double my income by writing during the day.

Garnet Carroll had originally intended for *The King and I* to be a cheap, fill-in production of only several weeks duration – a sort of Christmas panto. However, he had hired noted English director, Charles Hickman, and asked John Truscott to design the sets and costumes. Hickman and Truscott got together and persuaded Carroll to mount what became a sumptuous production that ran and toured for more than two years.

I was a little nervous about being fitted for costumes by John Truscott, given his earlier infatuation, but happily he had passed on to new sexual fantasies and was friendly but businesslike. His designs and costumes were lavish to the extreme.

Garnet Carroll made a shrewd move in casting busty, gutsy contralto, Sheila Bradley as Mrs Anna. She became blonde, soprano and lady-like (in the part, anyway!), and the transformation was symptomatic of her considerable skills as a performer.

Our 'King' was American import, Jeff Warren, who had worked extensively on Broadway, and in London's West End. He had a fine tenor singing voice which he had to downgrade to 'The King's' brutal rasp.

I soon became aware of the intimate family atmosphere that develops in the large cast of a long-running show. Despite the glamour and excitement onstage, backstage, behind the sumptuous sets, bereft of those dazzling costumes, witty lines and surging music, a village exists. A village of inhabitants that – unlike the villagers of *Brigadoon* who only surface once every one hundred years – materilises every night of the week. There are spats, love affairs, friendly bonding and down-right hate-fests. So many categories of human behaviour, and all embodied in the cast of a big, long-running show.

In *The King and I*, the offstage happenings far outweighed the drama nightly presented before the footlights. All the girls were required to have black dye jobs on their hair. Us 'boys' were instructed to get rid of all visible body hair. Thank God for that word 'visible.' Since waxing was unheard of, some used the razor, some depilatory creams. I used both. Unfortunately, in using a depilatory cream to get rid of my chest hair, some of it got onto my nipples and burned them. After that, even wearing a thin shirt was painful for weeks. We were also required to have the equivalent of what are now known as 'buzz cuts" and the remaining stubble dyed black. In those days just before The Beatles, before any kind of extreme fashions for men, our 'look' caused quite a stir, and some thought it extremely sexy.

For one of us, it would be the last haircut he ever had.

The show was an unqualified success. We settled in for a long run.

We opened mid-week, and at the end of the following week one of my five colleagues gave a party after the Saturday night performance. Not everybody was invited, because to have every member of that huge cast plus their other halves, you'd need to hire a hall!

The following morning, Sunday, the radio news bulletins headlined a sensational item. "Young actor from *The King and I* found dead this morning" Though it didn't articulate in so many words, the inference was suicide. No name was given. The first Roger and I heard of it was when we arrived at a Sunday brunch, and were greeted with pop-eyes and gasps of relief. Everybody crowded around repeating the awful news. What I couldn't understand was that some of them had automatically assumed that the unnamed actor was me. I didn't know why. I had everything to live for.

His name was Malcolm. I don't know why he had been chosen to be one of our group of six. He'd had little or no stage experience and to me, had no discernable talent. Malcolm hadn't been invited to that

Saturday night party. Someone later reported they'd heard him say "It seems I've been sent to Coventry." There was also a rumour that instead, he had spent the evening with one of our male leads. This was never confirmed, and neither was talk of a cover-up, financed by the Carrolls.

On the Monday evening, our first performance after Malcolm's death, we gathered in the dark of the wings, we priests who were now five not six. It seemed that somewhere, in the dark corners, behind the brilliantly-lit sets, Malcolm was still around. It was an eerie experience.

One Saturday, there was an earth-shattering scream during the break between our matinee and the evening performance but this had nothing to do with suicide. Sheila Bradley had just been told that one of the alternating cast of kids who played the King's children that afternoon had been diagnosed with measles.

Sheila was pregnant.

She hadn't found out about it until well into rehearsals, and for the time being, had kept it to herself. Now, when she heard about the measles, her resounding scream equalled any top note she'd hit as the sexy Lalume in the West End production of *Kismet.* Now, everyone knew her secret.

Fortunately, she didn't catch the infection and continued on in the part. John Truscott's incredibly voluminous crinolines, kept her increasing size hidden. But the famous Bradley breasts also grew bigger, and our show became a breast-perv's delight, so I was told, with certain gentlemen of the town repeatedly coming back for more.

Our body make-up, Texas Earth, was another problem. In the middle of a Melbourne winter, we had to strip off and daub ourselves with this red liquid, all over our bodies. And there were other discomforts. First of all, once applied, we couldn't wash it off, not completely. It looked great onstage, because it had a metallic ingredient that made our half-naked bodies seem glowingly bronze.

But there were side effects.

The girls found their everyday items of underwear, bras and panties, were turning orange and, more ominously, rotting. I had a sauna one day in an effort to sweat myself completely clean, and was shocked because what looked like blood was drizzling out of my pores. We all came to the conclusion that Texas Earth had to be bad for us. If it rotted our clothes, what was it doing to our skin? Efforts to gain compensation from the management had no effect. We eventually sued Garnet Carroll, through our union, Actors Equity, and it actually came to a court case which we won, and achieved a loading of about ten dollars a week which was supposed to enable us to cope with the effects of this damaging make-up. The sensible thing, of course, would have been to insist on a less drastic make-up. But we settled for the loading and continued to apply Texas Earth, subject our hair to harsh black dyes, and shave our bodies. In retrospect, we were stupid – but we were in a hit show, everybody loved us and hey, guess what, there was worse to come!

Since the Siamese tradition was that nobody could be taller than the King, everyone was on their knees most of the time, and the choreography incorporated routines that kept us, not just kneeling, but moving on our knees. This was particularly worrying for our girl dancers, all trained to the hilt and naturally paranoid about keeping their legs in shape. Kneecap injuries started to happen, plus muscle disorders due to us all having to use our knees as feet.

I was understudy to the actor playing the King's secretary, Phra Alack. When he went off with an injury, I stepped in. Or rather shuttled in, on my knees! After the performance, I removed my pantaloons and saw it – a large egg-shaped swelling on my right knee. I was out of the show for three days. At least I learned a lesson. I got two brick-sized pieces of foam rubber and wore them under my pantaloons, strapped to my knees forever after in that show. And with cries of "Why didn't we think of that before?" a lot of the others then did the same.

Apart from all the ills and spills, it was a happy time. There was the security of a regular pay cheque, and I was free during the day to write special material for television

Usually, I only saw the pregnant Sheila Bradley during the show, like when she'd come off after the strenuous *Shall We Dance* number, and warn us "Careful where you step, kids, I think I just dropped something!" As our season progressed, the number had to be cut down to accommodate Sheila's condition. I met her coming into the stage door one evening and was astonished at how big she'd become. The crinolines had camouflaged it brilliantly, but we all knew that she would have to leave us when we moved to Sydney.

I'd had no intention of going to Sydney. Six months of being a chorus boy was enough for me. Then the management offered me the part I'd understudied – Phra Alack, the King's secretary – if I'd go to Sydney. And not only that. The actor who played Phra Alack, also understudied the King! I'd be out of the chorus and into the front line. I talked it over with Roger and we decided I should accept. He had his job, our friends, a comfortable home with my parents, and the prospect of visiting Sydney during our season there. So we agreed that it would work out.

We opened at Sydney's Tivoli Theatre on July 17th 1963, to the kind of smash-hit reviews we'd had in Melbourne. Our new leading lady was Susan Swinford, who won headlines every actor dreams of. Susan had arrived from England as our Melbourne season was ending, and it was for her and Jeff Warren, our 'King', a fortuitous and welcome reunion. Susan and Jeff had played the romantic leads in the London, West End production of a hit musical, *Wedding in Paris*, years before.

For me, playing Phra Alack was far less arduous than running on and off as an assortment of priests and guards, but I was now understudy to the King. So for starters, I had to learn that entire part, immortalized by Yul Brynner, and now being portrayed to great effect by Jeff Warren.

Typical of the procedures of Australian show-business at that time, I was taken through the awesome part of The King once, and once only during an understudy rehearsal, soon after we opened in Sydney. I was afforded one orchestral rehearsal. I sang *Is a Puzzlement* and *Shall We Dance* and a couple of the King's vocal soliloquies, with the moves I'd copied from Jeff. Down in the pit, Isadore Goodman waved his baton amiably but dismissively, and sounded my death knell.

"We don't have to worry about David. He's got it!"

And I never again had either a vocal rehearsal or an acting run-through.

You hear the fairy story of how understudy Shirley MacLaine went on at a minute's notice in *The Pajama Game* on Broadway, and wowed the Hollywood moguls who just happened to be in the audience at that performance and whisked her off to begin her fantastic movie career. Well, let me tell you, she must have been very well rehearsed. With one rehearsal and one orchestra call, I spent the entire Sydney season scared shitless that one night I'd be pushed on in that gargantuan role.

It never happened.

But in order to keep myself proficient in the part, I'd haunt the wings, aping Jeff's moves as he performed. Despite our friendship, he objected to this. He said he could see me out of the corner of his eye, duplicating his every move, and it was distracting. So I was banned from doing it. It was a ridiculous situation, but unfortunately, it was typical of theatre procedure in those days.

And I was writing as well, contributing material to the revues staged by producer Frank Strain in a basement, under the Copenhagen Restaurant, in Kings Cross

Next stop for "The King and I" was Perth where in that November-December of 1963, the hospitality was overwhelming.

I tottered back to our hotel early one morning after some all-night carousing. As the lift doors opened at my floor, I was confronted by about half a dozen of our girl dancers going down to breakfast.

Sprung! I thought. But then I saw they were all crying. I blinked my bleary eyes. Surely they hadn't missed me all that much? And then they asked me: "Haven't you heard? John F. Kennedy's been assassinated!"

Everyone remembers where they were when they heard that dreadful piece of news. So that's where I was – hung-over in a lift with six weeping chorus girls.

With the Perth season almost over, I came to a decision. Enough was enough. I'd been in *The King and I* for an entire year of my life, and much as I'd enjoyed the experience, it was time for me to leave.

I rejoined my real-life family in Thanet St, Malvern. I did another late-night, two-performance-a-week revue, and resumed selling material to television. The rewards were sporadic and meagre. I began to feel that though I was making a name for myself in Melbourne, it wasn't exactly the kind of glittering career I'd envisaged when I dumped journalism for show business, or dumped London for Australia. I was doing what I had chosen to do but it was beginning to look as if it wasn't going to get me anywhere.

Roger provided an unexpected solution. One afternoon he arrived home from work, near to tears. He told me that JB Were had offered him his own department – but in Sydney, not Melbourne.

"I can't transfer to Sydney," he said. "Not without you." My response was probably one of the most unselfish decisions I'd ever made. "You came all the way to Australia to be with me. The least I can do is go to Sydney for the sake of your career." I declared this with a bravado I didn't feel. Of course Roger deserved my support in this promotion. I owed it to him. But even though I hadn't been totally successful in Melbourne, at least I was known. To go to Sydney where I wasn't, gave my insecurities a field day. Yet in doing so, I jumped right into the lap of a lady called Mavis Bramston and one of the most prolific creative periods of my life.

Our first Aussie home- the Thomastown "Bungalow"

The primitive way to take a shower while the house was being finished.

Three happy migrants - me and my parents.

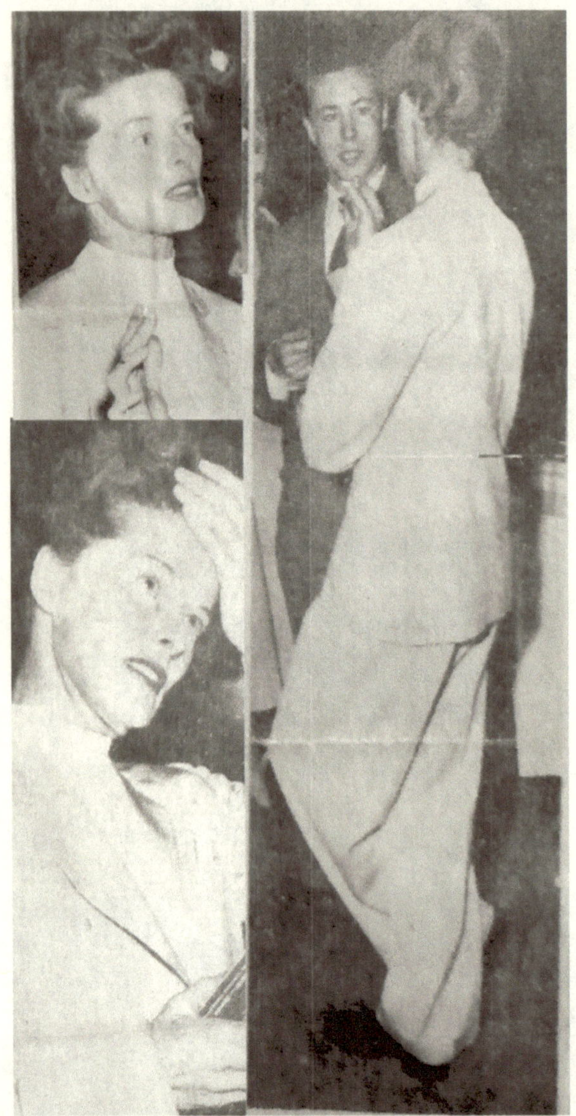

Katherine Hepburn and I make the front page

…and me!

Carol Raye and Hazel Phillips lie back and enjoy another stage hit

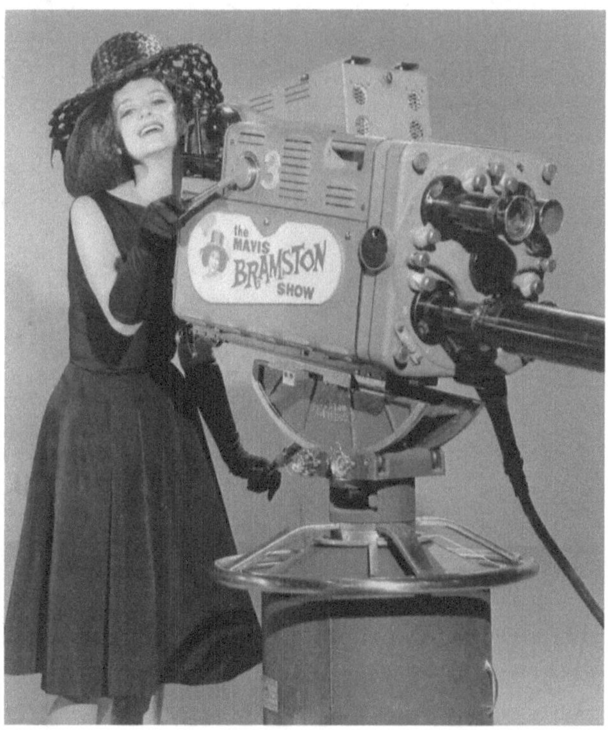

That lady! As played by Maggie Dence

"Togetherness"- Gordon Chater, Carol Raye, and Barry Creyton.

And now we go from the most famous lady in Australia to the most famous address in Australia.

The original residents of Number 96

Bev, (Abigail) makes a move on Don (Joe Hasham)...

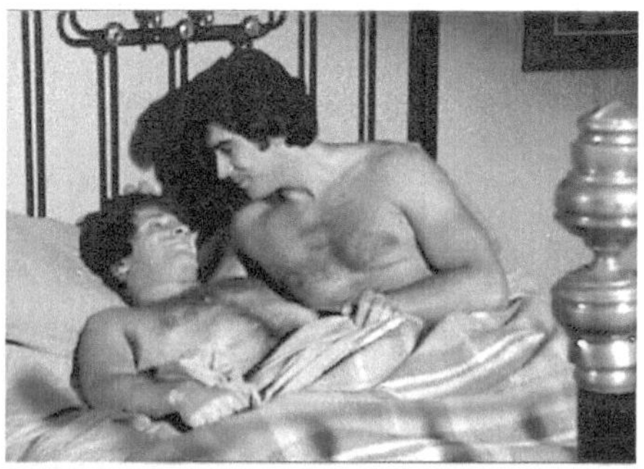

...but he seems much happier with Simon (John Orcsik). Wonder why?

LATE FINAL EXTRA

BIGGEST WEEK-DAY SALES IN N.S.W.

Daily Mirror

THE INDEPENDENT PAPER

TAB LATEST

BACK IN TOP FORM—SYDNEY'S BRIGHTEST PAPER!

Today's big 92-page issue of the Mirror is packed with bright, breezy news and entertainment for everybody. Just look what we've got for you...

CHICKEN KINGS!

The fabulous story of Jack and Bob Ingham, Sydney's "Chicken Kings", is told for the first time in a Pat Farrell special starting on Page 43 today.

THE SIX MILLION DOLLAR MAN

Meet TV's newest hero - P42

SUMMER SIZZLERS

1·8 MIL WATCH No 96!

AMAZING FIGURES

Our record ratings dominated the front page...

Fabienne bids to sell a TV sizzler from Down Under

NOT SO MUCH A PROGRAMME, MORE A WAY OF LOVE

MODEL Fabienne became a sales girl yesterday—and coolly stripped off her T-shirt as she got down to work.

...and topless in Cannes, Fabienne with Bill Harmon dominate Europe's front pages.

The varying moods of David Sale and Johnny Whyte.

Bill Harmon and me.

A night out – (from left) Johnny Whyte, Bunney Brooke, me, Del Harmon, Bill Harmon, and Pat McDonald

David's "Angels"- reunion at the "real" No. 96 after 40 years. (from left) Sheila Kennelly, Wendy Blacklock, me, Lynn Rainbow-Read, Deborah Gray, and Elaine Lee.

A recent chat about "Mavis" on Foxtel's "Playlist". Host Andrew Mercado, Carol Raye, and me.

Me with No 96's most distinguished fan, the Hon. Michael Kirby.

And the legend lives on. Two of the four popular DVD compilations.

11

Three eventful years later, there I was....a little dazed and numb having parted from *Mavis* and Channel 7, wondering if my career had peaked and my days of glory were over. I felt a bit like one of those Hollywood child stars when the 'cute' has worn off – and we all know what usually happens to them. I had time on my hands, and I began to socialize in earnest for the first time in years.

Roger and I had been keeping in touch with voice tapes – in those days, cumbersome reel-to-reels that had to be airmailed. All the months he had been away in England, and with my workload taking up so much time, it had been easy to remain faithful.

And then two weeks before he was due back, I became involved with a would-be actor. Having reached maturity with comparatively little sexual experience, and having spent the last seven years in a monogamous relationship, I was ripe for a bit of seductive flattery. I soon tumbled to the fact that he was an opportunist and a user, but unfortunately, not soon enough. I was still disentangling myself when Roger arrived back in Australia.

And that spelled the end of Roger and I as partners. Fortunately, there was no lingering animosity in our break-up, and he has continued to be my closest and dearest friend and plays an important part in my life to this day.

Alone in the apartment I'd bought in Neutral Bay, it was a time for me to coast along, basking in the afterglow of my *Mavis* success. 1968 saw nothing much happening career-wise except sporadic assignments like writing a weekly topical number for my friend Stuart Wagstaff to perform on his *Tonight*-style TV show, and special material for others. Strange offers of work materialized. Would I play the Joel Grey role of the compere in a revival of *Cabaret* at the Doncaster? No, I would not. Once you have held the reins, you don't go back to being one of the mules. Jon Ewing took the part and was far better in it than I could ever have been.

Toni Lamond invited me to her birthday party at a house she was renting in Bellevue Hill. It was a riotous affair, packed with show-biz people, but I remember it mainly for the moment when someone looking like a derelict who had wandered in off the street, approached me. "David? David?" I was at a loss, unable to recognize this gaunt, ravaged man dressed in dirty, crumpled clothes, his face obscured by long wispy hair and a bedraggled beard. He realized I didn't know him. "It's Peter," he said. "Peter Allen." I was shocked. I remembered him as the bright, clean-cut young performer who had come to the late-night revues I'd done in Melbourne. Now, he had split with Liza Minelli. His career was on the skids. And he was practically incoherent. I was making an effort to reminisce with him about those happy revue days in Melbourne when suddenly, someone thoughtlessly put a Liza Minelli disc on the record player. He swung around, staggered to the record player and swiped the arm of the player across the record causing an ear-piercing, gouging, screech that seemed to symbolize his pain. I marvel at the amazing resilience that enabled him to bounce back to the top from that period of utter despair, and that whatever angst caused him to react so badly to Liza's voice was soon gone. She was at his bedside when he died.

As I had no intention of ever going back to acting again, I switched agents, taking my leave amicably from Gloria Payton and signing with the international literary agents, Curtis Brown Ltd and its Australian representative, Peter Grose. And it was Peter that *Phillip Productions*, meaning the triumvirate of Eric Duckworth, Bill Orr and Paul Riomfalvey who had produced all the legendary Phillip Street revues, approached with an offer for me to 'devise and produce' a new stage revue to star Carol Raye.

I was flattered and delighted at the prospect of working with Carol again. In fact, I was delighted at the prospect of working, period!…*and* being entrusted to carry on the tradition of Phillip Street revues, the reason for my show business career to begin with.

Casting came first. Finding a male co-star for Carol proved impossible. Actors who can sing, dance, do comedy and look good were hard to find. Hugh Jackman wasn't around in those days. In desperation, I suggested that instead of having a male co-star, we have two actresses of equal strength. And this was how we came to team Carol Raye with Hazel Phillips in *Lie Back and Enjoy It*, a title I culled from the old saying 'If rape is inevitable….'

A strong supporting cast was assembled, plus a dance team of two guys and two girls. For material, I called on my tried and true colleagues, Ken Shadie, Bill Salmon/Harding, Ron Frazer and other talented writers.

It seemed everyone in Sydney's entertainment scene was waiting for the fireworks that might happen with two leading ladies vying for attention. Indeed, before rehearsals even started, I had a phone call from a concerned Carol. "I hope you know what you're doing, darling, with two ladies in the lead. They had dreadful trouble with the two Hermiones, Gingold and Baddely, when they did those West End revues together."

"Are you suggesting you're as big a bitch as Hermione Gingold?" I inquired.

"Well of *course* not, darling!" protested Carol, horrified.

"Then we have nothing to worry about," I said.

And we hadn't.

Whereas all previous revues had been a parade of unconnected skits, I resolved early to fuse this one into a cohesive whole, using style, colour and lighting. The urge to make it a visual experience as well as fun probably came from my recent television experience. Indeed, some critics saw this as a flaw, saying it made the production more of a television show than of the stage.

I was determined to avoid the last-minute chaos that always seemed to happen in revues, and to this end I assembled almost the full line-up of material even before rehearsals started. This enabled me to start the set and costume designers constructing and sewing well in advance. And as we went into rehearsals, I had two pillars of strength. My valued friend and colleague, Tommy Tycho was there to do the music and play for rehearsals, and spritely dancer Ronne Arnold, who was the choreographer. Both of them were wonderful assets and helped me cope with my inadequacies.

The only major worry during the four weeks of rehearsals was the lack of a strong solo number for Carol, particularly as Hazel had no less than three. I kept apologizing to Carol, who waved the problem aside, saying: "Don't worry, darling, you'll come up with something eventually." And finally, I did. It was a number called *I've Been Swapped*, based on the then-current wife-swapping craze. In it, Carol waltzed around in a floaty white negligee joyfully endorsing the custom because she'd got the best of the bargain – a virile young guy to replace her ninety-year-old husband. This number became the hit of the show.

Our public dress rehearsal before an audience of show-biz professionals was a disaster. The theatre was packed, there was an excited buzz, everyone was in a happy mood and prepared to…well, lie back and enjoy it! However, despite all my efforts at forward planning, the costumes and sets weren't finished, nothing seemed funny, the performances were off, and there were embarrassing glitches. I'll never forget Hazel dangling helplessly from the flies on a wire, like one of those gizmos they hang in the rear window of cars. She was supposed to fly gracefully across the stage as Barbarella – the Queen of the Space-Age Vamps, a send-up of the opening scene of the Jane Fonda movie, designed to show off Hazel's clowning, Lucille Ball-type talents. Unfortunately, it was a lot more *I Love Lucy* than we intended. The flying mechanism got stuck and so did Hazel. Valiantly, she sang the number like some sort of glamorous insect lurching and clinging to the top of the proscenium arch. They finally got her down, but she was so thrown by the experience – and no wonder – she misread the running order, dressed for what she thought was her next appearance, and had to do a sketch in which she was a suburban mum serving breakfast to her family, mistakenly dressed as Groucho Marx!

At final curtain, the applause was brief. The audience left hastily. Some of them told me later they were inwardly aching for me and the cast. It seemed to them we had spawned a disaster. After a harrowing post mortem, I went home and threw up several times during what was left of the night.

There's a show-biz legend that says a good 'dress' means a terrible opening night. The reverse also applies, and happily it did for *Lie Back and Enjoy It.* Magically, our opening night performance on June 18th, 1969 was a resounding success with not one of the failings that had afflicted the disastrous dress rehearsal. The crits were not only favourable, they were – in some cases – glowing.

"Cheers for the return of revue," wrote Frank Harris. "*Lie Back* rates with Phillip revue in its old top form which means, in first night terms, a happy preponderance of hits and a minimal presence of failures. Carol

Raye and Hazel Phillips team expertly as the stars with both showing a fine comic touch." "Revue Makes Happy Return", headed Griffin Foley's crit, and Taffy Davies wrote: "Revue returned to the Phillip Theatre last night. It might never have been away."

I was overjoyed to have maintained the high standards of Phillip Street. The show progressed into its season with healthy advance bookings. During the third week, the ever-hospitable Hazel invited everyone to her home for an after-show party. I drove to Greenwich where she lived and found Carol waiting for me in the front garden. It was mid-winter, close to midnight and she was shivering.

I grabbed Carol's icy arms. "What are you doing out here? Get inside – it's freezing!"

"I wanted to catch you before you went in. We've all heard you haven't been paid any money, and I wanted to say that if you're stuck for cash, I'd like to help you out."

It was true. The management had been tardy, but I reassured her that I was in no kind of financial trouble. And was knocked out yet again by the kindness I've encountered from ladies like Carol, Toni Lamond and Miriam Karlin in an industry supposedly inhabited by prowling, self-involved bitches.

Lie Back and Enjoy It ran for three months. It was not what you'd call a long run. The people who loved revue flocked to see it, but Sydney's long-term flirtation with satire was coming to an end. On television, *Mavis Bramston* had limped on, long after her popularity had been eroded by familiarity, a lack of cutting-edge skits and an unsuitable cast. Johnny Whyte had returned to London, and *Mavis* was replaced by *The True Blue Show*, which sputtered briefly like the last bit of a candle, then went out.

These were the dying days of revue. I wrote the title number for Ron Frazer's hit show *My Second Best Friend* at the Doncaster in Kensington. I did the same for a later show at the Silver Spade room in the Chevron

Hotel at the Cross, *Some of My Best Friends Are.* These were great shows with wonderful talent but basically they were there because Ron Frazer was the draw, rather than the revue elements. Ron had evolved into a star. There were no more revues in Sydney. Rather like intrepid warriors who won't surrender, two members of the Phillip Street hierarchy, Eric Duckworth and Bill Orr, retreated to Manly, where they established the Manly Music Loft. There, this last bastion of revue flourished throughout the seventies and eighties for the diehard fans who were prepared to travel. And they did. The Music Loft became an institution for lovers of clever, intimate shows in a restaurant setting. It is sorely missed.

After *Lie Back and Enjoy It,* came the question constantly confronting the freelance professional – what next? I didn't know it, but as the Seventies dawned, I was about to launch into the most diversified, creative period of my life. The downside was the threat of jail in a third-world country and the possibility of a scandal in Australia at the peak of my success.

They say you can't have everything

They're wrong.

12

I had been a journalist, an actor, a revue writer and now a producer/director for stage and in television. Every one of my recent assignments had been all-consuming and stress-related. I desperately needed to do something different and for advice I turned to the one person I could really trust in these matters, my agent, Peter Grose.

"What should I do now?" I asked him.

Affable. urbane, caring and down-to-earth Peter didn't even hesitate. "Write a book," he replied. "And *not* about television!" he added, anticipating the obvious. "There's already been one of those turgid so-called exposes of the industry written by one of your colleagues, and it bombed. So here's what you do. You write a book that has nothing to do with Australia, nothing to do with show business, and make it a sure-fire movie property."

That certainly gave me something to think about. I had just finished reading, and been knocked out by Ira Levin's *Rosemary's Baby* which fascinated me with its originality in the fantasy-thriller genre. I knew I could never be satisfied working on a run-of-the-mill plot – Plot 32B, as I came to label hackneyed themes. Like, how many books have been written about serial killers? Thirty years ago the subject was already getting stale. And yet, would-be authors who can't even write a laundry list let alone give birth to an original thought are still boring us with serial killer stories that all sound the same.

Not for me. If I couldn't be at least eighty percent original, I wouldn't bother. Having just been involved in the tail-end of one genre (revue), I decided to forge new ground by dabbling, not in science fiction but in science fact. This involved taking a new scientific trend and advancing it by asking the question: "I wonder what would happen if.....?" I discovered my ideal subject, an article on cryogenics, people being frozen after death to await the time when medical science could cure the disease that killed them, at which time they would be 'thawed out' and fixed up for another chance at life. Walt Disney was cited as one of the first subjects to submit to cryogenics, but this was quickly denied. However, there are those who still believe that dear old Walt resides in a freezer waiting to be re-animated, if you'll excuse the expression.

Nobody had written about cryogenics at that time, and I knew I had the basis for my plot. For the next three months, the only time I left my apartment was to buy groceries. I lie. I attended a couple of social functions I couldn't get out of, and spent the entire evening worrying about the characters I had left at home in compromising circumstances. They were more real to me than the people passing the salt. I hastened back home apologetically, to help them resume their fictional lives.

Everyone has heard of 'Cinderella' stories. This was a 'Rip Van Winkle' story. Beautiful 22-year-old marries rising young executive and gives birth to two daughters. She contracts a fatal disease, hubby has her frozen by a process in its earliest stages of development. Sixty years later, she's thawed out and revived. She's still twenty-two, but her daughters are in their sixties and her husband is an eighty-five-year-old senile millionaire. These were the ingredients I turned into an unusual thriller laced with black humour. I called it *Come to Mother*

I delivered the completed manuscript to Peter Grose, and after three months I was stir crazy. I jumped into the car and took off for the Gold Coast. I had a couple of very dear friends in Surfers Paradise, the entertainers Erris Venske and Kevin Byers, who always made me welcome in their home whenever I needed a break. They were the permanent attraction at the Grand Hotel, Labrador, and extremely popular with locals and tourists for the fun shows they conceived and performed themselves. These days, people do yoga to relieve stress. I had Erris and Kevin.

I spent a week lazing around in the sun, and then drove back to Sydney. But like the car, I was being driven. Another plot idea unrolled like a spool of film in my head....beginning, middle and end. By the time I reached Sydney, it was all there.

I rang Peter Grose. "I'm back."

"I read your manuscript. It's great," he said. "I'm sending it off to London."

"I'm starting another one," I told him.

"When?"

"Right now."

There was a pause. Then: "Sometimes, you scare me."

"Sometimes I scare myself!" I confided.

The Love Bite was prompted by an article I'd read about the world's food supplies running out. My plot dealt with cloning, again in 1970, something not yet touched upon in fiction. It combined cloning with cannibalism and a love story on an island in the Bahamas. Again, it was aeons away from the tired old stories about beautiful blondes being stalked by serial killers that continue to be churned out by mediocre copycats masquerading as thriller writers.

Like before, I was incarcerated in my apartment for three months until the manuscript was completed. By that time, Peter Grose had heard good news from head office in London. They loved *Come to Mother* and were about send it out to publishers.

I made a quick decision. I decided I wanted to be in London when *Come to Mother* was accepted by a publisher. "*If* it's accepted, don't you mean?" friends said. "No, *when*," I replied. I rang Johnny Whyte to tell him I was heading for London and he immediately invited me to stay at his flat in South Kensington. And, bless him, when I emerged from the formalities at London Airport, I found he'd assembled everybody I knew and had worked with into a welcoming party. All those familiar faces were there at the airport, and we piled into taxis and all crowded into Johnny's flat where more people arrived, Barry Creyton, Gordon Chater, Miriam Karlin and so many others. The party seemed to go on forever. This was a foretaste of things to come. Johnny loved parties, and he had many interesting friends. The character actor Richard Wattis who had played so many civil servants in movies and had worked with Marilyn Monroe in *The Prince and the Showgirl*, just wanted to quiz me about living in Australia, while I wanted to know all about Marilyn. Fenella Fielding, the gorgeously witty star of West End revues, was so funny she didn't need scripts. My bed was a couch under the grand piano in the living room. This meant I could only go to bed when everyone had gone. But when everyone had gone, Johnny always insisted on that one last nightcap, which always multiplied into three, four or five, and by the time I crawled under that grand piano, dawn was breaking along with my liver.

I loved being in London that summer. The weather was warm and placid. The West End was bursting at the seams with great shows. Carnaby Street was still flourishing, even though the swinging sixties were over, and I bought lots of the garish, tasteless clothes that defined the era. The parties went on, and I stayed in London until the autumn. I probably wore out my welcome with Johnny, but he never said a thing. Sober, he was a lovely guy and was extremely popular, with his London friends, with Australians and at the BBC where he worked on a freelance basis. A few drinks too many, and there would be an almost detectable metallic click in his eyes as Dr Jekyll switched circuits to become Mr Hyde. Anybody who crossed him then risked a ranting, vitriolic attack.

I saw this happen to others, but I myself was never at the receiving end of the tirade. We remained friends, drunk and sober.

Curtis Brown informed me that W.H. Allen had accepted *Come to Mother* for publication. I had brought the manuscript of *The Love Bite* with me to London, and I now presented it to the London office. They loved that one, too. My happiness knew no bounds. All the carousing became a celebration of my new career as an international author.

My thoughts were already on the next one. Typically, I didn't want to get stuck in the rut of just one genre. I began to research The Beatles. I gathered material on them from every available source in London and bought several of the scores of books that had already been written about them. My grandiose plan was to parallel the rise to fame of The Beatles with the story of four lads from Manchester (as apposed to Liverpool) drawing on my own early background. My 'Beatles' group would be called 'The Godforsaken', later shortened to *The Gods* which would be the title of my epic. I detail all this to illustrate how easy it is to veer off the track. I loved my concept for *The Gods*, I loved what was happening with my career, and I thought I could do no wrong.

Everything was wonderful, except I was feeling decidedly shaky. I was having palpitations, and periods of breathlessness. I went to Johnny's doctor for a check-up. "Sheer over-indulgence," he pronounced. I decided it was time to head for home.

I followed this sensible conclusion with one of my less-than-bright ideas. My plan had been to fly back to Sydney, with a short stop-over to see friends in Bangkok. Instead, I decided I would stay in Bangkok and write *The Gods* there. I was a writer. I could work anywhere, and part of the book was set in Bangkok, anyway. I obtained a three-month visa for Thailand, enjoyed one last big party to farewell everyone in London, and was on my way.

In Bangkok, I found myself a small apartment and moved in. I'd been helped in my search by a Thai friend of friends, Udom. He also helped me move in, did all the shopping to stock the kitchen, put me wise to everything involved in being a resident of Bangkok as opposed to being a tourist, and generally made himself indispensable. It also helped that we were instantly attracted to one another and he moved in, the better to look after me.

Udom loved to go dancing in the gay bars. I preferred to work nights. So every evening, after he'd cooked dinner, he would go out and I would work on *The Gods*. I scribbled away and the pile of manuscript pages grew at an incredible rate. Having someone to care for my every need released my mind to concentrate fully on the new book. After several weeks, Udom wanted to take me to meet his family, who lived in a village near the Cambodian border.

"You can't go there," European friends warned me, "it's jungle. There's fighting between rebel forces and it's terribly dangerous. Apart from that, you could be killed for something as trivial as your wristwatch and nobody would ever know!"

"Oh, I'll be fine," I replied. "I'll be with Udom. He'll look after me."

To get there, we had to travel twelve hours by bus, then hitch another ride out of the town of Udonthani. We were dropped off, as predicted, in the middle of a jungle. Udom's family lived in a house on stilts, not an elegant 'Queenslander', but a rickety structure between the rough floorboards of which could be seen pigs and other livestock in pens beneath the living area. As it grew dark on that first evening, we squatted in a circle around a single kerosene lamp, its meagre light casting sinister shadows and making every face appear malevolent. Nobody could speak English except Udom. I thought of the warnings I'd ignored and felt suddenly alone and threatened. All around, the jungle stirred ominously. I swear that if at that moment I'd heard the beat of toms toms, I'd have run off screaming into the night!

My terror passed quickly. I lived the following week in the most primitive conditions, in fact this made our early days in Thomastown without power, water or sewerage, like a stay at a luxury health spa. I didn't mind a bit. Udom's family, given the limitations of communication, showed me great friendliness and consideration, His mother chewed betel nut constantly. I remember she had a beautiful ruby red smile - and that was just her teeth! We slept on mats spread over the floorboards. Udom refused to let me eat what was cooked for the family and prepared all my meals himself. That sounds very grand. Actually, it was just rice and vegetables. I like to think he left out some of the more outlandish ingredients like frog-meat and spiders. One thing about serving spiders – everyone gets a leg! The 'bathroom' was a screened off part of the open deck. To shower, one just scooped water out of a huge earthenware pot, and Udom insisted I wear a towel around my middle while doing this. "Someone might see," he cautioned. It was terrible to throw water over oneself with a wet towel flapping around one's middle. One day, everyone had gone into the village, so I bathed without the towel. On his return, Udom glared at me. "You showered with nothing on!" he declared accusingly. "How do you know?" I asked. "Everyone was peeping," he replied, pointing to the wide cracks in the decking floor and the screen.

I was an object of fascination for the children of the village. I was the first Caucasian they had ever seen, and with their little button noses, they thought mine was enormous. I yelled: "You should'a seen it before I had it fixed!" Despite the primitive conditions, they were well-fed and healthy. A lot of this was due to UNESCO supplies. The local schoolteachers asked me to if I would take some photographs they could send to UNESCO to show how much their help was benefiting the children. I shot two reels of film, showing the various activities, the milk being doled out, the school stationary and books being used, things like that. Then I thought 'What the hell' and gave them the camera, too, so that they could do it themselves in the future.

Towards the end of the week, I became aware of much gabbling between Udom and his parents. Finally, he told me what it was all about. They wanted us all to go to a nearby temple, where Udom and I would participate in a ceremony that would end with us having ours wrists tied together with some kind of symbolic twine. The obvious dawned on me. It was a form of marriage.

"Not without a pre-nup!" I wanted to say. Even though by now totally immersed in a romantic tropical Dorothy Lamour/Maria Montez fantasy, some vestige of sanity prevailed. I smiled and managed to indicate my reluctance, possibly on religious grounds, while marvelling at their totally unprejudiced acceptance of me as a partner for their son. It also entered my addled mind that they saw me as a rather rich meal ticket to welcome into the family circle, with mother-in-law able to buy absolute harvests of betel nuts with the alimony flooding in from Australia.

We returned to Bangkok and the remaining weeks passed quickly. The first draft manuscript was finished. I was due to fly out one Saturday. On the Thursday night, I applied myself to filling out my airport departure forms, and I noticed a curious addendum on the three-month visa for Thailand in my passport. 'This visa must be ratified after six weeks'. Needless to say, I hadn't done it.

"Will it matter?" I asked my European friends on the phone. "Should I just turn up at the airport and say I forgot to do it?"

By now, I am convinced they thought I was quite mad. "You can't turn up at the airport with a visa that hasn't been ratified. They've had a lot of trouble with hippies blatantly and illegally over-staying. They'll throw you in jail!"

"What if I slip a few thousand baht notes into my passport when I hand it over?" I asked, ever the innocent.

"They'll take the money and STILL throw you in jail," my friends told me. “Here’s what you do. You cancel Saturday’s flight and book another for next week. Tomorrow, go and see the British Consul and ask him to write a letter explaining the situation, which you can take to Thai immigration.”

I followed instructions. The British Consul dictated a very sympathetic letter, explaining that I was ‘a famous author’ who had become so involved in writing his latest best-seller, I’d inadvertently allowed my visa to lapse. He thought that having a plane ticket back to Australia the following week would count in my favour. “But you’re not to go to Immigration until Monday. If you go this afternoon (Friday) they won’t want to be bothered and they’ll just throw you in jail for the week-end. And if you know anything about Thai jails, even a week-end would be too much!”

That word ‘jail’ kept coming up! With a further warning. "Don’t tell anyone about this. Someone might turn you in for a reward and they’d come and arrest you.”

For the entire week-end I was, as they say in film noir movies, ‘on the lam.’ We had to get out of the apartment, because the lease was up. So I spent Saturday and Sunday living with friends of Udom in the poor part of town, feeling like a crim on the run. Which I was. Frankly, I was scared to death. The British Consul told me that when I went to front up to Thai Immigration with his letter, I should have a friend stationed outside. If I did not reappear within two hours, that friend was to report my disappearance to him immediately. “People have gone missing,” he said ominously. “Sometimes we never locate them.”

Monday morning, I fronted up at the imposing building that housed the Immigration Department. I left Udom on a bench outside with strict instructions what to do if I failed to reappear, and approached the entrance with all the deadly resolve that must have impelled Anna Karenina to walk into that steam-belching train.

Inside, I was directed through a number of departments. Illegal Immigrants. Suspected Aliens. Unwanted Settlers. There could have been a final one called Dispensable Idiots, but maybe that's just in my mind. By the time I found myself in the wood-panelled office of some military chief, I was totally intimidated. So intimidated and frightened, that today, I would think twice about packing an aspirin on a trip to Bali.

A taut and terrific military man in full dress uniform faced me from the other side of the desk. He looked like Jackie Chan auditioning for the part of Mussolini.

Being in those days, a slave to nicotine, I immediately fumbled for a cigarette. As I lit it, he shoved a large glass ashtray towards me.

Saved! It was an act of courtesy, and it gave me hope that I wasn't going to be treated like some drugged-up dead-beat. Jackie/Mussolini strode around the room, proclaiming Thailand's reasons for keeping undesirables out, and if not out, then imprisoned as punishment for their blatant misdemeanors. I had a sudden feeling of déjà vu. It was like I was back in *The King and I* and this was His Majesty strutting around imperiously. I quickly rejected assuming the prickly role of Mrs Anna, and remained silent in my chair....more like the submissive Tuptim.

Finally, his tirade was over. After a long scruitiny of my passport, he put me out of my misery. "Your visa will be re-endorsed without penalty."

There was a tearful farewell with Udom at the airport a few days later, and I flew off in blissful ignorance of what had really been going on. While I had been working in the evenings, Udom had been working too – turning tricks, two or three a night, before coming home and sliding into bed with me. I had been shacked up with a male hooker and I didn't even know it. I'm grateful I survived this period without catching any communicable social diseases. I am even more grateful that AIDS hadn't yet reared its ugly head. As it was, in my ignorance

I kept in contact by letter and telephone, maintaining my emotional involvement and I didn't learn the truth until it was too late. Fate was saving that little bombshell for the future.

On my return to Sydney, my unit was still occupied so I accepted Roger's hospitality in the terrace house he had bought and renovated so beautifully in Kirribilli. He hosted a welcome home party the following week-end. A memory lingers of a small but voluptuous blonde who for reasons known only to herself had taken off her clothes and was lolling in a corner of the room in only her well-filled bra and panties. Eventually, she was persuaded to put on her dress and leave with the remainder of the guests.

I didn't know what she was doing there; I'd never seen her before. I didn't know her name and I don't even remember talking to her. But she was later to feature very prominently in my professional life.

After six months away, funds were low. Peter Grose had several possibilities lined up, but one he favoured was for me to write two or three episodes of a situation comedy called *The Group*. The original concept and pilot were goers, and the production team of Bill Harmon and Don Cash desperately needed writers for a projected series.

I was curious. "If they're so desperate, why do they only want me to write two or three episodes?" "They can't afford to pay your asking price for more," Peter replied.

I ended up writing nine episodes of *The Group's* thirteen episode season. Bill and Don must have raised my money somehow, and we developed a fruitful working relationship. Bill was impressed that I could turn out scripts in double-quick time. I liked the way he could invariably put his finger on the weakest part of a script, then come up with a positive suggestion to fix it. He was no writer, and his suggestion might not work, but it would lead me to think of something stronger. He was always utterly supportive.

The Group was based on the simple premise of five young people sharing an apartment together, three boys and two girls. It won a Logie for that year's best situation comedy. This was probably because it was that year's *only* situation comedy.

Along the way, I moved back into my Neutral Bay apartment. *Come to Mother,* was due for publication in London, six months hence, in June. But there were problems. W.H. Allen asked if a black character, a gigolo type who had affair with an older white woman, could be changed to a white man. The miscegenation angle, they warned, could lead to the book being banned in South Africa, losing me the sale of perhaps thousands of copies. I wrote back saying: "No way. I refuse to help the racist government of South Africa dictate what the rest of the world should read." My letter got delayed in a British mail strike. The next I heard from W.H. Allen was this: "Since we have not heard from you, we have made George white."

Telephones ran hot, cables flew but the publishers would not relent. I appealed to Curtis Brown in London to intervene, and it was from them I eventually had the good news that they had stopped the presses and George was being changed back into a Negro. In Sydney, *The Australian* covered the debacle under the headline: *When the Negro Turned White, David Saw* Red.

After I'd handed in my final script for *The Group*, Bill and Don took me out to dinner. At one point, I excused myself to go to the bathroom. When I returned there was a small box on my plate. It contained an expensive pair of cufflinks. I was extremely touched. I'd been well paid for my efforts and didn't feel this gesture was necessary, but I appreciated it. If they had an ulterior motive in getting me on-side for the future, they needn't have bothered. I was already on-side. Bill, a Jewish guy from Brooklyn, was the full brash New Yorker, tough but a softie underneath. His experience in show business was impressive, from working on television with big stars of the day such as Jimmy Durante and Betty Hutton. Don was more Conservative, always impeccably dressed, whereas Bill didn't own a tie. Don was the financial numbers man, bookish, intelligent and reserved. To describe them, I always coined what someone said about Spencer Tracy and Katherine Hepburn – "He gives her sex, she gives him class." And so it was with the professional partnership of Bill and Don.

My work on their series had earned me enough for my plane ticket to London for the debut of my first novel. I had organized for a friend to house-sit for me, and when he moved in, I moved out to Roger's in Kirribilli for the week leading up to my departure. With only five days to go, my agent, Peter Grose, telephoned.

"Bill and Don have invited us to lunch tomorrow. They want to talk about your doing another series for them." I didn't want to be bothered. "But I leave on Friday." This was Monday. Peter persisted. "They want you and they won't be happy with anyone else."

"How much are they paying?"

"Two hundred dollars."

"For a treatment? You'd pay more for a treatment for hives!" Even in those days, it was peanuts. But Bill and Don were such nice guys. I was wavering. "Where are they taking us?"

"Beppi's" Peter replied.

That won me over. It was my favourite Italian restaurant. I guess you could say I was seduced by visions of mussels meuniere and spaghetti marinara. When people ask "Are you ruled by your head or your heart?" I would have to reply: "My stomach." And it was that decision that totally changed the course of my life for the next six years and gave me possibly my biggest success.

13

A lot of misinformation has been printed about the groundbreaking television series entitled *Number 96*. Similarly, there have been many claims of participation in the creative processes leading to its success that have no basis in fact. These are some of the reasons why I decided to put the details of my life and the creation of *Number 96* on record, together with as much background information as I can recall. I was there before *Number 96* even had a name. I was there during its incredibly successful run. I was there behind the scenes while it was in production, and I was out there when it was acclaimed in public. What I write is accurate.

The misinformation predates even my lunch with Bill and Don, before I knew anything about their new project.

In one publication, an alleged review of Australian television, Ken James who appeared as one of the young people in *The Group* recalls an intimate conversation I had with him on the set of that show, in which I confided that I was writing a controversial new series and I planned to call it *Number 69*. "Oh no," he recalls warning me. "That's far too suggestive." And as a result of this warning from a sage, tender in years but far more mature in matters of morals (and sexual practices), I apparently had second thoughts, and switched the numbers.

This story is absolute rubbish. It never happened.

The possibility of my participation in another series for Cash-Harmon did not occur until well after my chores for *The Group* had been completed. Furthermore, I would have no more engaged Ken James in a confidential exchange, than I would Bobo the Clown.

I detail this to illustrate that whatever crap goes into print becomes history, and that is a danger. This same dubious publication has me as one of the creators of *The Mavis Bramston Show* – again, incorrect. Neither of the two compilers of this travesty of historical facts bothered to contact me to confirm any of the information they connected with my name. Which is why I sympathise with today's superstars when they complain of the totally unfounded rubbish that is written about them in the trash magazines.

My agent, Peter Grose and I met up with Bill Harmon and Don Cash at Beppi's. They told us that Channel Ten had commissioned them to come up with a concept for a continuing series. A soap, in other words, but in this instance, a night-time soap. I was still unimpressed. Loved the food, didn't care about the rest. My sights were set on London and the publication of my first novel. All Bill and Don had was one idea – people living in a block of flats.

"Like a perpendicular *Coronation Street*? A high-rise village?" I ventured. Something inside of me twitched, and I didn't know whether it was an idea or one of the mussels was off.

Bill and Don pounced. "We can show you the location." We all piled into a car and went to Moncur Street, Paddington and the unimpressive block of flats that was to become the most famous address in Australia. My brain started to clock in as we drove back to the city. I was working on it, even though I didn't quite realise it. "There'd have to be a tremendously diverse cast of residents to maintain the storylines," I ventured. "Yeah, yeah," Bill nodded enthusiastically. Ideas began to flip over in my mind. A migrant couple from Lancashire, like my parents. A sticky-beak old man like the one in my block in Neutral Bay. And the two shops that fronted the building. Maybe one of them could be a Greek delicatessen? And as for diversity, fuelled by a good lunch and the fact that I was having a book published in London and I didn't give a damn, I asked: "And how about putting two homosexuals into one of the flats?"

To his credit, Bill didn't bat an eye. "Great," he rasped. "Give me homosexuality without any deviations!" I never quite worked out what he meant by that, but I took it as a yes.

They eventually dropped me off back at Roger's house in Kirribilli. Roger was preparing to go out for dinner. Left alone, I grabbed a half-bottle of scotch and went and sat on the floor in a corner of his living room with a pad and ballpoint. Ironically, it was the corner the blonde who'd divested herself of her clothes had propped herself up in at my welcome home party there.

I started to write. My presentation was different to the usual bald statement of facts. I decided to take the reader by the hand and lead him/her into the world of my concept, as if we were taking a stroll around the neighbourhood.

"Walk down any street in that once-unfashionable suburb near to town, where you wouldn't have ventured ten years ago," I began.

"Walk there now because it's safe, it's pleasing to the eye, and you get a vicarious thrill because now it's 'in' and it's the part of the city where the smart set rubs shoulders with the old die-hards who have lived there for years.

"Notice the refurbished terrace houses…peer into the windows of smart shops….gaze upwards at the modern blocks of units that push their way inbetween the one and two story relics of yesterday's housing with superior aloofness."

And so I continued, conjuring up the sights, smells and sounds of Paddington in colourful detail until finally: "Walk on until you see a small block of apartments. Let us move inside and meet the people living there, flat by flat."

Oh, those characters. At the time, it seemed all the people in the American sit-coms we were inundated with were presented as perfect specimens: perfect morals, perfect manners, perfect families, perfect hair, perfect clothes. I decided that the characters I invented for this new show of mine would all have faults and peculiarities – but doesn't everyone in the Real World? I based a Lancashire migrant couple on my mother and father, and I even used my own mother's name Lucy. My father loved Australia, but to provide conflict, Alf Sutcliffe would have to be a whingeing pom. I thought of the sticky-beak old geezer in my own block of flats, and did a gender change making him an overbearing woman with a compliant hubby. They had owned the original house on the land, and when they sold to developers they had been given one of the flats. Therefore, in their mentality, the ownership factor still kicked in. I had recently met a guy who worked in the financial sector. He was blonde with rimless glasses, short but very attractive, and he was the epitome of the discreetly-living gay. I based the character of Don on him, the young law student living with a more flamboyant bisexual fashion photographer who was also involved with a media-manipulative older woman. I mixed in Bev, a sexy Harbour cruise hostess, and a shady lady called Vera Collins, who was everybody's friend, including a succession of totally unsuitable men.

None of these characters had names at this stage. I hauled the Sydney telephone directory down on the floor beside me and without looking, began to flip the pages, prodding my biro down, and using whatever name the point had landed on.

It was getting close to midnight. The scotch was getting low, so I started on the storylines for these people. They were all so interesting and diverse, I had no difficulty in writing four pages of plot ideas which were still being drawn upon two years later.

The summary of my treatment that I have quoted above is the finished article. But that night, when it was all just scribbled notes, I had no title. I decided on a temporary label. Anne Deveson and I had reduced the title of our Carol Raye sitcom to 7D, so I went for numbers again. I thought that I could think up a clever title if and when my treatment was accepted. In the meantime, I would stick an identifying number on it, the street number of the apartment block. I rolled it over in my mind, going for alliteration, given that 'N' was the first letter of 'Number'. The possibilities rolled past. *Number Nine....Number Nineteen......Number Ninety*. Finally, *Number Ninety-Six* seemed to have the correct rhythm. I settled on that, without a thought of what connotation would be placed upon it later.

The next day, I typed it all up and sent it off to Bill and Don. And the following day, I flew out to London for the publication of my first novel.

I have set out the process by which the series that became *Number 96* evolved for a good reason. The published November 2012 obituary of TEN's then Director of Production, Peter Skelton, written by his son, named Skelton "co-creator of the hugely popular series *Number 96*". And later in the obituary: ".......with TEN's Program Director, Ian Holmes, conceived *Number 96*."

Note the use of the words 'co-creator' and 'conceived', both indicating an artistic, inventive and creative flow of ideas into a project that was already brimming with life. This, of course, never happened. All these gentlemen did, faced with a Channel TEN that was hopelessly in the red, was ask – or 'commission' if you want to indulge in the grandiose expressions of television executives – the independent producers Cash-Harmon to come up with a continuing drama series that, somehow, would grab the ratings. Nothing more. At that stage, there was no concept, no characters, no situations, no title, nothing. So how can you 'co-create' or 'conceive' something that doesn't even exist? Bill Harmon and Don Cash contributed the idea of using the block of flats in Moncur Street. After that, I was on my own when I settled down that evening – with no input from anyone else, least of all from television executives – and poured all my ideas into an original treatment, a copy of which I have to this day, and which conforms exactly to what eventually ended up onscreen.

I never even met the two gentlemen I've named until after the show premiered on air. Despite their later claims, I always found them able guys and certainly a cut above the usual run of TV executives. But as for *Number 96*, it premiered exactly how I alone had conceived it, and with scripts written by me and without studio intervention.

Leaving all that behind, I again stayed with Johnny Whyte in London but this time I was only there for a few weeks. Johnny's drinking had started to affect his health, and one day I arrived home to find him in bed. He had collapsed in the BBC canteen. "How awful!" declared Fenella Fielding in mock horror when I told her. "Everybody must have thought he was auditioning!"

Come To Mother was published without any fanfare, not even a launch. All I knew was that it had been delivered to all the major book stores for release on the date stipulated. Much to the horror of the people at W.H. Allen, my publishers, I announced my intention of visiting as many of these stores as possible to introduce myself. You'd have thought I planned to parade down Piccadilly stark naked hurling copies of the book at passers-by. "It's just not done, dear boy," they said in shocked but muted tones. According to them, the bookshops hated authors turning up, because authors always complained about their books not being displayed to advantage.

I gave an assurance that I wouldn't complain, I would merely thank the bookshop staff for stocking my novel, and move on. To my mind, it was good public relations, and this proved to be so. Most of the staff I encountered responded to my genial, undemanding attitude and I believe this influenced them to recommend my book to their customers.

This, then, became the pattern of my days in London, doing the rounds of the bookshops. In the evenings, I went to shows. One I saw was *Cowardy Custard*, a pastiche of Noel Coward songs at the Mermaid Theatre in Puddle Dock. At interval, I was chatting with friends when somebody said something funny. I roared with laughter, stepped back – and felt my foot tread on something. I turned, and found myself face to face with Ginger Rogers. I couldn't have been more surprised had I suddenly spotted Mother Theresa in a singles bar. To make matters worse, I'd stepped on Ginger's toe. Oh my God, even Astaire had never done that! I just gaped like an idiot, for once stuck for words, until I mumbled an apology. She flashed a wonderful smile, amused by my incoherence and obviously accustomed to people just gaping, and said a few words to put me at my ease. That entire foyer seemed suddenly to be in shades of black and white while Ginger with a mane of admittedly brassy blonde hair, bright red lipstick and pearly teeth, seemed to glow in glorious technicolor. That's me. The everlasting, tragic movie fan.

I had come to London telling everybody in Australia I wanted to be there, not only for the book's publication, but also when it was bought for the movies. Like one year before, everybody said: "*If*". I repeated: "*When*." Talk about the power of positive thinking. Two weeks after publication day, Universal Pictures bought the screen rights of *Come to Mother* for forty thousand dollars. That sum was a lot in those days. Come to think of it, I wouldn't knock it back now!

A strange ritual followed. I had to sign the contract at the American Embassy in Berkley Square. For some legal reason, the deal had to be closed 'on American soil.' The contract was thicker than a brick, and more overwhelming in its detail than the charter of the United Nations. It covered not only the screen rights of *Come to Mother* but every form of media variation and interpretation up to and including the musical version in outer space. I signed willingly. And then, to make that magical day complete, the telephone rang and it was Bill Harmon calling from Sydney.

"Jeezus, David, everybody at TEN loves your treatment!" he shouted.

And pleasantly surprised too, I now assume, since nobody at the studio had 'co-created' or 'conceived' what they'd now been presented with. "They've given us the go-ahead, no changes, no nothin'," Bill continued. "Write the pilot on the way home."

I followed instructions, and the pilot of this quintessential Australian series was written by a Pom in Naples and Bangkok and typed up on the hotel typewriter in Hong Kong.

Oh yes, I certainly had a stopover in Bangkok on my way home, but besides working on *Number 96*, my main purpose was a reunion with Udom. He was passionate in his desire to get out of Thailand, and implored me to facilitate his entry into Australia. I wanted desperately to help him, and promised to do all I could once I was back home.

When I stepped out of Customs at Sydney Airport, the flashbulbs popped and the reporters closed in. Having a book published in London didn't count for much, but having it bought by Hollywood a mere two weeks after publication had created quite a buzz

It was August, and by this time *The Group* was showing on Channel Seven. Terminally-mordant critic Phillip Adams wrote a piece on it. As if pontificating from the heavens, his usual approach, he ripped into that week's episode of *The Group* and in particular, the script. "Sale's script was banal and witless – far too many words, far too few ideas." And more, in wounding, scathing terms.

There was just one complication. The episode he referred to wasn't mine. I had not written it. I was on to my agent, Peter Grose, in a flash. Peter, in turn, began talking 'defamation' with solicitors. And then Bill Harmon called. The mistake was Cash-Harmon's. My name had been erroneously put on the episode in question. Therefore, it was not the fault of Phillip Adams that he had attributed it to me. However, some form of retractment was called for, and this was given in grudging terms by Mr Adams the following day. Unfortunately, this did nothing to erase the impression that I had been responsible for something below standard.

I had flown home in high spirits. In London, everything was positive. *Come to Mother* was selling well. The initial reviews were favourable. And it had been sold to the movies. Now, in Australia, I was being made to look like some sort of amateur. Sound familiar?

The next blow came from Bill Harmon. The pilot episode of *Number 96* I had written on the way back didn't work. "You've tried to cram too much information into it," Bill said. And then he came up with one of his brilliant suggestions. "Write Episode Three. Then work backwards."

It sounds crazy, but I followed his advice. And it solved the problem. I had been contracted to write the first six episodes myself, and this occupied me in the coming weeks. Only one of my original characters failed to make it. I had designated the other ground-floor shop as an establishment selling antiques. "Let's keep that shop vacant," Bill suggested. "It gives us plenty of options." It did indeed. That shop later became a supposedly incest-ridden pharmacy and then Norma's Wine Bar. Bill's instinct hit the bulls-eye, yet again.

I used the movie money to pay off the mortgage on my unit in Neutral Bay, and to finance a trip back to Europe for my parents, not only to see their relatives in England but also to see Europe in style. I had a ball assembling their itinerary, which took in Paris, a cruise on the Rhine past all the fairytale castles of Austria; Switzerland, and Spain, making sure they had the best of everything all the way. I think that alone made the success of *Come to Mother* worthwhile.

Meanwhile, as 1971 drew to a close, and using my character run-down and the episodes I'd just written, Cash-Harmon started auditioning actors and actresses for the major continuing roles. I had cast several of the parts myself, merely by tailoring them especially for actors I knew. I wrote the part of Aldo Godolfus, the Greek delicatessen owner for Johnny Lockwood, whose work I greatly respected from our time together on *Mavis*. Closer to production, he rang me and asked could he play the character Hungarian Jewish because he couldn't do a Greek accent. I told him sure, but forgot to change the name. No Hungarian Jew ever had a name like Aldo Godolfus, but nobody ever noticed.

While writing *The Group*, I'd been shocked to find a favourite actress of mine, Bettina Welch, had been cast in a small part, too insignificant for her talents. "I'll write you a great big juicy part in whatever I do next," I promised her. And Maggie Cameron, the arch-bitch business-woman, kept her in work for the next six years.

Ronnie Shand, with whom I'd worked years before in *The Wizard of Oz* at the Tivoli, was a natural for Herb Evans, and Elisabeth Kirkby had played a character in *The Group* with such a convincing Lancashire accent she was the only one I ever had in mind to play Lucy Sutcliffe. Bill Harmon cast the rest, and brilliantly, too, even if at first sight some of his choices seemed inappropriate.

Just before production began, Bill and Don hosted a getting-to-know-you cocktail party, a tentative gathering of rather nervous, anxious-to-please actors who had no idea that in a matter of months they would be household names and that their faces would be recognizable all over Australia. I hadn't sat in on the casting, so I went along interested to see whom Bill had chosen to bring my characters to life. When Bill introduced me to Pat MacDonald and said: "This is Dorrie," my first reaction was: "Oh, but you're far too young." I had visualized her as a tiny grey-haired lady, the regulation image of a pensioner. Pat was a stylish middle-aged lady. But Bill's unerring instinct proved right. Dorrie, as played by Pat, was always well-groomed, within the limits of her pension. She became a poster girl for our senior citizens. But that first remark of mine must have remained in Pat's mind. Poignantly, just before her death years later, she told someone: "David never really approved of me." It's sad that my first surprised reaction left such a lasting, but incorrect impression. I thought her Dorrie was perfect. Joe Hasham was dark, being of Lebanese descent, and not a bit like my blonde vision of Don, the homosexual. But he, too, was perfectly suited to the role. In fact, everyone was. There was a moment of embarrassment when I saw a petite but buxom blonde and uttered the clichéd line: "Haven't we met somewhere before?" "At your welcome home party in Kirribilli," she replied, in a light, lilting voice, scrunching up her delicate features. "I got a bit sloshed and took off my clothes, but don't let's ever talk about that again." She was so sweet, I nodded in agreement. This was my Bev Houghton, and she had but one professional name, Abigail. We never referred to my welcome home party again, but taking off her clothes became quite a habit.

Abigail was only in *Number 96* for a relatively short period of its run, but she had a tremendous impact as its sex symbol and has always been the one person people tend to ask me about. I just used the word "sweet", which is not a description usually pinned to sex symbols, but that's how I always found her. In company, she gave the impression of being quiet and rather shy. She would never make a flamboyant entrance at a party, for instance. You might be there for a while and wonder if she'd arrived, only to find her sitting quietly in a corner. She loved to laugh and had an infectious giggle. She spoke fluent French and was a far better actress than she ever had a chance to prove. She was also extremely intelligent but unfortunately, not in aspects of her private life, nor in her subsequent career choices. Britain's Diana Dors was labeled a sex symbol from her mid teens, but in later years she overcame this with some gutsy character work onstage. It's a pity that Abigail was never given the opportunity to do the same.

Apart from cast members of a more mature age, all the younger ones were required to sign contracts with a nudity clause. They did it without a second thought. Nudity…even partial nudity on Australian television? Forget it. You didn't even see much flesh on the cinema screen in those days, except in art house movies from France or Italy.

And as for America, Barbara Eden wasn't even allowed to show her navel in *I Dream of Jeannie*.

We had other plans. I had launched the 'adult' concept of our show by suggesting and including a homosexual relationship – a world first in a TV series - as well as having Aldo's teenage daughter have sex with the frustrated husband of a heavily pregnant wife. I also had her being gang-raped. Not the sorts of things people do with their clothes on. And Bill Harmon encouraged this. "If someone has to take a shower, show 'em taking a shower. If people are in bed having sex, they're not even in their underwear. We'll show it like it is!'

This was how the subsequently labelled *Sex 'n' Sin* show evolved. We wanted to present a gritty picture of life as it was being lived in the seventies in an inner-Sydney suburb. Yes, hard as it was to believe, guys were actually shacking up together in same-sex relationships. Yes, people showered and had sex in the nude. Yes, frustrated husbands with pregnant wives whose libido was on hold sought relief elsewhere. And yes, unfortunately, girls were getting gang-raped. But being the person I am, with an irrepressible sense of humour, I tried to lighten the proceedings with some laugh lines or witty remarks here and there and the diversity of my characters helped in this regard.. I knew from the start that undiluted bathos wouldn't make it.

Cash-Harmon's office was on the first floor of a North Sydney building over an undertaker's parlour. That in itself was what is called 'gallows humour.' It was impossible to go there to a conference without seeing coffins or passing grieving relatives. But it was up there, in that office that the bombshell dropped just as we were going into production, early '72.

The telephone rang. Bill answered it. Listened. Replaced the receiver. Up until then, we had been scheduled to air two nights a week. Bill looked at us. Ian Holmes, Director of Programs at Channel 10, had convinced the network to take the most important gamble in Australian television history. "They're gonna strip the show, Monday to Friday at eight-thirty," Bill told us.

My immediate reaction was *failure*. Nobody was going to stay home five nights a week to watch a half-hour show. I honestly believed the decision sounded the death knell of our projected series.

And how could we possibly make five episodes a week? It was unheard of.

The answer was the genius of Don Cash. His shooting schedules were revolutionary. There were just two flats on the studio floor to represent the eight. Plus the two shops. Don's solution to shooting five episodes a week, was to dress one of the flats as Number One, and shoot the entire week's scenes in that flat, all the scenes in the five episodes. Then dress it as Number Two, and shoot every scene in the five episodes in that flat. And so on. This resulted at week's end in an enormous reel of tape filled with disconnected scenes that had to be edited into their correct episodes. But in terms of efficiency, it worked. It required great concentration from the cast, who maybe had to do a scene in Episode One in Flat One, and then jump to a scene three episodes later on the same set. Continuity, in terms not only of dramatic feasibility, but visually in terms of costumes, made great demands on cast and crew but they all responded. Thanks to his meticulous scheduling, Don's idea worked, and was subsequently adopted in the production of every other multi-episode soap.

There were other repercussions. As creator, I was to be paid a royalty of $50 per episode. My royalty payments immediately jumped from $100 for two episodes per week to $250 for five and I was also paid at a higher rate for the episodes I wrote. Bill wanted me to be script controller, but after my taxing workload on *Mavis Bramston* I shied away from any executive position. All I wanted to do was stay home and write scripts.

"Bring Johnny Whyte from England," I suggested. "After doing *Mavis*, he's familiar with Australia, he loves it here, and even better, he once wrote for *Coronation Street* so he knows this scene backwards."

Johnny was on the next plane.

A couple of nights before the show premiered, Channel Ten took over the ballroom of a top city hotel for a launching party. It was more of a lynching party! There were so-called celebrities, media representatives and flocks of the usual rent-a-crowd types and everybody behaved as they usually do at these affairs in Sydney, consuming as many drinks and eating as much food as possible, while paying not the slightest attention to the real reason they've been invited. The first episodes were being run on a dozen strategically-placed screens, but nobody really watched. Every so often, somebody would catch sight of what was happening onscreen, and let out hoots of derisive laughter, as if it was all a big joke.

I was appalled, and began to dread the first airing of the show.

March 13th, 1972 dawned. Channel Ten's clever publicist, Tom Greer, had hit upon a fabulous promotional gimmick. He placed enormous ads in all the newspapers proclaiming "Tonight at 8-30, Television Loses its Virginity!" Some of the more straitlaced ones refused to run the ad as submitted, and substituted "Innocence" for "Virginity". Even so, who could have resisted checking out an announcement like that? Obviously, not the majority of viewers.

Our opening night was a smash. The public loved what they saw. And those who were disgusted loved it too! Needless to say, the critics loathed it and said so in no uncertain terms. Just like *Mavis*, parts of the screen were blacked out in other states, to hide covert 'hands up the skirt' moves and bare nipples, but these attempts at censorship just raised the curiosity of the deprived viewers to fever pitch as they wondered what they were missing.

When the ratings figures came out for our first week, they confirmed what had been indicated by the clamour of public debate that had greeted our debut. We had romped home with incredibly high ratings that beat all the opposition. And we continued to do so. The other channels threw everything at us except nuclear weapons. They programmed hit blockbuster movies, imported series that had been wildly successful overseas, 'A' list specials, the lot. But nothing could shake the domination of that nightly 8-30 – 9-00 timeslot by *Number 96*.

Up until then, Channel Ten had been in the red, a late starter in the television industry, limping along behind the other channels after the overblown opening in which I had participated as one of the extras. Now, the revenue started to pour in, as it does with hit shows, so what did they do? Invest all that money into the creation of other hit shows to build upon their success, to help them stay in the black? Pay the best creative talent available to capitalize upon *Number 96's* success? No way. First priority was to turn the first floor executive offices at Ten's studio complex into the kind of panelled, deep-carpeted, luxury suites occupied by Hollywood moguls. It became a fantasy world for wankers.

Then having surrounded themselves with expensive trappings, they settled back in their leather upholstered chairs, puffed on their cigarillos and proceeded to stretch their limited intellects by attempting (a little late in the piece) to tell us what to do next with our hit show. Apparently quite at ease with our saga of infidelity, incest, gang rape and racism, they wanted to tinker with the ingredient that really offended them: the homosexual character Don Finlayson. This objection was coming from people in an industry that was already swamped with gays, which says a lot about their perception of the real world. Let me reiterate, that Donald Finlayson was no wrist-flapping effeminate queen of the type that had only been allowed, up until then, to surface in movies and stage farces, as an object of derision. I had written Don as an ordinary, decent guy, a law student who happened to be attracted to men instead of women.

Bill called me into the office over the undertakers. He was seated behind the 'double' desk that he and Don Cash had commissioned, their one concession to success, a piece of furniture that symbolized their business partnership. Don Cash's place was unoccupied. He was becoming increasingly absent because of health problems.

"Jeezus, David, they want us to turn the queer straight," Bill told me in his usual less than subtle way. I had grown accustomed by then to him starting every sentence with an explosive 'Jeezus!'

"No way," I said.

"And that's what I think, too." Bill fixed me with his eyes and suddenly became intense. "You're gay. It took me a long time to figure it out, but it doesn't matter. It's not important." He was really striving to make himself understood. "And you know what? I don't care." He actually laughed as if he'd been released, and reached over to grab my hand. "I don't care!"

"So when I say you can't just turn someone who's gay into a heterosexual, I'm speaking from experience," I told him. "It's not a matter of choice, like flipping a coin."

"I know that. And there's no fuckin' way I'm gonna let this happen"

True to his word, Bill Harmon fronted up to the Channel Ten executives and said if they tried to force the issue of turning Don Finlayson into a heterosexual, he would take *Number 96* away and offer it to Channel Nine. Needless to say, they capitulated. Then, as now, TV executives had fear in their eyes. They are scared of losing their status. If commissioning a new show, they say "We want something like…." mentioning a hit show and wanting a nice, safe copy, instead of saying "Give us something original, fresh and new." They want to hang onto their precious high-paid jobs, and not be held responsible for something that might fail. Therefore they have to play safe. They cannot afford to take risks. They are what stagnates television. Then and now. They are accountants, and solicitors, advertising execs, sports identities. And they know as much about the entertainment business as Forrest Gump. Obviously, thank God, there were a few exceptions, which is why *Number 96* made it to air in the first place.

Bill Harmon had the guts to challenge the naysayers. I called Bill and Don Cash 'buccaneers' because they were freewheeling guys who knew what they wanted and fought for it, stood up for what they believed in and resisted interference. It's a pity there aren't more of them around today.

With Johnny Whyte to bounce off, I began to enjoy doing the show a lot more, particularly in the early stages. Our story conferences were full of rollicking fun, wisecracks and private jokes. As a result, we began to inject more comedy into the storylines and characters. Johnny invented Arnold Feather to help Aldo in the delicatessen, and I brought in Mrs Claire Houghton, Bev's mother, who lived in Buckingham Lodge, Point Piper with her over-the-top snobbery and politically incorrect remarks. I wrote her specially for the noted radio and stage actress Thelma Scott who made Claire one of our favourite characters because of her *grande dame* delivery of gasp-inducing remarks like: "We all feel as deeply as you do about Aboriginals…. just as long as they don't come to live in Point Piper!"

Dorrie's malapropisms multiplied to outrageous proportions. Catch phrases and recognizable modes of address, used perhaps once or twice, were then adopted as identifiable verbal traits for every major character. It got so that you could obliterate the names of characters on any page of script and still identify who was saying what merely by the speech patterns.

This should have made it easier for any new writers to latch on, but this was not the case. Writers joined and left our team in rapid succession in those early days. Some were young and inexperienced, others had major track records. Writing for *Number 96* was specialized. It required writers who were adept at both comedy and drama, and who could imbue scenes with bits of business, have characters move around, and not just sit or stand there verbalizing the synopsis. Every episode had anything from twelve to twenty scenes, each of which had to end on some sort of mini cliff-hanger, with the major cliff-hanger coming at the end of the episode. Johnny Lockwood described it as 'dramatic vaudeville'. In vaudeville, rapid-fire blackout sketches followed one after the other in quick succession. If you didn't like one, you scarcely had time to think before the next one had started. Lockwood's summing up was very perceptive.

As far as television drama went, it was a whole new ballgame. The Grundy production company, already adept at duplicating overseas quiz games in Australia, was rumoured to be obtaining copies of our scripts. Then, it was alleged they would have analysts breaking down each episode, counting the number of lines, tabulating the number of comedy situations as opposed to dramatic ones, timing with stop watches the length of each scene. In other words, trying to duplicate by mechanical methods what we were doing instinctively. I never found out whether these rumours were true or false, but when Grundys began churning out their own soapies, there was a bland, assembly-line quality about them, reliant more on pretty young faces both male and female, than any inventiveness of plot or character. Certainly, I became accustomed to seeing quite a lot of our plots and characters recycled in other soaps, but usually only the least controversial of our stories.

Crawfords jumped on the bandwagon with *The Box* a so-called sexy series based on the behind-the-scenes activities at a television studio. It became a formidable rival. but never quite reached the iconic level of *Number 96*. Bill Harmon, now a pro-gay heterosexual, was outraged that the Crawfords effort had a gay character who was a stereotypical effeminate type, going against everything we had done to give homosexuals a little dignity.

We continued on our merry way. Every week, the ratings came out confirming our supremacy with the biggest viewing audience ever on Australian television. Everybody connected with the show was joyous, but still in a state of disbelief. Strange stories, some weird some gratifying, started to filter back to us. Apart from the usual condemnation from the pulpits (something I had become accustomed to in my *Mavis* days), we heard that Leagues Clubs and pubs were assuring patrons that TV sets or extra screens were being installed, because so many people were staying home to watch the show their business was being affected. There was no doubt that people were watching, but some still complained, with the result that the Broadcasting Control Board demanded the right to vet all episodes before they went to air, and sometimes ordered censorship cuts. This continued for a while, the first time it had happened since television was introduced in Australia, but eventually the Board just gave up bothering and conceded the public's right to watch the country's most popular show uncensored.

We were also surprised to learn that *Number 96* was the most popular-rated show with children and teenagers. With regards to young children, we wondered about the lack of parental discipline in letting them watch, after all we were in an adult time-slot. Then we learned that kids were creeping down from the bedroom and watching the show from between the banisters or concealed behind furniture. This actually happened. In later years, I have been told by so many grown-ups that this was what they did when they were kids, and it was their indoctrination into the raunchier aspects of 'real life.' In addition, teachers were complaining that we were perverting their efforts to teach children to speak correct English because playgrounds were full of mini-Dorries parroting that they were quite 'ardamant', and that they were going 'beresk'. I wish the teachers today were as vociferous about their pupils adopting the slang of American ghetto kids or the whining upward inflections of California's 'Valley' girls as personified by Paris Hilton.

On a more positive note, I personally had a letter from a mother who said that *Number 96* had restored valuable communication to her household. Now, the whole family, including her teenage children, gathered to watch the show, and afterwards they all discussed the various contentious topics raised in storylines. "We are actually talking amongst ourselves again," she wrote, "whereas before it seemed we had nothing in common." Joe Hasham was receiving letters, too. His came not only from ardent, if confused, female fans offering their services to 'change' his sexual orientation, but also from closet gays isolated in country towns who up until then had believed they were utterly alone in having same-sex inclinations. Joe shared some of the letters with me, and we were both moved by the tales of utter loneliness and desolation from young men, some of whom had been close to suicide, who now realized that they were not freaks, not the only ones in the world to have these feelings, and who now knew there were so many others like them. To Joe's credit, he personally answered every letter in sympathetic and positive terms.

More disturbing were the letters from misguided people who actually wanted to move into the block of flats. "Please let me know when one of the flats becomes vacant to rent" ran a typical appeal, "because I lead the kind of life that would fit in perfectly, with enough happening to give you plenty to go on."

I'd had creepy letters from weirdoes while doing *Mavis*, but these latest ones took viewer confusion to a new level. And it was down, not up. We were forced to acknowledge that there were people out there who believed that what they saw on the box every night at eight-thirty was actually happening. Some were content to sit at home and enjoy what they saw. Others wanted to join in and participate. Not only did they send in these letters inquiring about the availability of flats, the actual apartment building in Moncur Street, Paddington, became the focal point for visiting fans at week-ends. They crowded on the pavement outside, in the hope of seeing Dorrie and Herb, or Vera, or Alf and Lucy Sutcliffe. The real-life residents complained about intrusion of privacy and Cash-Harmon, who had obtained a clearance from the building's owners right at the start, had to do some fancy diplomatic moves to keep our location intact.

Another strange story of viewer indentification: Bettina Welch, who had invested my gift to her of Maggie Cameron with realistic forcefulness, jumped into a taxi one evening. The taxi driver looked at her amazed as she gave her destination. "You're....Maggie Cameron, aren't you?" Bettina nodded graciously, avoiding the argument that no, she was just the actress *playing* Maggie Cameron. The taxi driver checked his watch, then looked at her, with an utterly dismayed expression. "Then.....why aren't you *there?*! .....*Doing* it?"

These were the days before video recorders. The viewing public had no access to pre-taping techniques. This 'innocence' added to the nightly reality of the show, the assumption that what they were seeing was actually happening that day.

Another example: When we turned the empty shop into a pharmacy, actress Lynn Rainbow was cast as Sonia Vansard, one of the brother and sister owners. A plot development had her disappear unaccountably. Everyone was asking: *Where is Sonia Vansard*? Lynn Rainbow attended a surf life-saving carnival at Bondi Beach one Sunday afternoon. The switchboard at Channel Ten was inundated with calls. Breathlessly, and with utter conviction, caller after caller informed the switchboard girl: "Quick, if you want to find Sonia Vansard, she's at Bondi Beach watching a surf carnival!" And these were not hoax calls. These people actually believed they had located the missing girl. Despite the frequent claims of critics that our series was unreal and phony, obviously a lot of viewers disagreed.

Sadly, I have to admit I think our series was probably a foretaste of what I see as the current curse – so-called 'Reality Television'.

It's a wonder this abomination wasn't introduced right after our series folded. The public had shown it wanted to participate in other people's lives. Forget the 'sex and sin' component, viewers loved the compatability of the characters in *Number 96*, the way they met on the stairs and invited each other in for coffee, the way they shared their problems with each other in a way that didn't happen in real life. There were a lot of lonely people out there in the seventies,(and still are, for that matter!), flat-dwellers in sterile high-rise apartment blocks who didn't even know their next-door neighbours; even mothers with big families that weren't communicating. They loved feeling that they were a part of this vertical village, and were perhaps a little envious, too.

It's sad, even pathetic, that today's substitute for a tightly-scripted series, performed by professional actors and actresses, is some vehicle starring bitchy would-be cooks and home renovators, aspiring models who look like skeletons and fat people who resemble over-inflated balloons. Oh – and talent shows. Not one. Dozens.

It may seem creaky and dated now, in retrospect, but our series was made to appear real and believable by a team of great writers and experienced actors. And it enticed viewers into this web of believability, simply because it was constantly entertaining. Nobody could abide missing an episode. If they did, they rushed up to people in the supermarket or at a cocktail party to find out what happened the previous night. On another level, there was the snob element. I lost count of the number of times people came up to me at parties and announced imperiously that they wouldn't be caught dead watching the show. Given a few drinks, they were back again, asking the inevitable "what's going to happen to…?" questions. The snobbery was not only directed at the show itself but at the people involved. Once, at a wine and cheese function held by the Writers Guild, I overheard a lady who had contributed to *Mavis Bramston* proclaiming: "I don't know how David Sale can associate himself with such rubbish!" The following year, she joined our regular team of writers – and was happy to do it!

Sometimes, the caustic rhetoric about the show demanded a rejoinder. At one cocktail party, I was the recipient of a tirade of criticism by a suburban would-be Noel Coward. I kept silent, because I did not want to instigate a slanging match that would ruin the party. Finally, when he ran out of snide comments, he paused to draw breath and asked: "And what, pray, are you intending to write next?" "Hopefully, your obituary," I replied. The laughter completely demolished him. Unfortunately, I wasn't always ready with a devastating quip, and most times I just had to bite my lip and keep silent.

This wasn't the case at our script conferences. Johnny Whyte and I tended to be completely irreverent, and I believe this general air of light-heartedness imbued itself into the fabric of the show. The more outrageous the suggested plotlines, the better, and every one had to have 'legs' - in other words enough strength to keep it running for several weeks. I remember one well-meaning writer, new to our team and trying to be 'relevant', suggesting that Vera Collins – because of her rather active and varied love life – should contract a social disease. Johnny and I fell about with hoots of laughter. That poor writer. "And what does that give us in terms of a story?– One scene with her doctor and two more of her taking pills?" we hooted. "That's not a plot, it's a consultation!"

The scripting set-up was in two stages. Every twelve weeks, the production team and the writers would have an all-day barnstorming session at the Cosmopolitan Hotel in Double Bay. The coffee would percolate all day long, and Bill Harmon made sure we all had an excellent buffet lunch. During the day, we would progress from flat to flat, suggesting, talking over, and sometimes arguing over plotlines that would keep the characters busy over the next three months. A synopsis writer would take copious notes, and it would then be her/his job to split up all these plots into the scenes that would be the skeleton upon which every future episode would be fleshed out. Each week, the designated writer would turn up to debate the five sets of synopses that would be his assigned week's episodes. There was usually a team of four writers at any one time, of which I was always one, and we each wrote a block of five episodes a month.

One complication was that no actor could appear in more than three of the five episodes a week. This always meant some juggling of plotlines. It didn't matter how serious a situation a character might be in, if it was in his/her third episode that week, we had to script around it until the following week.

Our procedures quickly settled into a well-oiled, smoothly running machine, except no machine ever emitted the gales of laughter that came from our team. But the gales, as gales do, blew in some dark clouds and the first one was entirely of my own making.

The success of the show, and my greatly enhanced financial state, induced in me a heady feeling of largesse. I did a stupid thing. I succumbed to Udom's constant entreaties and flew him to Sydney. This involved my being a guarantor on his visa – the authorities would only approve one of three months - and I had to open a bank account in his name with five hundred dollars in it. In my one moment of sanity, I made it a joint account to which I also had access.

Behind my back, my friends were throwing up their hands in horror, seeing the foolhardiness of such a move, but nobody had the nerve to actually tell me. Apart from the emotional and physical bond, I really wanted to do something to improve his life. I thought that if he perfected his English, it would enhance his chances of rising above Bangkok's overwhelming unemployment situation and he would qualify for a job with some multinational company there. So before he arrived, I enrolled him in an English-speaking course at a college that specialized in teaching Asian students. Note 1: I was still not aware that the ability to speak perfect English was not an issue in his chosen profession! Note 2: I was dumb!

He arrived in Sydney and did all the right things for a week, then totally disappeared. Correction. After five days, he'd already sussed out King's Cross, and stayed out all one night. *Then* he disappeared, along with his bags. I was frantic, particularly after I rang the Language College to see if he was still attending lessons. No, the principal told me. Udom hadn't been in since the first two classes. Where was he? I came up with a quick excuse..."I think he's moved in with some Thai friends he met at your College." "He can't do that, he can't change addresses," the principal boomed. "Your name is on his visa and he should be at your address! You are responsible for him, and if there is any problem, I shall have to inform the Immigration Department." I blubbered something or other and put the phone down. I was frantic. Here I was, creator of the immensely popular 'sex 'n' sin' show, threatened with a real-life sex' n' sin scandal.

I remember going to a script conference at which the main point of discussion was Sonia Vansard's unaccountable disappearance. "Jeezus Christ, David," Bill Harmon exploded, "where the hell would she go? People don't just disappear." With a sly wink at me, Johnny Whyte, in whom I'd confided, said: "Oh yes they do, Bill, they certainly do!"

I was scared to death. If the College principal contacted the authorities, I was in trouble. I fled to Surfer's Paradise, and made Erris and Kevin's life hell by pacing the floor every night, unable to sleep. You cannot leave your troubles behind; you take them with you. I drove back to Sydney, and the first phone call I had was from a very carefree Udom telling me he was working at a hamburger joint at Circular Quay. "But you can't work," I spluttered. "You're on a visitor's visa. If they find you, they'll arrest you!" "Oh, that's all shit," he replied airily, "everybody does it and nobody gets caught." He invited me down there the following night, and in his break from flipping hamburgers in full view in the window of the shop, we sat down over coffee where he casually confessed to me his preferred means of making money and the fact that already he was doing very well with a growing Sydney clientele. There wasn't a hint of any concern for me. I had served my purpose and now

I was being dispensed with.

I spent the next eleven weeks petrified. I drew out the money from the joint bank account and terminated it, but that didn't help. I was tortured, night and day, by the fear that he would be picked up for violating the terms of his visa, or worse, for prostitution. In my writer's mind I visualized him being pushed into a corner and, forced to save his own skin, blurting out that David Sale had imported him for sex. It wasn't at all like that. He had pleaded with me to bring him over. I believed we had a strong relationship. I wanted to improve his chances at life by enrolling him in the language course. And, of course, I could see it coming - 'Thai boy', one of the racist slurs that reduce Asians to underage pawns. Udom was twenty-three, an adult, and a lot more streetwise than I. But he would be the victim and I would be the predator in any scandal.

On the outside, I was rejoicing in the immensely successful TV series that I had created, public acclaim far outweighing critical disdain. Privately, I couldn't hit the pillow without a deadly cocktail of scotch and valium, because if I didn't pass out immediately, there was the horror of lying there, looking at the ceiling and anticipating what might happen if Udom was caught. It wasn't only the danger to me – it might reflect disastrously on the show.

Somehow, I got through those three months, immersing myself in a heavy workload that not only included my responsibilities to *Number 96*, doing another draft of my next novel *The Gods*, but also writing the title number and several other pieces for the Ron Frazer revue *Some of My Best Friends Are* at the Silver Spade cabaret room of the Chevron in Potts Point. At that same venue, Hazel Phillips was signed as support for American singer Tommy Leonetti. She asked me to write her act. She was such a chatterbox and totally inimitable in the way she phrased things, I knew I couldn't just put my own words into her mouth. So I hit on the idea of recording her talking about the numbers she had chosen for her act, and then edited her words into a script, also interpolating some gags and reminiscences she had related to me on other occasions, so that it was always Hazel talking, not me.

Opening night, all was going well until – typically Hazel – she couldn't resist departing from my format to slip in a filthy joke which as one critic wrote: "…scorched the tablecloths." I was practically *under* the tablecloth with embarrassment, thinking she'd just ruined everything, but blithely, she segued into a sentimental number and all was back on track.

Poor Tommy Leonetti. Hazel wowed 'em, and stole the notices.

At last, the three months period stipulated on Udom's visa was up and I felt I could breathe easily again. A few days after the visa expired, it was a Sunday and I was on my way over to the eastern suburbs to dine with friends. As I drove up Macleay Street towards the El Alamein Fountain, I saw a familiar figure. It was Udom, sauntering along as large as life. I almost crashed the car.

I called on the assistance of friends in checking around and discovered that some other sucker had renewed Udom's visa for another three months. I didn't like that at all, but at least my name wasn't on the current visa and we had not been in contact at all since the evening at the hamburger joint. I felt I had ceased to be responsible for him, and fortunately I was going to be off the scene for a while. This was June, 1972, and my second novel *The Love Bite* was about to be published in London. Again, I took off for London, this time with five synopses so that I could write my quota of *Number 96* scripts while I was away.

As I had done with *Come to Mother*, I made the rounds of the leading bookshops, a chore made easier than the year before because the first novel had sold well, and had garnered favourable reviews. But it wasn't all celebrations. I had sent the manuscript of *The Gods* in advance and everyone at Curtis Brown thought that it was totally unsuitable to push as my third novel, as it was in a vastly different genre to my first two, and therefore would confuse and possibly alienate what they called my fan base. Also, there was the opinion that the time was not right for a salacious saga based on The Beatles. Their reign was not yet history, and they were all going strong, if in different directions.

I decided to worry about that later. I was bound for Hollywood!

14

Michael Ludmer, the Story Executive at Universal had been a prime mover in the studio's purchase of *Come to Mother*. During the intervening year, he had kept me posted on the travails of bringing my novel to the screen, and had invited me to visit Los Angeles on my way back to Australia. I needed no further urging.

If there is one thing Hollywood studios know what to do well besides make movies, it's how to treat people who are in favour with them. I marveled at the effusiveness with which I was greeted. After all, I was just one of many authors whose books had been bought as possible movie properties. But I was a little different, I have to admit. I had a tearaway hit show running on Australian television, and nothing appeals to Americans more than success. They can sniff it on you like an expensive after-shave. And with all this going for me, I had another endearing quality. I wasn't looking to take over somebody's job, which in Tinsletown is a constant threat.

Good news travels fast, and Hollywood had already heard of *Number 96*. An article in *Time* magazine augmented the buzz. It featured a rear shot of a naked Elaine Lee rising from a bed to confront Norman Yemm. The caption was "You could be arrested for what you just did to me!" The reason for the quote was rape within marriage, another of our controversial themes. The accompanying article left no doubt that

Number 96 was not only controversial by American standards, it was also Australia's top television show.

I'd hardly settled in at the Beverly Wilshire Hotel, when an invitation came from the studio to attend a private screening. It was a made-for TV movie titled *That Certain Summer* and it starred Hal Holbrook and Martin Sheen. Divorcee Holbrook has his adolescent son for the school holidays, attempting to keep from the boy his homosexual relationship with lover Martin Sheen. It was a beautifully crafted delicately presented movie, so delicate in fact that Holbrook and Sheen never even lit each other's cigarettes. let alone touched. At drinks afterwards, I was approached by the director, Lamont Johnson. I started to congratulate him, but he interrupted with wide-eyed perplexity. "How do you do it?" he asked. "I know about *Number 96* and your regular homosexual character who's become so popular. I always assumed Australians would be narrow-minded."

"Not if something's presented to them in a truthful way," I replied. "They call it 'giving it a go.'"

"This is just a preview," Johnson told me. "But purely on advance publicity, I have a mound of hate mail this high." His hand was at shoulder level. That incident illustrated the profound difference between Australia and the United States at that time. And their stitched-up attitude continued for years.

A limousine arrived to take me to the studio for a day with Michael Ludmer. His offices were at the top of what was known as the Black Tower at Universal. Like most of the up-coming executives in Hollywood, he was well groomed, darkly attractive, around thirty-five and utterly charming. He had also been associated with Alfred Hitchcock, helping in the famed director's constant search for interesting properties. "Hitch would have loved *Come to Mother*," he told me. "He's in London filming *Frenzy* at present, but….." he shook his head, "frankly, he's slowing down and I doubt he'll make another picture." (Hitchcock did manage one more, *Family Plot* four years later). Ludmer handed me a script. "We assigned your novel to producer Harry Tatelman, and he's come up with this script."

"I'll read it this evening," I said, "and get it back to you when ----"

He interrupted me. "Don't bother. When you've read it, throw it in the wastebasket."

"What?" I was perplexed. This was my introduction to Hollywood's perpetual state of intrigue and subterfuge.

"That script stinks," Michael told me. "Tatelman's off the picture, but he won't be told until we get Joseph Stefano interested. In the meantime, I'd appreciate it if you'd go down to Tatelman's cottage and talk to him as if everything's fine. He's expecting you." So now I was turned into a barefaced liar, which I found to be a pre-requisite of survival in Hollywood.

Feeling distinctly uncomfortable, I was escorted down to Tatelman's cottage, which is what they called the small individual production offices scattered around the Lot, by a guy who could have been Michael Ludmer's younger brother – well groomed, darkly attractive and utterly charming. This clone, Jeffrey, was a studio courier waiting to be a movie star. I've looked out for him since, but never spotted him, so he must have waited too long.

Tatelman was more the 'old Hollywood' type – overweight, elderly and blustering, puffing cigar smoke like an ancient steam engine. The inside walls of his 'cottage' were decorated with posters of cheesy 'B' grade movies, all produced by him. I began to feel better about what I knew.

"Wait'll you read the script," he enthused hoarsely, "You're gonna love it." He paused for dramatic effect, his arms reaching upwards, his hands clawing as if for an unattainable Academy Award. "It's been written by a 22-year-old Rhodes scholar!"

I attempted humour. "I wouldn't care if it's been written by a 22-year old road sweeper, just so long as it's good." He didn't get the joke. Just like he wasn't going to get the movie.

Michael Ludmer rewarded my duplicity by talking me to lunch in the studio commissary and introducing me to a languid Henry Fonda who, when he walked away, did for jeans what Monroe did for clinging gold lame. Now I know where Jane got it. I also met a rather intense Greer Garson. The erstwhile *Mrs Miniver* was clad in turn of the century costume, and when she learned I was from Australia, she grabbed my hands and drew me down with an intensely searching expression as if I had the cure for cancer. "Tell me about your cattle," she implored huskily. It flashed through my mind that she and her Texas millionaire husband, Buddy Fogelson raised a rare breed of cow on their ranch. I thought *she* was a rare breed of cow to assume that just because I came from Australia I was an expert on livestock. I carefully explained that most people in Australia lived in cities along the coastline and knew nothing of what went on in the outback, least of all the cattle. I felt her grip loosening as she lost interest in me as quickly as if I'd been an unpedigreed calf.

"What do you want to do for the rest of the day?" Michael asked after lunch. I told him I wanted to see the studio, not by means of the commercial Universal Studio tour, but to actually visit working sets to observe their methods of production. It took time, but he obtained a clearance for me. Jeffrey materialized again, and off we went. At one point, we stood on the sidelines for the shooting of a scene for the big Western series of the time, *Gunsmoke*. All the regulars were there – plus, as guest star, none other than Greer Garson. At one point during a break, while someone was fussing with her sadly thin red hair, she caught sight of me and waved vaguely. I tried to hide behind Jeffrey. I dreaded her coming over and asking how we Aussies treated hoof-rot.

I was in movie-fan heaven when I returned to Michael Ludmer's office for a late-afternoon drink. "About the studio car," I ventured.

"Could it take me to Santa Monica instead of just back to the Beverly Wilshire? I'm going to Kathryn Grayson's house for dinner."

Michael almost coughed up his dry martini. "You Aussies!" he exclaimed. "Here I've lived all of my life in Hollywood, and never met stars of her magnitude, particularly one I've adored since I was a kid, and here's you going to dinner with her!" He was really distressed.

I told him that I had met Kathryn briefly after a concert she'd done in Sydney through a mutual friend, entertainer Tracy Lee, who was now her house guest. Michael was still shaking his head enviously when I left.

Kathryn's house was the full Tudor mansion set in its own grounds on La Mesa Drive, with twin radio-controlled gates and a half-moon drive. She told me MGM helped her buy it in the nineteen forties, when she was a teenager, trilling her way to stardom. It appeared to be overrun by dogs, actually four. This glamorous star of MGM musicals such as *Showboat* and *Kiss Me Kate* looked exactly the same twenty years later even without the benefit of heavy studio make-up. Black skivvy, black pants, hair brushed casually, perfectly-glowing skin, she was the antithesis of today's Botoxed Beauties. After dinner, she insisted on driving me back to the Beverly Wilshire Hotel – "driving at this time of night, is the only way to really enjoy it here". Before the day of my flight back to Australia, she telephoned me. "I know you have to book out before midday, otherwise you have to pay more. Come to me, spend the rest of the day, and I'll drive you to the airport." I really couldn't believe this kind of consideration from a lady I had sat in the Metro, Collins Street, and adored.

I had other things to do before my departure, so I landed on Kathryn with my luggage, late afternoon. The house was sizzling with tantalizing odours. "I'm roasting a leg of lamb," Kathryn announced. "I know you Aussies like lamb." But she was unaccountably sad. I asked her what was wrong, and she told me that the late Mario Lanza's wife, Betty, had died that day. When Mario died suddenly, in 1959, his wife had gone into a decline. Kathryn scooped up the children and looked after them for months until Betty Lanza was ready to resume parenting. Kathryn had made two movies with Mario when she was an established star and he was a newcomer. "Mad Mario" was how she described him to me. "When we made *That Midnight Kiss*, he tried to make it a tongue-kiss. During *The Toast of New Orleans* he actually chased me around the set trying to rape me. He was crazy and uncontrollable, but he had such a wonderful voice, and I feel so sad for the children, now they've lost their mother as well as their father." Kathryn served me the lamb roast and then she drove me to LA airport. I relate this, not as an exercise in name dropping, but to illustrate that some immensely successful stars do manage to survive with their humanity intact.

I arrived back in Australia to find that *Number 96* was still topping the ratings and demolishing all opposition. Everybody seemed to be talking about it. Bill Harmon should have been on top of the world, but I detected a strange melancholy in him. Then, abruptly one day, he telephoned me. "David, I gotta talk with you. Let's have lunch. Tomorrow." Something in his tone indicated to me that we wouldn't be enjoying the meal.

He ordered drinks as soon as we sat down, and wouldn't speak until he had the drink in his hand and had swallowed half of it in one gulp. I was horrified to see he was on the verge of tears.

"Listen David," he said, his voice near a whisper. "I have to tell you something, and you must keep it to yourself and not tell anyone else, not even Johnny. Don's dying. He has cancer and there's nothing they can do about it."

It was my turn to gulp my drink. I knew Don Cash hadn't been well and had been in hospital, but I never suspected anything like this.

"We have to go on like normal. I know, Don knows, Nancy (Don's wife) knows and now you know. I need someone in the team to talk to, and you're it. But for obvious reasons, it mustn't get out."

And so began another phase in the sweet and sour saga of my life with *Number 96*. Udom eventually went back to Bangkok, so I heard. Good riddance, said I. How sad that he felt the only thing he had to trade was his body. But now, more predominantly than his treachery, there was the constant burden of maintaining outwardly the joy of our success, while witnessing the physical decline of the fine, upstanding Don Cash, into a gaunt shell. Colleagues noticed his appearance and commented and asked questions. "Do you think it's easy to keep a show like this on the road?" I'd tell them belligerently.

We ended 1972 on our first spectacular end-of-year cliffhanger. Chemist Gordon Vansard, drunk-driving with his mistress, totalled his car in a crash that was staged in the grounds of Channel Ten. It was quite a stunt, and the entire cast applauded it when we watched the playback at our Christmas break-up party. I remember how happy everyone was. The actors, secure in their continuing roles, were almost delirious with success. The crew, too. We had the New Year to look forward to, and the continuation of a hit show that was dominating the ratings. All I could see was a pale, thinner Don Cash. There, with Bill, where he belonged but not for much longer.

"What's the matter with you?" Johnny Whyte demanded waspishly, having had several drinks. "You're never happy and never satisfied."

"I am," I protested, and proceeded to drown my sorrows.

Don died early in 1973. I never had the sense that he was gone because there was no funeral and no memorial service. Instead, his widow threw a big wake at their home in Bellevue Hill. It was a celebration of his life rather than mourning his death, and on me it had the effect of his always being around.

It was tragic that Don didn't live to see the show go on to greater success than he'd ever imagined. And Bill Harmon was never quite the same. The feistiness was still there, and the drive, but underneath, there was insecurity. Bill attempted many other projects, spin-off TV series, specials, movies, but nothing ever got off the ground. Bill and Don had also been two of the driving forces behind one of the best Australian films ever made, 1971's *Wake in Frigh*t. Without Don, the magic generated by really special partnerships had gone.

It lingered, however, in *Number 96*, which with time has now come to be regarded as an accurate depiction of life in the 70s. While critics were using words like 'preposterous' and 'trashy', Eleanor Whitcombe a respected writer who was one of our original contributors, went on record to describe it as 'the most professional, well-organised and integrated show' she had ever worked on. The actors had become unbelievably popular and the public lapped it up. And I was in the euphoric situation where work seems like play and you can do what you want to do and still get paid.

Unlike current soaps, we packed in a wide diversity of plots, races and ages. Our characters ranged from pensioners to teenagers. They were Australian, South African, Jewish, Indian, African-American and Aboriginal. How they lived ranged from slapstick comedy to melodrama. It mirrored our country's social mores and its multiculturalism, sometimes exaggerated, sometimes almost too painfully real.

Behind the scenes, there was occasionally as much drama going on as before the cameras. By this time, Abigail had become Australia's first sex symbol, but to balance the flashy glamour, we had made her appear vulnerable by cleverly revealing that her character, Bev Houghton, was still a virgin, with an inherent frigidity just waiting to be thawed out by the right man. Practically every straight male in the country from schoolboy to old fart wanted to be that man!

Unfortunately for the actress, however, the gravy train began to wobble off the rails.

Later in the year, rumours surfaced about a series of photographs showing the actress in, let's say, some highly intimate situations. These rumours became stronger and Bill Harmon actually acquired copies. "Oh yeah, they're definitely Abigail," he told me. "We're gonna have to do something, before this hits the papers."

What Bill did was call in Abigail, and her manager-fiance Mark Hashfield for a meeting in his office. Bill asked me to be there, too. Since Don's death he had tended to want me around in moments of crisis. To Abigail's credit, and I believed her implicitly, she had recently left her handbag in the back of a taxi and it was never recovered. She had filed a report to police of the missing bag and its contents, a list that included 'a roll of undeveloped film', so that the incident was on official record. Obviously, whoever ended up with the film, had it developed and.... well, we knew the rest. She insisted to Bill that the shots had been taken for strictly personal viewing.

But with regret in his voice, Bill told her: "We're gonna have to let you go, honey." Abigail had done nothing wrong. The undeveloped negatives of a few photographs, intended to be kept private, had unfortunately fallen into the wrong hands. Compared to the exploits of some of today's celebrities who survive the scandal of widely-circulated 'sex tapes' it was a minor ripple indeed. But times, despite the free-wheeling antics depicted in our show, were different then.

She was our biggest drawcard, but Bill had told me time and time again that nobody was indispensable. "A girl can walk into the kitchen to make coffee, and a different girl walks out holding a cup. If it's a hit show and the match is good enough, nobody gives a damn."

And nobody did. Although Abi's departure, softened by vague references to a future part in a big screen movie, was featured in headlines from Broome to Bendigo, a million or so viewers kept tuned in and saw Bev Houghton transform herself from Abigail to Vicky Raymond, whose sister Candy was already playing a character in another flat. Vicky was no less lovely and well-proportioned than her predecessor, but the mystique of the character – overtly sexy, but still a virgin had been weakened when Bev Houghton, still played by Abigail, was sensitively deflowered by jolly Jack Sellars, and later crawled with more than sisterly affection into the bed of her crippled brother. Vicky was reduced to playing just another dime-a-dozen blonde sex bomb, which was a shame. She soldiered on for six months and was shot as a Christmas 'go-out' for her trouble. Her passing went virtually unnoticed.

Another backstage problem manifested itself when Bill cornered me. "Pat wants us to write in a friend of hers, Bunney Brooke. Do you know her?" I remembered Bunney – an acknowledged lesbian from my days at the Melbourne Little Theatre. An accomplished actress, she was very popular with theatrical acolytes, dispensing wisdom about the profession like some sort of guru. But this persona tended to split and divide. If Bunney was in a cast, then there was a very definite division of camps, pro-Bunney and anti-Bunney.

I told all this to Bill, who decided we should discuss this with Pat. She dismissed it totally because, although she didn't admit it, she was enmeshed in an intimate relationship with Bunney and to her, Our Miss Brooke could do no wrong. Bill, the softie, capitulated. "Write her in," he ordered. And so Flo Patterson entered into the lives of Herb and Dorrie Evans and certainly enriched their existence in terms of on-camera plots. Unfortunately, history repeated itself, and off-camera Bunney had a disastrous effect on our hitherto united cast. With as much precision as if she'd been wielding a surgeon's scalpel, she slit it into two separate camps, those who sat at her feet and those who disliked her. It was a situation with which we had to work. Bunney had the power to hypnotize with her theatrical knowledge, but even Elaine Lee who became one of the followers, eventually saw the light. "Thank God, before Pat died, I sank to my knees and apologized," she says today.

Johnny Whyte's duties as script supervisor seemed to be getting to him in various ways. For one thing, never exactly a teetotaler, he began drinking even more heavily. I noticed his hands trembling at morning script conferences, and a faint sheen of perspiration crossed his forehead and upper lip, even when the weather was cold.

His involvement with the show increased in its intensity. Script supervisor was a responsible job, and one I'd ducked because I knew the concentration it needed and after *Mavis* I didn't want that kind of pressure any more. But Johnny's involvement quickly began to get obsessive. AND possessive. It became impossible to get him to talk about anything else but the show, even in social situations. He explained away the morning tremors by saying he'd had to sit up all night, rewriting scripts. ("So and so's latest batch of scripts were awful," he'd confide) Let me say that we had a team of talented writers whose work would ordinarily need little editing. But Johnny wanted everything to be his way, and if a scene didn't flow as he saw it, he wouldn't tinker with the odd line. He would totally rewrite the whole thing, even if it took all night. His dominance of the scripting reached its nadir when he ordered that writers' names be removed from scripts. This would have been actionable had it been reported to the Writer's Guild, but nobody dared. It was just Johnny being Johnny. The reason he did this was because the cast welcomed the work of certain writers. Some writers wrote best for some characters, and actors recognized this. They'd say "Oh, Derek Strahan's scripts were good this week, they're always good." And similarly enthuse about the work of others.

This infuriated Johnny. He maintained that once scripts had gone through his sausage machine (my admittedly flippant term to describe his editing process) all scripts should be divested of the writer's personal embellishments and stamped with his overall view of the show and the characters.

It didn't succeed. Actors still sneaked up and whispered to me, for example: "They were yours this week, weren't they? We'd know your writing anywhere." And I'm sure they said this to the other writers.

Nobody can really erase the intensely personal input of a writer, nor the generous desire of actors to complement the writers they believe provide them with good lines. But this situation added a nasty conspiratorial element where it was unnecessary.

Johnny's growing obsession with the fictional world of *Number 96* extended to a weird dominance he felt he had over the characters he, himself, had introduced. Arnold Feather was Johnny's invention. This erudite, bumptuous, uber-efficient and more than slightly camp young man became a huge favourite in the series, as portrayed by Jeff Kevin. And he so embodied Johnny's fantasy that late one night, after many drinks, Johnny confided: "I don't know who I'm in love with more – Arnold Feather or Jeff Kevin." Maybe in trying to resolve this dilemma with the real-life actor, the response was negative and therefore displeasing to Johnny. He had Arnold's leg blown off by a letter bomb. It had all the elements of some kind of revenge. He was so determined that this should happen, he already had a wonderful storyline all thought out, in which a recuperating Arnold would fall in love with his nurse. We went along with it. Unfortunately, when Arnold married the nurse, Patti, Johnny took an immediate dislike not only to her, but the actress playing her, Pamela Garrick, and probably to the idea that his fantasy male was sleeping with a woman. He took great satisfaction in nominating her as the next victim of the Pantyhose strangler. It seemed like he was starting to blur reality with the fiction of the show. His manner became extremely volatile. If there was a party with members of the cast, one of them might make a remark he found objectionable, and he would sack them on the spot. He 'sacked' lovable Sheila Kennelly in a hotel corridor after the Logies, and she came to me in tears. I assured her all would be forgotten in the morning. He wrecked a dinner party thrown by Joe Hasham and his new wife Sue, and rang me the following morning to confirm their address so's he could write them a thank-you note. "Thank-you note?" I exclaimed. "You should be sending them an apology!" He didn't remember a thing, and was appalled.

Unlike Johnny, I had other interests and at least tried to keep my life reasonably balanced. I had met a fellow I liked, an English migrant like myself called David Beedie. And there were similarly happy couplings happening around the show. Joe Hasham met his future wife Sue who worked in Channel 10's publicity Department, and married her soon afterwards. Big-hearted Bill Harmon advanced money to Tom Oliver, who played Jack Sellars, to divorce his wife, from whom he was separated, so that he could marry Lynn Rainbow, the actress who played our troubled pharmacist, Sonia Vansard. Sadly, neither of these marriages lasted as long as my relationship with David Beedie.

I had another opportunity to step off the relentless treadmill that was *Number 96*, when I was required to fly to London for talks with the representatives of Senta Productions, the company which had taken out a year's movie option on my new novel *The Love Bite*. They were the creative team behind Michael Apted's just-released film *Triple Echo*, in which a sensitive story was backed up by a high-powered cast led by Glenda Jackson and Oliver Reed. It all sounded major league to me, and I flew to London full of high hopes, with five synopses of my usual monthly quota of *Number 96* scripts, just to keep me grounded.

Before I left, I talked with Bill about an up-coming storyline. I had suggested the germ of the idea, a witchcraft cult in Kings Cross, because of my ongoing fascination with *Rosemary's Baby*, at our last brainstorming session. Since then, it had been expanded with the creative input from our other writers, so that its connection with our building and its characters would come from a lady who moved in with Vera Collins, a lady who was a practising witch. "Don't let's cast her as a Morticia Addams or" (mentioning a real-life, self-confessed Kings Cross witch) "someone odd-looking like Rosalie Norton," I pleaded with Bill. "Let's go against type. Let's have this evil lady totally normal, warm and lovable on the surface. Bill, get Toni Lamond!"

I had a hidden agenda. I knew Toni was going through a difficult time in her life and needed work. That is no reflection on her enormous talent, it happens to everyone in show business at one time or another. I thought casting her as the devious witch would be good for the plot and also a tremendous opportunity for Toni to show her versatility as an actress. Bill loved the idea. Already he was a fan of Toni's, and welcomed the reason to have her in our show.

I flew to London, not knowing that I had planted a land mine that threatened to blow up the show I'd created.

My talks about the movie version of *The Love Bite* in London were less than satisfactory. The people from Senta Productions seemed to have a totally wrong take on the novel. I kept my mouth shut, as I had with Harry Tatelman and the 'Rhodes scholar' script of *Come to Mother.*

That, incidentally, was such a cheapening of the story, with 'mother' rising from her coffin in a crypt and other hackneyed horror film clichés, I'd had great pleasure in consigning it to the waste-basket, as instructed. Now, I foresaw a similar situation with *The Love Bite*, but as these people had only a one-year option on my book, I figured I was in a good position to reject any extension if I didn't like what they came up with.

By the time I returned to Sydney, the 'witchcraft' story had been taped and shown, and had proved to be the most disliked storyline in the short history of *Number 96*. It seemed the viewers would accept any of our outrageous situations except the fact that there could be a coven of witches in Kings Cross, holding the occasional Black Mass to sacrifice a naked virgin. My parents put it in a nutshell. It was all 'too unsettling' they told me, with distaste on their faces.

It was also 'unsettling' for the actors involved. Toni Lamond, who was required to recite the Lord's Prayer backwards, was so spooked, she refused to consign this perversion to memory, and read it from a printed board, placed off-camera. Elaine Lee used her South African background when she was supposed to lapse into mumbo-jumbo while under hypnosis. She resorted to Swahili swear words which, had they been translated, would have put us off the air forever. Sadly, the savage demise of Peter Reynolds, who had played the Satanic priest Vernon Saville, was also linked with this farrago. In real life, he burned to death in his bed, and reports of the tragedy made special mention of one of his last appearances as the Devil's tool.

Fortunately, this one unpopular storyline had no effect on our ratings. It seemed *Number 96* was unstoppable. Sometimes, however, it was hard to sustain our long-running characters. At one stage, we almost had to drop the character of Don Finlayson, but not because of any moral objections. We just seemed to run out of storylines for him. He was now a solicitor, dedicated to his career and his friends. His being a homosexual now seemed universally accepted and, in terms of our show, he had become just plain boring. We emerged from one of our periodic brain-storming sessions with no ongoing plots for him. We were very depressed. We were all fond of the actor Joe Hasham, and Don Finlayson was one of our most popular characters. Over drinks afterwards, the general gloom continued until our Floor Manager, Ted Jobbins, suddenly came up with the solution to our problem. "Why don't we bring in Don's *Auntie Mame* to brighten up his life?", Ted suggested. Johnny Whyte and I looked at one another and cried in unison: "Carol!" Within minutes, we were on the phone to Carol Raye in London, and within a matter of weeks she had returned to Australia to play Don's effervescent Aunt, the Baroness Amanda Von Pappenburg. That one bright idea, from a valued member of our team, not only perpetuated the character of Don right through to the end of the series, but brought Carol Raye back to our shores in one of her most delightful roles.

Putting my reservations about the movie versions of both my novels aside, I not only settled back into the routine of storyline brainstorming, script conferences, and writing my quota, I actually got my private life on a settled course. David Beedie, who at first had seemed rather aimless, got his act together, enrolled in a Travel and Tourism TAFE course, and landed a job with Japan Airlines. He told me he'd done it for me. I was glad he'd done it for himself.

Satisfied that I wasn't nurturing another Udom, we became a couple. David was an unassuming, gentle guy who demonstrated his unswerving devotion to me in many ways. First, he got his own career on track, then he guided me in directions I would never have gone without him. The wonderful view from my Neutral Bay unit had gone. The three houses on the other side of the road had been replaced by two ugly twelve-story high-rises, despite the North Sydney Council's policy of a three-story limit in the area. Policies mean nothing when palms are greased, and that Council in the early seventies was as corrupt as they come. One Council member who was a supporter of the developers actually visited me one evening, masquerading as someone who opposed the high-rises. I was fairly high-profile, and obviously had to be sounded-out about my opposition to the ugly development. This devious councillor engaged me in earnest discussion as if he hated the whole idea, while assessing the strength of my objections. Was it any wonder that despite opposition and petitions, the high rises went up?

My fabulous view had gone, apart from 'glimpses' of the harbour on either side of the new buildings. I suffered the biggest hazard of Sydney living – losing your view. I wanted to get out, but I thought I would never recoup my financial input because the view was lost. We were confronted by a patchwork of windows, and it became a game to focus binoculars on this façade in a reality version of Hitchcock's *Rear Window*, and just as fascinating. I often wonder what became of the young man who stretched out on his bed to masturbate with his right hand, while his left arm cushioned a rifle like a lover. I knew there were weirdoes out there from my 'fan' mail, but this guy was something else!

I put the unit up for sale. I'd had enough of apartment living and began to look around the inner city for a house. Then I noticed that David B. was circling places on the Palm Beach Peninsula. "You don't have to worry about peak hour driving. You can be a writer at home, in beautiful surroundings." he told me. And so, our search for a home extended to the northern beaches.

Everything worked out fine. I sold the unit at a profit, and bought a house on a hillside, on Bilgola Plateau overlooking Pittwater. We moved in, quickly acquired a German Shepherd called Kurt and a black kitten called Daisy. Kurt and Daisy. ("Gert and Daisy" was an old-time British music hall sister act). I bought a Volvo sedan, because Gwennie Plumb said living so far out I'd need a strong, safe, dependable car, and I had a swimming pool installed which was actually level with the roof of the house, because it was higher up the hill. There was a long, steep drive leading down from the road, and after trudging up its daunting length one Sunday after lunch and reaching the pinnacle, Carol Raye said: "I feel I ought to plant a flag!" But that location, on the hillside, surrounded by gum trees and with its view of Pittwater, gave me the peace and privacy that I'd wanted but didn't know it. David B. had been right, as he was in so many ways. At last I had what I had yearned for. A family-style relationship with someone who was utterly supportive, dependable, always there for me, someone who loved making guests feel welcome and for whom no good turn was too much bother.

At last I was reaping the rewards of lots of tough and sometimes financially precarious creative work. A sunny, happy period had started, and there was a lot to look forward to. They'd already filmed big-screen versions of such classics as *War and Peace*, and *Gone With The Wind*. Next on this illustrious list? Why, what else but *Number 96 – the Movie*.

15

I have described the making of the movie and its premiere earlier. And while it played to packed cinemas and drive-ins all over Australia, back at the studio, the juggernaut rolled on, gathering more comedy characters as its momentum increased.

After Dorrie and Herb had been joined by Dorrie's best friend, Flo Patterson, the chemist shop and its troubled occupants had been replaced by a wine bar run by Norma Whittaker and her husband Les,(Sheila Kennelly and Gordon McDougall) who also worked nights as a hospital orderly. What with his gory tales of what went on in the emergency ward and his crackpot inventions, and her ebullient barmaid quality, complete with a blonde wig she only wore in the bar, the Whittakers provided endless fun. They were joined by Dudley Butterfield, who became Norma's assistant in the bar and also did the catering. He was another gay character, but charmingly camp rather than flaring. Johnny enriched the character by making him a film buff who was mad on movie musicals. Everything seemed to remind him of one musical or another which made him then ask "Did you see it? Oh, it was ever so good!" Wickedly, this was Johnny's jokey dig at me and my addiction to MGM. As played by the very heterosexual Chard Hayward, who had appeared as a near-nude extra in one of our earliest episodes, Dudley quickly became of our more popular characters.

And so did the wonderful Mummy and Daddy. Skilled actors Wendy Blacklock and Mike Dorsey attacked these characters as they would a hearty meal. They moved into *Number 96* with their daughter Marilyn (Frances Hargreaves) and son Dean (erstwhile pop idol Marty Rhone). But when the kids moved out, Mummy and Daddy were joined by the gaudily boisterous club entertainer, Trixie O'Toole. She was practically a mirror image of the inimitable club entertainer, Jan Adele, who played her. I had met Jan after seeing one of her performances, and thought she (or her character) would be perfect to inject a little mayhem into the staid, respectable lives of Mummy and Daddy. Trixie barged in like a souped-up 4WD roaring into a nunnery. I talked a lot with Jan and her show-biz mode of speech (she had started as a Tivoli showgirl) was so funny and colourful, I began taking notes. Typical quote: "Yeah, I once recorded a twelve-inch lp. Only trouble was it had a ten-inch hole. It was like a licorice pizza!" Jan fired off this repartee with the precision of a machine gun, and I diligently recorded it all. I transferred my notes to the scripts I wrote for her first appearance in the show and she immediately felt at home. "It's like I'm playing myself," she said. She was.

Trixie O'Toole moved in with Reg and Edie whenever she was in a quiet period between gigs and usually brought chaos into their lives. They were a bizarre trio, but the chemistry worked like magic.

Writing our kind of comedy was not a matter of being able to come up with a string of jokes. We did not need the kind of quick-fire gags that some writers specialize in, like Kathy Lette for example, who seems to go through life with a pun in the oven. Our comedy came from the fact that the characters themselves were innately funny, and therefore the situations they got themselves into were funny, too.

Less amusing but nonetheless fascinating was when we recruited transgender entertainer Carlotta to come into the show. Nobody knew outside our cast and production crew that Vera Collins's new flatmate

'Terry' was being played by a sex change, so convincing was Carlotta. We even engineered a romance between her and Arnold Feather, which reached a very funny but poignant conclusion. In later years Carlotta complained of the way she seemed isolated on the set, how distant everyone was. In actual fact, she was purposely kept under wraps because we didn't want the public to guess her secret before the denouement.

We kept a lot of secrets from our viewers, particularly during our 'murder mystery' plots. First, there was the Knicker-Snipper, a mixed-up psychopath who delighted in cutting up women's underwear. Then there was the Pantyhose Strangler, who disposed of several of the building's residents. Finally, the Hooded Rapist ran amok. We kept these plots going for as long as possible, because, like all good mysteries, they kept the viewers guessing. Then, when we could string out the plot no longer, the perpetrator would be revealed in an Agatha Christie-type surprise climax. Of course, many viewers would claim "Oh, I knew who it was all the time." The point is, even we didn't! We never decided who was going to be the villain of the piece until practically the end of the plot. Then we'd review our cast of characters, decide who we wanted to get rid of, then make that person the culprit. I'm sure there were many occasions when our chosen culprit couldn't possibly have been in a particular place at a particular time, or gained entry into a particular flat, but nobody ever bothered to check up.

We were a lot more responsible when it came to our more serious themes. We tackled many social issues, in fact a person no less than Dr Sarah Williams, the then senior psychiatrist at North Ryde Hospital went into print, declaring that there were several areas in which the program had helped change community attitudes for the better.

Perhaps the most dramatic change was the public's view on homosexuality, which became much more informed and acceptable thanks to the portrayal and presentation of our gay solicitor, Don Finlayson, who did more to achieve a more universal acceptance than all the gay lib groups put together. In an oft-told story, I was once travelling by bus and heard one little old lady say to another: "Oh, I do hope Don gets back with his boyfriend."

Women were made more conscious of the threat of breast cancer when the much beloved Lucy Sutcliffe discovered a lump in her breast. The night she was told the lump was benign achieved the highest ratings in the entire run of *Number 96*. So much for sex and sin!

This plotline was introduced at the request of the Anti-Cancer Council. Although we had become adept at coming up with our own takes on social issues, we were more than happy to comply if we were asked by vested interests to bring certain subjects to the public's attention.

The Autistic Children's charity rarely got decent contributions, and they felt this was because the public didn't know enough about autism to warrant donations. So we had Dorrie forcing Herb and Flo into a ballroom dancing competition to aid autistic children, even though Dorrie herself misheard the charity and thought it was for *Artistic* children (She had been a Shirley Temple fan!) This enabled us – through the plotline – to inform her (and the viewers) about the reality of autism, and also gave us a lot of funny sequences of her rehearsing Herb and Flo. "They're coming on like a regular Fred Astaire and Ginger Meggs!' she proclaimed delightedly. In fact, they won the competition, and actually presented a real cheque for $500 to a member of the Autistic Society on camera.

A request from the Police Department for us to highlight the growing use of drugs by schoolkids gave us a powerful storyline. In this, we had a schoolgirl tempted into mainlining by a wayward friend. The scenes that showed her shooting up, were actually supervised on the set by two members of the Police Drug Squad. Of course, some of the critics labeled this as gratuitous, not knowing of the circumstances, but judging from the influx of mail, we had certainly alerted a lot of parents to the dangers threatening vulnerable teenagers.

Our only other brush with drugs had been much earlier, when a niece of Dorrie's came from Coff's Harbour to stay, bringing a marijuana plant which she told her aunt was just a herb. So, when Dorrie had to take a salad to a Senior Citizens bring-a-plate function, she practically stripped the marijuana plant and scattered the leaves amongst the lettuce. Like all the senior citizens who ate the salad, I'm a bit hazy about what happened, but despite the fact that no liquor had been served, several pensioners were arrested for being 'drunk and disorderly', one respectable lady had removed her clothes and was dancing in the streets, several others were observed attempting to bring their late-life sexual fantasies to reality, and Dorrie and Herb arrived back at *Number 96* definitely off the planet.

Our high ratings, the constant public attention, and the elevation of practically anybody who appeared on *Number 96* to instant recognition, tempted a lot of 'names' to appear. My *Mavis* compatriot, Noelene Brown, joined us briefly. A strange rock star, who in a previous life had been the 'Clark' teamed with Barry Crocker in the performing partnership 'Crocker and Clark', turned up in his new persona, Count Copernicus. Needless to say, in Dorrie-speak, she referred to him as Count Copper-Knickers!

We were even graced by the illustrious presence of the Duke and Duchess of Bedford. They were in town for the twin purposes of plugging their stately home in England to potential tourists, and her autobiography about becoming a Duchess, *Nicole Nobody*. To publicise their appearance in *Number 96*, Tom Greer organized a harbour cruise with as many of us who could be spared from the shooting schedule on board. Duchess 'Nicole' and I found we had a publisher in common, W.H. Allen, who had published my two novels and her autobiography. We both had axes to grind about how we had been treated, so we sat there on this gloriously sunny day, peeling prawns and drinking white wine and aired our grievances. I talked about how thin-lipped they were at my insistence on visiting booksellers and introducing myself. Nicole, a charming, attractive Frenchwoman, was concerned about their parsimonious attitude. "Twice they had me there for discussions which extended over the luncheon period. But never once did they suggest we eat." The third time she was invited for a late morning conference, she and her secretary took in a picnic basket. As the talks reached midday, the Duchess and her secretary – still talking – produced the picnic basket, and unloaded fresh rolls, pate, a dismembered roast chicken, containers of salad and fresh fruit onto the W.H. Allen executive's desk. And proceeded to devour it all, in front of him, while continuing their discussions.

This was a lady after my own heart, feisty and earthy and inimitably French. The Duke and Duchess's appearance on our show required them to turn up in Norma's Wine Bar in search of Baroness Amanda Von Pappenberg (Carol Raye). There was a brief exchange between them and Carol and then they left. Two intriguing points. It was felt necessary to remove the 'nude' portrait of Norma Whittaker from the wall of the bar during their scene. Whose cringing, forelock-tugging idea was that? And, as the Duke and Duchess had to join Actors Equity to deliver their speaking parts, they were entitled to a basic appearance fee.

They collected it. And, tucking their $200 into their pockets, they departed our shores.

International cabaret and TV star, Lorrae Desmond also joined us as a Mrs Robinson character, straight out of *The Graduate*, a glamorous older woman who had a fling with Arnold Feather. She – the actress and the character – delivered perfectly what I consider is one of the wittiest and clever lines of the entire series. We joined them on a water bed after an apparently less-than-successful sexual encounter. Arnold, we gather, suffered from premature ejaculation. When the phone rang and she heard her husband was on his way home, Arnold jumped out of bed, frantically began pulling his clothes on, and urging her to phone for a taxi. "Do you think it will come quickly?" he asked.

"If the rest of the evening is anything to go by, it'll be here before you get your pants on!" she replied.

I didn't know Lorrae well at that time. She'd refused my offer of a week on *Mavis* several years before, we waved at each other in restaurants, and I'd been to see her clever one-woman show at the Manly Music Loft. Fate decreed that we would become much closer in the years to come.

On Wednesday, October 9th, 1974, Sydney's afternoon tabloid 'The Daily Mirror' featured a glaring front-page headline:

1.8 MILLION WATCH 'NUMBER 96'

Based on surveys by the McNair-Anderson Analysis team, the story revealed that our show was still the most popular on Australian television, with an audience 350,000 greater than its nearest rival, the biggest ratings number in TV history. These figures featured in the annual report of Federation of Australian Commercial Television Stations. The story also stated that *Number 96* had achieved an unprecedented level of employment for local talent. During the past year, the show had used 1,957 actors; 35 writers; and 57 technicians and crew members.

None of the other channels could break our muscular hold over the 8-30pm time slot. They threw everything at us, even 'The King' Graham Kennedy. And missed. It must have been the first time in his career that Graham Kennedy didn't pull the biggest audience.

Our success signaled the start of merchandising. There was a *Number 96* cookbook; Abigail, still clinging to her sex symbol status, recorded a breathy album of songs, as did – in a more homely old-fashioned way,- Pat McDonald and Ron Shand, with a collection of nostalgic standards. Other cast members leapt onto the bandwagon. Joe Hasham recorded an album. Even actor Norman Yemm, transferred his reviled character as Harry Collins, Vera's brutal husband, to disc in a revolting single called *Darlin' Vera*, a sentimental hymn of praise to the wife he'd deserted and subsequently barged in on and raped.

There were *Number 96* T-shirts, and paperback novel tie-ins written by people who had nothing to do with the show. Tom Oliver fronted a wine bar in Kensington called, in a switch on his character's name, *Jack's Cellars*. Everyone was capitalizing on their new-found stardom in a frenzied rush for riches. And I was enjoying every minute of it.

I had a hit show on television, two successful novels both bought for the movies, a very happy relationship with David Beedie, and a comfortable home on Bilgola Plateau. We entertained frequently. I loved to cook. David B. enjoyed looking after guests. Our home became a gathering place for everyone associated with *Number 96*.

There was one party around this period of my life that ended badly for me, but set a behavioural pattern for the rest of my life. It was the end-of-year break-up party held on the set of Norma's Wine Bar at the Channel Ten studio on a hot summer evening. For some reason, David B. didn't come, which was a pity because, being a light drinker, he usually did the driving on these occasions. As proceedings became jollier, red wine accidentally splashed across the white blouse of one of the guests. A bucket of water was produced and the lady took off the blouse to dunk in the bucket, which left her in her bra. Ever the gentleman, I took off my shirt and offered it to her as a cover up.

This left me naked from the waist up, and it was in this less-than-sartorial state that I was arrested for drunk driving on the way home. More inebriated than usual, I had let the car stray over the middle line going around the tortuous Bilgola Bends and knocked corners with an oncoming vehicle. Stupidly, because I was conscious of the way I was and the way I looked, I kept driving, and made it home. I didn't even have the chance to get out of the car. The police were already there. They wouldn't let me go into the house to tell David B. They breathalysed me, arrested me and took me off to the lock-up in Collaroy. It was nearly 4am before I was allowed to telephone David and ask him to come and bail me out. By that time, I had gone through the full arrest procedure, and been locked in a cell. They not only took the laces from my shoes and my belt, but also my glasses, so that meant I really couldn't see anything. When the glasses were returned to me as I left with David B., the first thing I saw was the despising look the officer-in-charge gave me. No wonder. I'd sobered up, but I was baretop, scrunching the waist of my pants to hold them up, shuffling in shoes with no laces and red-eyed from weeping. I have never felt more ashamed.

I arrived for my court appearance in Manly in the New Year, carrying several references from important people attesting to my good character. But nothing could erase the fact that I had been over the limit and had left the scene of an accident. I knew I thoroughly deserved any punishment meted out to me. My only worry was that it would get into the papers and count against *Number 96*. Fortunately, there was just a brief item in the Manly Daily, and no mention of the show.

My license was cancelled for six months, I was fined $500, and ordered to pay for the repairs to the other car. When added to the repairs on my own car, my costs amounted to $2,000. This was a less-than-severe punishment. The knowledge that I could have seriously injured or even killed another human being sat heavily on my conscience. I had learned my lesson. To this day, I have never driven a car after even having had just one drink. I've faced what could happen, and it's not pretty.

I was still suffering the humiliation and inconvenience of this experience when in early 1975, Bill Harmon told me: "Keep April-May free. We're gonna sell *Number 96* to the world at the TV Festival in Cannes!"

Bill's invitation came at just the right time. Living on the Peninsula without transport unless David B was available to be chauffeur meant I spent a lot of time at home. Now I would be away for the latter part of my license suspension.

I joined Bill and his wife Del at the Carlton Hotel in Cannes the third week in April. Nancy Cash, Don's widow, was also along, so that made four of us, ready to sell *Number 96* to buyers from seventy countries attending the Festival. New Zealand had already refused to air the show, and we put that down to what could be politely termed the extreme conservatism of the straitlaced Kiwis. Little did we know we would get the same reaction from the rest of the world.

Comparing the TV Festival to the legendary Film Festival which immediately followed it was like comparing the drab spinster sister who arrives at the church first, before the gloriously radiant bride who comes later. Frankly, in those days it was a curtain raiser to the main event. Nonetheless important, given television's growing supremacy in the entertainment stakes, it was just duller. No glitz, no glamour, no international stars – they were waiting in the wings for us earnestly-committed TV types to vacate our suites at the Carlton so that they could move in. Even so, it was tremendously exciting to be there, at what was, for a few weeks, the hub of the world's entertainment industry.

The orderly palm-lined seafront with its luxury hotels facing their private sections of the beach, the restaurants, a climate like warm perfume, all combined to whisper wealth, exclusivity and opportunity, and the magical chance to attain all three. It wasn't just about trying to achieve success. That place, that ambience makes you believe you can.

There were two or three glamorous receptions, one hosted by the Australian contingent. But basically, it was a gruelling exercise in hard sell. Like an Ideal Homes Exhibition, we all had stalls in the Main Hall, called the *Palais de Festival*. There were private screenings of episodes of our show for the visiting buyers. And late afternoons, when I'd done my stint, I quickly changed and joined the leisure set on the Carlton's barricaded stretch of beach and sipped long drinks served by bikini-clad waiters. Lying there, on an allocated *chaise longue* in an orderly line of *chaise-longues*, I ruminated on the difference in beach culture. I was used to just running onto Balmoral, Bondi or the beaches Whale and Palm on the Peninsula, and throwing myself down on the sand. There was something quite homogenized and artificial about this Riviera experience.

Bill soon got restless. "We shoulda brought Tom Greer to stir up some hype. We shoulda brought Abigail!" he grumbled. Despite having unloaded Australian TV's first sex symbol, Bill still had a soft spot for her – or maybe a hard one! "It's all so fuckin' dull." He surveyed the Australian contingent, all running around earnestly and busily, writers, directors, producers, independent documentary makers, representatives of the commercial network product. "Nobody knows who we are or what we represent. There's none of that show-biz pizzazz!"

He decided to rectify the situation. At his suggestion we went out and bought half a dozen white T-shirts and a roll of bright red material. Suddenly, the Harmon's swanky suite at the Carlton became a sweatshop with Del and Nancy expertly fashioning the *Number 96* logo with strips of the red material, and all of us helping to stick the results on the front of the T-shirts. The finished product, I might say, was dazzling. The four of us put them on and marched out onto the Croisette. The reaction was immediate. We became the focus of attention. Passers-by stopped and asked: "Excusez-moi, what ees theez Numbaire dees-neuf sees?" So then we told them that it was the title of Australia's most popular TV show.

We feared that the rest of the Australian contingent would think us as brash as our show, but it had the opposite effect. Suddenly, our fellow-countrymen began sporting outsize name-cards emblazoned with the title of their product.

As far as Bill was concerned, that was only the beginning – but there was no way anyone else would try to copy his next move.

"David," he said, as we took a rare hour of relaxation to have a lunch break on the beach, "I want you to do something for me. See all these girls going bare-top?" He indicated several nubile girls on the public beach, at the other side of the barriers fencing off the Carlton Hotel's section of sand from the hoi polloi. "Go ask one of them if she'll strip for us to advertise the show."

"What?" I exclaimed. "Where?"

"Just parading along the beachfront," he said casually, pointing to the Croisette, "I'll spread the word to the international press; she'll appear wearing a *Number 96* T-shirt, then she'll peel it off. Bingo! Instant publicity!" I had to laugh at the hutzpah of this man. "You can't do it," I told him. "Bare-top on the beach is okay, baretop anywhere else, particularly on a public thoroughfare, is illegal. We'll all be arrested." I shook my head. "No, I won't do it."

He turned to his delightful wife, Del. "Honey, you go talk to them. I can't – they'll think I'm a dirty old man. David won't do it. You go, honey. They'll trust a woman."

And, unbelievably, Del scampered off to the barrier. She squatted down and began crooking her finger, gesturing. My God, I thought, they'll think she's a lesbian on the loose! A willowy blonde with breasts like pumpkins wandered over to Del. They had a conversation through the wire screen, like convict and girlfriend in an old Warner Brothers gangster movie. Then Del came back all smiles. "She's interested," Del told us. "So I invited her for cocktails."

The girl turned up, had a couple of drinks and agreed to Bill's concept. She was very good looking, charming and intelligent, too. After she left, we all had another drink and toasted our success, even though I thought it would lead to us all being thrown into jail. We were just about to leave to have dinner when the phone rang. It was our bare-top damsel. She had told her husband about the job, and he'd forbidden her to do it. She hadn't mentioned a husband to us, so it was left to us to wonder whether that was just an excuse, or whether it had dawned upon her that we were actually a gang of white slavers, poised to whip her off to Macao.

Bill put down the phone solemnly and relayed her withdrawal to us. Then he looked at me. "The ball's in your court, David. I came up with the idea, Del did all she could, now it's your turn. You gotta find us a sexy broad."

Feeling like a cut-rate Florenz Zeigfeld, I went out late that night to enlist the aid of my only hope, the Cote d'Azur's leading drag entertainer, Les Lee. I'd been given an introduction to Les Lee, who had his own very popular cabaret room in Cannes, and had sat through his act and later had supper with him a couple of nights previously. He was my only contact, and I felt if anybody could help me, Les Lee could. He said he would.

The following day, I met him for lunch at a beach café, and he introduced me to a beautiful 20-year-old self-professed 'model' named Fabienne. Despite her good looks, she appeared quiet and unassuming. Nevertheless when I requested her, with a panache I certainly didn't feel, to remove her top, she complied with a casual shrug and a smile to reveal a pair of small but perfectly-formed breasts.

Bill was delighted at my discovery when I took her to meet him after lunch, and decided to do the stunt later that afternoon. He began to telephone the list of press representatives we'd been given. He wasn't the most lucid of communicators at the best of times, and in his state of high excitement, he was having great difficulty in making himself understood during one call. "Excuse me," he bawled into the receiver, waving an arm wildly, "I don't speak English!" He was prone to these funny mixed-up sayings. Another time, when discussing a difficult actor, Bill exclaimed: "He's cuttin' off his balls to spite his face!"

Promptly at three, we all assembled on the Croisette....Fabienne in a *Number 96* T-shirt, and a bikini bottom and Bill in his T-shirt, with reporters and photographers clustered around, and Del, Nancy and I on the sidelines waiting to be arrested. At a given signal, Fabienne gracefully pulled the T-shirt over her head, then bare-top – and almost bare-bottom - she walked along the seafront handing out *Number 96* brochures. One old lady actually spat at her. An elderly gentleman waved his walking stick. At least, I *think* it was his walking stick.

As instructed by Bill, Fabienne made her way to the steps of the Palais de Festival where, by this time crowds had gathered to admire the view. At the top of the steps, she turned, still handing out the brochures. The photographers were going wild.

And then I saw them. Two gendarmes approached the steps and began talking to Fabienne.

This is it, I thought. She's going to tell them who coerced her into this stunt and then point me out. Then the two of us, if not all of us, would be flung into the local equivalent of Alcatraz!

Fabienne gestured for Bill to join them. I was puzzled. They were all smiling. Then Bill handed over the girl's discarded T-shirt. Evidence, I wondered? Then the gendarmes departed with the T-shirt, smiling broadly. I found out later they'd approached Fabienne merely to ask where they could obtain a copy of the T-shirt for themselves – and that was all.

They got the T-shirt; we got a million dollars-worth of publicity.

The next day, we had the entire Page 3 of London's *Daily Mirror*. Photographs of Fabienne disrobing and walking along the croisette were headlined: "Not So Much a Programme, More a Way of Love," with the sub-heading: "Fabienne bids to Sell a TV Sizzler from Down Under." The text told readers about Australia's controversial nightly serial, which was described as 'the frankest TV show in the world.' It quoted me as saying: "You could say it's *Crossroads* with sex!" (*Crossroads* was Britain's idea of a soap and about as sexy as corn plasters). I was particularly amused by the last paragraph: "Mr Sale and Mr Harmon both patrolled the Cannes seafront in white T-shirts with *Number 96* emblazoned in red. But Fabienne attracted more attention…without anything on her chest at all."

Other newspapers also had full covers of the stunt, but in Ireland, 'full cover' literally meant covering Fabienne's nipples with a black bar. Another London paper headlined its photographs with "Too Hot for Us!", and added an old publicity shot of Abigail, with a prurient depiction of *Number 96* as something that made *Deep Throat* look like a Disney release.

We didn't employ a cuttings service so God knows what was printed about us in the European newspapers we didn't get to see. The following day, the *Daily Mirror* again gave us its entire Page 3. This time, building on my quote of the previous day, the headline was: "X-Roads! Or What Goes On – And Comes Off – In That TV Show From Down Under." This article was illustrated by a huge picture of Tom Oliver with a naked Rebecca Gilling in the shower scene from the movie.

But already, the general reaction to our show was negative. "…the sexy sizzler has really fizzled out in Britain – yesterday it got a swift 'No Entry' sign from the BBC and ITV." Tactfully, they pointed out that they would be unlikely to be interested in such a program…even though they had not seen it. ATV, the company responsible for *Crossroads,* said: "Perish the thought that our family serial should be associated with this program in any way."

You could almost see the pursed lips and hear the clipped, superior, disapproving tones. And this from a country that happily embraced the dirty schoolboy antics of Benny Hill chasing scantily-clad girls young enough to be his grand-daughters, and the lavatorial nudge-nudge wink-wink style of the *Carry On* movies. Nowadays, they're churning out explicitly sexy numbers like *Footballers Wives* and *Hotel Babylon.* It took them thirty years to catch up.

Meanwhile, in a bizarre reversal, the Brits happily embrace the homogenized vision of Australia as presented in *Neighbours* and *Home and Away*, an always-sunny suburbia inhabited by (usually) blonde, blue-eyed Caucasians with not an ethnic in sight, acting out (although 'acting' is frequently beyond their capabilities) laundered versions of re-cycled plots.

The same applied to America. We know how much the Americans admire success, and they were reduced to the state of ravening wolves by the ease with which *Number 96* had won its status as Australia's top-rated show. They wanted to duplicate it, and tried. But nothing worked. How could they translate our scripts, which were an accurate depiction of Australia's cultural mix and the problems engendered by this mix? How could they duplicate the humour, which was so typically Australian? And how could they depict our open approach to sex? But they tried, even though American TV was governed by the legendary Black Book. This was a hallowed manual that listed all the do's and don'ts, what was to be avoided, what would be unacceptable in certain regions. One of the main regions was what is termed the Bible Belt, inhabited by fundamental Christians living in rural communities. In short, red necks. Their hang-ups would negate fifty percent of our storylines. Another region, the Deep South with its history of racism would not accept any interaction between our people of colour, African Americans, indigenous Australians, a character from India. Forget mere interaction, we even had an inter-racial love affair!

Their attempts to launderise our show and make it acceptable to American audiences were ludicrous and, of course, they failed. It took the Americans at least another fifteen years before they could come up with a reasonable facsimile. And that was *Melrose Place*.

Just a few years ago, I was asked to address a visiting team of literary students from Boston University. They were in their early twenties, and I was told they were inclined to giggle at what was being presented to them in Australia. I decided to show them a segment from a video compilation of *Number 96* to illustrate my talk. I faced them well prepared. I had selected a scene where African American Ronne Arnold confronted a couple of racists in the local pub who wanted to get him out of the apartment building, and sent up the whole "I hate blacks" syndrome with humorous but very biting dialogue.

"I'm going to show you an excerpt from a series we did in the seventies," I began in a reasonably quiet tone. "It's in black and white, and it may appear a little creaky, but I would like you to understand something." I dropped the ingratiating delivery and started to get hard. "While we were doing this" (I began to yell at them) "YOU LOT WERE DOING THE BRADY BUNCH!"

That shut them up. They saw, they gasped, and they took the ensuing discussion seriously.

And it's not only people from overseas that we have to convince about our groundbreaking efforts. The cultural cringe still exists. We have broken down barriers years before other countries. We have been more outspoken and we have been more daring. But we forget, or are hesitant to claim that we did it first.

I was overwhelmed when the Australian Writers Guild honoured me with an Achievement Award for Comedy several years ago, particularly as I wasn't headed for the grave, as these gestures sometimes indicate. I used my acceptance speech to point out how we should claim our achievements, instead of kow-towing to the Americans, praising their belated efforts years later when they merely have followed our lead. I repeated my story about the talk to the Boston literary group. That highlighted how we had confronted racism in our country. But in this case, I used the fact that we had tackled the subject of homosexuality sympathetically and seriously twenty years before *Will and Grace* and *Queer as Folk*, and we should claim that breakthrough as our own.. Too often these days, we have young writers in the media, too lazy to do their research, crediting America with breakthroughs we pioneered in this country. They should wake up and stop thinking the world only came into existence the day they were born.

Back in 1975, Bill, Del, Nancy and I realized from the reaction we'd had in Cannes that our 'in your face' drama was just too advanced for other countries in those stitched up times. It was disappointing, but I had other fish to fry. Once again, I was Hollywood-bound.

16

I flew home from the Cannes TV festival via Hollywood. Kathryn Grayson was interested in doing a TV series and asked me to come up with a concept for her, something fun and different with a little excitement and mayhem in it. What I came up with was *Katie*, in which she was to play a retired opera singer with a propensity not only for getting involved in murder mysteries but also for solving them. Every episode was to be a potted Agatha Christie-type puzzle with a surprise denoument. I sent it over to Kathryn a couple of months later, but nothing came of it. Angela Lansbury had great success with practically the same format, several years later, in *Murder She Wrote.*

While in Hollywood, I also looked up Michael Ludmer, the Story Executive at Universal, who told me the exciting news that a made-for television feature of my novel *Come to Mother* was about to happen from a teleplay by Joseph Stefano of *Outer Limits* fame.

Several months later, after its airing as ABC Suspense Movie of the Week, I read the review in *Variety*. It began: "Interesting concept turns sour..." and ended: "The shame lies in the waste of talent and a good idea." I got some consolation from these phrases because they acknowledged the worth of my original story. However, in typical Hollywood fashion they'd changed the title, the plot, the characters and the location. Called *Live Again, Die Again*, it had little to do with *Come to Mother.*

Having ditched Harry Tatelman's trashy 'B' grade horror approach, one would think they'd have returned to my novel as the basis for a smart, off-beat thriller with touches of black humour. But that's not the way Hollywood works. They settled for "a melodramatic binge, in which director Richard A Colla opts for heavy-handed helming of his cast as they try swimming upstream against a flood of bathos…" as another critic wrote.

Back in Australia, I continued with my regular script-writing commitment to *Number 96,* but became aware of a rising discontent behind the scenes. Johnny Whyte was becoming more and more autonomous and possessive of the show. He was already removing the names of writers from the scripts, so that the only name on them was his own as Script Editor. Threatening to resign to go back to England was another ploy. He nursed grievances like they were ailing relatives. He also circulated scathing letters to our team of writers, obviously penned in the small hours when alcohol had nourished his evil twin. He never sent one to me, but judging from what I was told about the insulting and demeaning tone of the letters, it's a wonder we kept any writers at all. At the time, I confronted Bill Harmon with Johnny's behaviour. He waved his arms ineffectually. "Well, David, you keep goin' away, and someone's gotta hold the fort," completely ignoring the fact that my last absence had been to go to Cannes at his invitation.

I decided to throw a party in an attempt to revive the jolly spirit of the series, not just any old party, but a big, lavishly different one. I hired one of the Palm Beach ferries, invited the cast, studio crew, friends and my parents, and with around a hundred people on board we chugged off into a Pittwater sunset. It was a riotous success.

Despite this, the prickly atmosphere surrounding *Number 96* continued. The botched movie version of *Come to Mother* had disappointed me greatly, and now I suspected my second novel *The Love Bite* was in the wrong movie hands, too. Bill Harmon said: "David – you need to do something new. Name it." I grabbed at an urge, an idea. I wanted to regain the fun of the early revues I'd written, and now I wanted it on a larger scale.

"I'd like to do a TV special with Jill Perryman. I want to turn her into Australia's Carol Burnett." *The Carol Burnett Show* was a ratings hit wherever it was shown, and showcased its star in an entertaining mix of broad comedy and song.

Bill responded positively. Jill Perryman, just out of the long-running J.C. Williamson's stage hit *No, No Nanette,* was signed by the new company formed to do the special, Sale-Harmon. Bill argued: "Why not my name first?" I told him: "This way it sounds better." And privately, with my black sense of humour, I thought that if Bill had died instead of Don, this could have been a Cash-Sale production, which would have put a retail slant on the entire enterprise.

Jill Perryman was at that time Australia's leading musical comedy actress. An angular streak of a woman rather than conventionally beautiful, she had a big wide smile, a great singing voice and a gift for comedy. The camera hadn't been kind to her in earlier TV outings, but I was determined that in my special she would look her best, and ensured this in discussions with Ted Dunne, the costume designer, and lighting and camera technicians.

Jill asked for another theatrical powerhouse performer, Gloria Dawn, as her principal guest. With these two ladies on board, I recruited the male Aussie sex symbol Jack Thompson, to provide some beefcake.

My admirable *Mavis* colleague, Ken Shadie, was now writing for *Number 96,* so he was on hand to help me write the special material, and our beloved maestro Tommy Tycho was with us to provide his musical magic.

For a one-off special, *Jill* rated exceptionally well. The TEN network immediately ordered a 13-week series of one-hour shows. We were all ecstatic. Bill Harmon envisaged another hit series to consolidate his success with *Number 96*. I was delighted to be back in the world of song, dance and comedy. It appeared everyone was happy with *Jill* but Jill. She had never looked better on camera, never been supplied with so much specially-written material, and never been presented so strongly on television. Yet, unaccountably, she turned her back on a series that would have extended her popularity to the vast television audience, and opted instead to accept fifth-featured billing in the next J.C. Williamson production, *A Little Night Music*.

We were all shattered. Bill Harmon bounced back with typical hutzpah. "Okay, David, so we go with Gloria!" Bill adored Gloria Dawn's raucous performing personality, as I did, so we began to formulate another special for her along the lines of *Jill*. As with Perryman, I gave Gloria the opportunity to choose her guests. Always a more solo performer, Gloria didn't seem at all interested, except to ask if her daughter Donna could do a spot with her. I agreed, and was glad because the teenaged Donna Lee's appearance gave us a preview of another generation of her family's gift to entertainment.

Sadly, *Gloria* didn't rate as well as *Jill* had done, therefore there was no offer from the network for a series. The pity of it all was underlined by the critical accolades earned by *Jill*. A consortium of Melbourne critics, in their review of the television season awarded us: Best Variety Show – *Jill;* Best costumes: Ted Dunne; Best Variety Producer – David Sale. A friend in Melbourne sent me a cutting listing these awards. I immediately sent a copy to Jill Perryman at Her Majesty's Theatre. I never heard back from her.

Even though I was doing the specials, every month, wherever I was, whatever else occupied me, I always filled my quota of one week's *Number 96* scripts. The writing team seemed to change constantly, as Johnny Whyte became more demanding. His obsessions with Jeff Kevin/Arnold Feather had soured the previous year, resulting in Arnold's leg being blown off. Johnny had this way of penalizing the characters played by out-of-favour actors. Now, Arnold was supposedly fitted with a prosthetic limb which required Jeff Kevin to limp through his part. We all got rather tired of this, Bill included. He finally said: "What the hell, the leg grows back!" Arnold stopped limping, and no mention was ever made again about the missing limb. A miracle had occurred right before our eyes.

As new writers were taken on board, some were surprising blasts from my past. David Phillips became our synopsis writer. Actress Susan Swinford joined us, too, as a writer. As a boy, David Phillips had played Mrs Anna's son, Louis, to Susan's Mrs Anna in the lavish production of *The King and I* in which I'd also worked. And so, all those years later, Phillips, Susan and I were reunited in very different circumstances to the court of the King of Siam. But unlike *The King and I,* our current show was in trouble. The ratings were sliding just as surely as melting snow slips down a mountainside. At script conferences, writers were complaining about the difficulties of coming up with new stories for some of our well-worn, long-established characters. Aldo and Roma. And Les Whittaker, whose Johnny-Whyte-inspired inventions ("This'll make us a fortune, Norma!") had become just plain irritating. We had a crisis meeting. We were still eleven weeks ahead in scripting, so any changes we decided upon would have to happen in slow motion – or so it seemed. The meeting progressed into and well after the cocktail hour. We were all drinking quite heavily in our frustration.

In my usual flippant way, I said something like: "Let's blow 'em all up and make 'em disappear in one swell foop!" I snapped my finger and thumb. It was meant as a joke, but Bill latched onto it. "Yeah, why not?" he mused. As we callously considered his idea of a bomb to dispose of some of our beloved but extraneous characters, I was still thinking eleven weeks ahead. "No," Bill burst out. "If we're gonna do it, we do it now!" This involved massive tinkering with eleven weeks of episodes, changing everything involving Maggie Cameron, who was to plant the bomb, and the reworking of two weeks of episodes leading up to the fatal explosion, plus major adjustments in the episodes following the bomb blast. I took this on as my job and worked on those scripts solidly and swiftly until I had them all blending seamlessly into the bomb episode, which was expertly written by Derek Strahan.

It was September, 1975. It was a Friday. And the bomb, planted by Maggie Cameron in some cartons delivered to the delicatessen, exploded. Nowadays, they would duplicate the façade of the apartment building in a paddock and blow it up, or perhaps just create the devastation by computer. In those days, they actually did it in the studio, the week before. Explosives experts set charges. The floor crew were evacuated on a countdown. Robotically-controlled cameras, their lens protected by sheets of shatter-proof glass, were focused on the fake front of the building. The studio had been emptied of people. And thank God it was, because when that famous explosion happened, the blast was so unexpectedly strong, it blew out the studio doors!

It also blew everyone's mind. Like a lot of other things associated with *Number 96*, the explosion garnered an incredible burst of publicity. It was headlined on the front pages of all the leading newspapers as if it was a real-life disaster. Lists of the dead and injured were published as if real people had been killed or hurt. Rival television networks, including the ABC, ran footage of the moments before, during and after the bomb blast on their news bulletins. Co-incidentally, Lucy Sutcliffe was nearing the culmination of a pregnancy. It worked perfectly for us when dovetailed into the bomb sequence. The shock sent Lucy into labour, and the birth of the Suttcliffe's baby daughter introduced a little positive humanity into the otherwise depressing scenes of death and destruction. Aldo and Roma Godolfus were killed in the explosion, as was Les Whittaker, who'd tried to alert the residents of the building and ended up in the delicatessen when the bomb ticked off its last moments. A fourth casualty was a minor character played by actor Scott Lambert.

The disaster also robbed us of one of our strongest characters. Maggie Cameron, who owned the block of flats, wanted to redevelop the site, and had planted the bomb to frighten everyone away. She had not meant to kill anyone, and so had planted a warning note that was discovered too late. She was pronounced insane, and thereby disappeared from the series, until we found a logical reason to bring her back.

As a precautionary measure, just before the bomb episode went to air, Bettina Welch, who played Maggie Cameron so convincingly, was shipped off to her homeland of New Zealand, more or less to hide out until the anticipated furore had died down. We all loved and respected Bettina, who in no way resembled the rapacious, vitriolic woman she was asked to play. However, she had made her character's nastiness so believable, we were scared some of the weirdos out there in viewer-land, would attempt revenge. We were all immensely relieved to have her out of harm's way. Bettina's Maggie Cameron was television's first glamorous but evil bitch, a character later duplicated again and again in other soaps. And to be honest, I had copied her too. I based Maggie on the strong women Bette Davis and Joan Crawford had portrayed in their movie hey-day.

But the 'bitch syndrome' first happened on television – like a lot of things – in *Number 96*. Later incarnations included 'Pat the Rat' in a Grundy opus, and Alexis Carrington in *Dynasty*.

The abrupt, callous and cataclysmic explosion not only shocked the nation, it also gave a much-needed boost to our ratings. And, despite the negative outcomes of our specials with Jill Perryman and Gloria Dawn, Bill Harmon was once again induced to expand into other series. Unfortunately, none of his efforts succeeded. I begged off being associated with any of them. One, *The Unisexers*, about a group of young people designing jeans, actually made it briefly to air. The rest were mostly attempted spin-offs from *Number 96*, which Bill, in tightwad mode, tried to justify financially by shooting the scenes as part of the show's budget, then expecting them to work when they were removed from *Number 96* episodes and assembled into plots that didn't hang together. Suddenly, our regular characters began to behave rather strangely in certain scenes, which must have been confusing for our faithful viewers. For instance, the gentle, gay solicitor, Don Finlayson, started to appear tough and Clint Eastwood-like, because certain scenes from his spin-off private eye drama *A Law Unto Himself* were shot and shown in *Number 96*. Similarly, with a Mummy and Daddy spin-off, which had Reg and Edie going to work for an advertising agency. For *Fair Game* Vera Collins (Elaine Lee) suddenly – in *Number 96* – started associating with two other divorcees, and swapping so many double entendres, their scenes together made the average *Carry On* movie look like something by Chekov.

It was sheer madness, and in the process must surely have damaged the ratings boost the bomb blast had given our show. And of course, none of the 'pilots' hastily assembled from scenes shot as part of *Number 96* emerged as the kind of smartly scripted and edited vehicles that networks would have snapped up. I'd tried to explain this to Bill while it was happening, but he wouldn't listen. The outcome – dismal failures, every one of them – came as no surprise to me.

We were now into 1976. The movie option on my second novel, *The Love Bite,* was dropped by Senta Productions but almost immediately, British director Douglas Hickox showed an interest.

Having learned my lesson with Universal's botched job on *Come to Mother,* I told my London agents that any deal would have to include at least a first draft screenplay by David Sale. Douglas Hickox agreed to this, and a very lucrative contract for the screen rights was drawn up.

Emboldened by this looming boost to my finances, David B and I began searching the Peninsula for a more lavish abode. We found it at 325 Whale Beach Road, Palm Beach which was everything a slum kid could dream of. At the end of a long, sweeping drive, it was a low one-story brick structure. The entire back was floor-to-ceiling glass overlooking undulating lawns to a cliff edge, then ocean to the horizon. Buying it was a stretch for me, and I had to take out a mortgage but I wasn't particularly worried. *Number 96* was now being shown in a different format. Instead of five half hours a week, it was currently going to air in two one-hour episodes a week. I still had my royalties coming in, and now there was the promise of greater rewards from the movie version of *The Love Bite.*

When David B and I moved into that house on Whale Beach Road, we moved into our dream. It rapidly became a nightmare…..a career freefall, a relationship disaster, and an eerie supernatural influence which might or might not have caused it all to happen. There, in that beautiful setting, things got ugly. Extremely ugly.

17

Our first few months in the new house were idyllic. I had never lived in such a blissfully tranquil environment and neither had David B. It was also good for Kurt and Daisy, with spacious grounds for them to romp around in. Every day, I listened to the ocean washing against the cliff and I was reminded of how far I'd come from Newton Heath, Manchester.

Work-wise, my relationship with Johnny Whyte worsened. Occasionally, when happily inebriated, he would revert to his old kind and funny self, but this was happening less and less. I wrote my quota of scripts and attended plot and script conferences, suggesting new storylines and stamping my foot at anything I didn't like. However, in relinquishing any executive role with the show, my influence had weakened. I recognised this and in all fairness, I had to accept it. Whenever I quietly had a grumble to Bill about the way the show was progressing, he would shrug: "Well, David, with all his faults Johnny's there for the show night and day."

He was absolutely right. We still held the majority of the viewing audience, though some of them must have been deluded that it was all real. Every week-end, crowds of sightseers would gather outside the block of flats in Moncur Street, Paddington that we used in our title sequence, somehow expecting to see our characters going about their lives. In a strange way, they were anticipating Reality Television thirty years before it became fashionable. Even so, at the time it illustrated that some viewers were just plain crazy. Although, maybe crazy viewers might have been preferable to some of the new characters Johnny introduced.

I loathed it when he invented a bumbling psychiatrist and his overbearing foul-mouthed grandmother. The actors cast to play this unattractive duo were as charmless as the characters. Johnny had also thought up the ludicrous situation of having the psychiatrist actually using the living room of the flat as a consulting room, a notion that was beyond the bounds of reason, not to mention the local by-laws. Added to this unpalatable mix was a stream of 'patients' , including the much-talked about Miss Hemingway, who had a compulsion to remove her clothes, usually on camera. Despite what had gone before, this was the introduction of no-holds-barred full frontal nudity to *Number 96,* and it smacked of desperation.

In hindsight, I rank this as the beginning of the end. At the time, it just added to the discomfort I was feeling about the show. Therefore, when Douglas Hickox offered to fly me to London and provide accommodation while we spent two weeks formulating my first draft screenplay of *The Love Bite,* I readily agreed.

For the first time, I bowed out of my usual quota of *Number 96* scripts while overseas, explaining that I wanted to concentrate fully on the movie discussions. In actual fact, I wanted a complete break from the show. Maybe distancing myself from it would enable me to take a fresh look at it when I got back and come up with some ways to halt the ever-present threat of dipping ratings.

I flew to London in February, 1977. Amazingly for that time of year, the weather in London was fine and sunny for the entire two weeks I was there. Douglas Hickox's offer of accommodation meant him giving me his mews flat in Kensington, while he moved out to stay with his girlfriend. I felt as if I was stepping into one of those daffy English movies of the 1950s. The mews was familiar because it had actually featured in a number of British films, notably in the classic *Genevieve.* Just behind Harrods, this narrow row of garages and former stables with living quarters above was the height of picturesque chic.

Douglas was a similar delight. He was immensely experienced in filmmaking; he had grown up in the movie industry. His early experience had been as a 'gofer' at MGM's Boreham Wood studios, back in the early fifties when MGM was using its European profits to finance such blockbusters as *Knights of the Round Table* and *Quentin Durward.* He had a fund of stories about those days and we bonded immediately. Our work schedule involved daily discussions to get a scene-by-scene run-down on paper, upon which I would base my screenplay, to be written on my return to Australia. We made some changes, including a new ending, but they were all improvements on the plot of my novel. It all boded well for the movie version.

Along the way, Douglas introduced me to his business partner in this venture, a cameraman called Ozzie, and Ozzie's girlfriend, the actress Rita Tushingham. It turned out Rita was responsible for the whole thing – she had bought *The Love Bite* to read on a flight to Rome, and had been so impressed by its possibilities as a movie property she had passed it on to Ozzie and Douglas. This alone would have been enough to endear her to me, but I'd admired her ever since her debut in *A Taste of Honey*, which established her status as one of the 'new-age' actors in Britain's era of 'kitchen sink' dramas. Rita, by 1977, had certainly moved away from the kitchen sink, mostly in the direction of the boudoir. She had slimmed down and glammed up since her early days, but still retained her fun, down-to-earth quality. Both from North of England working class backgrounds, we behaved like naughty kids in the smart restaurants and clubs where we wined and dined.

Having asked Hollywood refugees Joan and Casey Robinson to

house-sit at Palm Beach, David B arrived towards the end of my two-weeks in London. Douglas and I finished the treatment to our mutual satisfaction. We parted regretfully, with my promising to start on the script as soon as I got back to Australia. Before that, however, David B and I spent time visiting friends in Zurich, Geneva and Majorca. I couldn't really put the movie out of my mind, and made many notes along the way, so that when we arrived home I was in good shape to start writing the first draft immediately.

I rang Bill Harmon and Johnny Whyte to let them know I was back, but told them I had to concentrate on the screenplay for a while. Which is exactly what I did. Writers have to immerse themselves in the work at hand without any distractions. Palm Beach was perfect for that. My work extended into the evenings. A night-cap looking at the ocean, a snack and bed, summed up my only time away from the typewriter. I was too tired to watch television, but I was kidding myself that despite the unpleasant characters Johnny had introduced, the old faithfuls like Dorrie and Herb, and Arnold, Don and Norma Whittaker, plus the funny new owner of the delicatessen, Giovanni, played by the occasionally explosive Harry Michaels, would keep the appeal of *Number 96* afloat.

After a while, with the script going well, I felt I could say hello to the real world again, and tuned into *Number 96*. I missed the opening titles and thought I had the wrong channel. What I saw were swastika flags hung on walls lit by flames and ravening, leather-clad bikies intent on violence. I flicked the remote….ah, now I saw Dorrie and Herb. Maybe I'd tuned into some Z-grade cheapie by mistake. But no. Suddenly, the bikies were back and now they appeared to be crucifying Giovanni. Sickened, I snapped the 'Off' button and rang Bill at home. I kept it short. "May I come in and see you tomorrow?" Any other conversation at that moment would have had me exploding.

The following day, Bill and I met in the office where we'd had so many happy times. Bill sat behind the double desk he had shared with Don Cash in the good old days. But unlike he'd been in the past, he now appeared sheepish, vulnerable and not disposed to argue.

"I can't even recognize the concept I created," I told him. "Bikies. Swastikas. Crucifixions. Whatever happened to storylines like Lucy Sutcliffe's breast cancer scare that got us our biggest ratings? They were plots that appealed to our audience. Who are you aiming at now – neo-Nazis?"

All Bill could do was shrug. "You go off on your own projects. I have to go with what Johnny comes up with." Strong in some ways, Bill always needed someone to lean on. Someone to guide him through intellectual or creative issues. For years it had been Don Cash; for a brief time I'd been the one; now it was Johnny. "If you allow the show to continue along these lines, it'll be off in six months!", I told Bill. And I turned and walked out, slamming the door behind me in an exit any drama queen would have been proud of. It put me on the outside in more ways than one, because it effectively severed me from the show I had created.

I'd given *Number 96* six months. That proved optimistic. It was off the air in three.

Following my confrontation with Bill, I bunkered down at Palm beach and concentrated on my screenplay for *The Love Bite*. Occasionally, Douglas Hickox would telephone from London to ask how I was going, always supportive. My London agents also communicated with me that the publishers W.H. Allen had heard about the upcoming movie and wanted a paperback version of *The Love Bite* based on my screenplay. I was excited by this and mentioned it to Douglas, the next time he called.

Occasionally, fortified by a few drinks, I would tune into *Number 96*. I was usually appalled by what I saw. Every new development signaled desperation. One of the worst was turning gay movie-buff

Dudley Butterfield straight...Dudley, whose image was prime mince! It beggared belief. This miracle of gay-into-straight should have rocked the world. It should have sent the hierarchy of the Catholic Church out to dance in the streets, rejoicing in the knowledge that homosexuality could be reversed by the mere stroke of a scriptwriter's pen. Instead, it was greeted with indifference. By then, *Number 96* had as much credibility as a Three Stooges short. Bill, who had violently opposed the move to turn Don Finlayson straight in our early days, had obviously given up. I'm surprised that after what seemed to be several hundred heterosexual affairs, they didn't turn Vera Collins into a rampant lesbian. But they didn't. They just dumped her.

They dumped Norma Whittaker, too. And Norma's cosy and convivial wine bar became – in a misguided effort to be trendy – Duddle's Disco, where deafeningly amped-up music at least served the purpose of drowning out terrible dialogue, and reduced every scene shot there into an incomprehensible barrage of noise.

For every warm, recognizably human character dropped, another with no redeeming features was shoved in to take their place. My original concept had been built on life-like characters, some of them flawed but despite their shortcomings, endearing and believable. Now, following the lamentable psychiatrist and his grandmother, the oft-naked Miss Hemingway and, with a loud burst of toxic exhaust fumes, the Nazi bikies, Johnny revisited his earlier fantasies by introducing 'Chook' Feather, Arnold's long-lost twin brother. This plot-twist was draped in so many cobwebs, it could have been plucked from the tomb of Edgar Allen Poe. It had already been used unsuccessfully to bring back actor Gordon McDougall as the deceased Les Whittaker's cousin, and it hadn't worked. So, if at first you don't succeed, try the same disaster again. With all due respect to Jeff Kevin's skills as an actor, the couple of scenes I endured had him struggling with Arnold's butch, coarse alter ego, and the result was embarrassing. And when 'Chook' became involved in the inevitable violence that now appeared to be the solution to every plotline, I stopped watching altogether and finished the screenplay.

I switched on again for the final episode. David B was away and I was alone at Palm Beach. It was Johnny's conceit, a last laugh I suppose, to turn Edie McDonald into David Sale because the last, the very last scene in the whole saga had Edie – as miraculously transformed into a writer as Dudley had been turned straight – typing the words of her first novel...."Once upon a time, there was a building called *Number 96......*"

Then followed a curtain call of practically every actor who had ever appeared on the show. This part of the farewell was Johnny's tour de force and it worked brilliantly. I watched them come in and take their bows, and the memories flooded back. Everybody who had ever been connected to the series was invited to be there.

Everybody, that is, but me. The creator had not been asked.

I shed tears. And I wandered outside to look at the ocean and revisited all the great years, relived the wonderful roller-coaster ride that had been *Number 96*. And I wondered how it could have worked out differently.

Maybe I should have taken an executive position and stayed with it 24/7, as I'd done with *Mavis*. But I'd had that kind of all-consuming involvement, and never wanted it again. Instead, I'd stepped back, having presented the original concept, still having a say in things, but also following other projects, attempting to have a life and advance my career in other ways.

I came back inside and looked at the blank TV screen. I felt as though I'd just been a spectator at my own funeral.

18

A grizelled and ancient veteran of wars and Australia's droughts once told me: "Don't ever get too happy, David, because that old bloke in the sky has got a bucket of shit and he's just waiting to pour it all over you."

The demise of *Number 96* brought this to mind, but it didn't seem appropriate. Sure, the hit show with my name on every episode had gone, and with it, my lucrative royalty payments, but I still had the upcoming movie of my novel for which I'd just finished the first draft screenplay, a beautiful home, and a loving relationship.

But the bucket had started to tip.

I sent off my first draft screenplay to Douglas Hickox in London. He rang me soon afterwards, and having read it, gave me a list of minor adjustments which I told him I'd be happy to incorporate into a partial rewrite of the draft. I was just about to hang up when he lobbed a hand grenade into the placid meadow of our working relationship.

"Er...David?" it was a tone he hadn't used with me before. Hesitant, and unsure. He hesitated, then started again. "I...er...have a suggestion. Um...as long as you'll be busy making these adjustments on the script, I wondered if you'd mind if somebody else took over writing the paperback version of your novel?"

I was puzzled. "What do you mean....took over?"

"Well.....that they write it."

I thought he was joking.

"Douglas, let's be clear about this," I told him. "Nobody writes my stories but me!"

Our conversation ended awkwardly. And after I'd replaced the receiver, I sat looking at it a long time, still finding it hard to believe what I'd just heard. I made the adjustments to the script Douglas had requested and mailed the new pages to him within the week.

I never heard from him again.

The movie never happened. The affable, friendly, totally easy collaboration between writer and producer ended right there. And to this day, I still don't know whether our disagreement about the paperback version had something to do with it, or just the myriad problems he may have encountered in getting the movie on the road. The last I heard of the movie rights to my novel was that they ended up owned by some group called the Serprocor Establishment in Lichtenstein. I have referred several inquiries from interested producers who see the book as a great movie property, but they always hit a blank wall.

I immediately did a partial rewrite of my original book for the paperback edition of *The Love Bite*, dispatched the manuscript to W.H. Allen in London, then sat up and looked around. Strangely, nobody was banging on my door with job offers. A top Los Angeles lawyer friend was amazed when I told him this. "If you'd had the success you've had with *Number 96* here in the States, you'd have a stampede of producers begging you to repeat the magic." As it was, I just accepted anything that came along.

Fellow writer Michael Lawrence's concept for a children's show called *Carrots,* had been green-lighted by Channel 7. He approached me, almost with cap in hand, asking if I'd possibly be interested in writing for it. He needn't have been so obsequious. I'd never written for children before and I was delighted at this opportunity. It was certainly fun while it lasted. The fun faded a couple of years later when the situation was reversed. I was desperate for work, Michael Lawrence had a hit series *Return to Eden,* which I would have loved to write for, and I tried to contact him. He never returned my calls.

Then TV mover-and-shaker John Collins signed me to produce and write a local version of an English show called *That's Life* which had become enormously popular with British audiences. Basically, it was a satirical expose of consumer rip-offs, a concept recently revived as *The Checkout*. Our version was hosted by the ebullient Noel Ferrier and it reunited me with my old *Mavis* buddy, Barry Creyton who led a panel which also included actors Bernadette Hugheson and Doug Scroop. A headline previewed it as "David's Sale of Laughs." It was hard but stimulating work because as with *Mavis Bramston* it required an hour's original material every week.

After our first show, we were inundated with tip-offs, contributions and consumer problems from viewers eager to air their grievances or reveal anomalies and fraudulent business practices.

All this might have been worth the effort had we delivered a hit show. I think we did. But like so many ill-advised network decisions, we were defeated by the time-slot TEN decreed. Six-thirty on a Sunday evening was hardly a time when the average viewer needed the stimulation of our show. It's a feet-up, veg-out time, after a day at the beach in summer or sports in winter, and a time when not everyone wants to exercise their brain with the kind of sharp content we presented. The response we got in the avalanche of contributions and tip-offs was amazing. We had touched a nerve. People welcomed an outlet for their grievances. But overall, the ratings didn't justify extending our initial season of thirteen weeks.

I was surprised when my agent passed on a summons from the Grundy Organisation. On a scale of bizarre invitations, this ranked with Dita Von Tease being invited to hang out at the Vatican. They had some kind of medical 'soapie' in preparation. Strangely enough, even in the planning stages of this new venture about young medical students, ironically titled *Starting Out,* they were running out of plot ideas, hence this invitation to their one-time arch-rival to attend one of their brainstorming sessions. A new show, fresh characters, an original situation....the storyline opportunities should have been boundless. I found out why they weren't when I arrived and was presented with a list of directives regarding unacceptable subjects. I almost laughed out loud at the first two on the list. No ethnic characters. No terminal diseases. In a medical series? In racially-diverse Australia? The rest of the list of no-no's continued to read like a recipe for pasteurization. I went home and concocted two pages of plotlines involving blond blue-eyed Caucasian medical students battling such health crises as teenage acne, ingrowing toenails, split ends and buck teeth, and they actually paid me for this rubbish. None of my suggestions was used, but the ones that went to air weren't much better. It's amazing that this cobbled-together collection of old clichés even lasted 84 episodes to air. Unfortunately for me, my swift response to their summons, evidently stirred some reaction in the Grundy hierarchy. I had responded to their stupidity once, maybe I was one of them after all, and maybe I could do it again.

The need for money influenced my decision, and as the only viable alternative was armed robbery, I accepted this next offer from Grundys, which was to produce a TV special purporting to be an investigation of the supernatural. I should have advised them just to train the cameras on some of their own employees, who flitted around like ghosts with fear in their eyes. They even had their own haunted castle – Grundy House, a concrete horror on the Pacific Highway, which was to be my prison for the six weeks it took to boil up a stodgy porridge of mind-readers, conjurors, faith-healers and card-sharps. I must say they were infinitely preferable to the Grundy staff who treated me as if I were an alien from outer space. I tried to be my usual bright and breezy self, but it seemed like the regular employees of that time had attended refresher courses on how to be disagreeable. I had worked there for three weeks before I found out that all the staff gathered together for Friday night drinks in one of the boardrooms. This discovery led to a grudging invitation to join them, and I went along misguidedly thinking I could break down barriers and forge new friendships. What actually happened was that a girl from Accounts got very drunk and, waving her arms crazily at the assembly, screeched: "David Sale gets paid more than anyone else in this room!" This really endeared me to the crowd. The rest of the evening was as fun-filled as a Ku Klux Klan reunion. If somebody had brought a rope, they would have lynched me.

I gritted my teeth and went on with the show. My introductory ploy to anyone being considered for an appearance was: "I guess I'm the right person to produce this program because I suspect the house I live in is haunted." This wasn't a trick to gain their confidence, nor was it a figment of a writer's feverish imagination. Although I'm one to greet any over-the-top claims regarding the supernatural with a healthy dose of cynicism, I had to admit there had been some strange, inexplicable goings on at 325 Whale Beach Road.

When we first moved in, actresses Gwen Plumb and Thelma Scott identified the property as what used to be "Evelyn Gardner's old home." "This is nobody's old home," I replied. "it's almost brand new." Gwen and Thelma explained that Evelyn Gardner, once a reigning star of Gilbert and Sullivan operettas, had lived in a house on this site with her faithful dresser, Annie. Floor levels and layout were practically identical. Obviously, the architect had followed the same basic plan of the original house and built on the foundations, even incorporating some walls into this reconstruction.

It started with a tumbler sliding across a glass-topped coffee table. David B and I were sitting there and we watched its progress. I jumped up to catch it when it fell off the edge. It stopped at the edge.

"Condensation," I said, picking up the glass and looking at its base. Completely dry. And when I checked, there was no tilt to the table.

Other glasses were not as fortunate. We began to find them, always broken. A wine glass, its stem snapped. A tumbler, cracked in two places. A glass serving plate that looked as if it had been sliced in half. The sun, sparkling on something at the cliff edge, attracted our gaze. It was another broken wine glass, lying in the grass as if it had been thrown there, and yet there had been no party, no instance of drinking outside. I knew I wasn't responsible for this stream of breakages and David B was equally adamant.

Like Vera Collins, her character in *Number 96*, actress Elaine Lee had developed a talent for reading Tarot cards. I wasn't a total believer, but I figured at this stage of my career, any good news might help. Elaine played out the cards, making some vague forecasts. Then she looked at me, puzzled. "Who's your lady house guest?" she inquired. "We don't have anyone staying with us," I replied. Another shuffle of the cards. "There she is again." It happened a third time. Elaine pointed to a particular card and gave me a knowing glance. "Come on – who've you got there? Somebody famous you're trying to keep a secret?" "There's no-one but David and me," I protested. Elaine paused, thoughtfully. "I'm sorry, but the cards say there's definitely a lady in your house. A very strong-minded career woman….with reddish-gold hair."

When I got home, I acted on a hunch. I telephoned Gwen Plumb. "That Evelyn Gardner who lived in the house this one replaced – what colour was her hair?"

"Reddish-gold," Gwen replied. "Tell me more," I said. It transpired Evelyn had retired in 1960, and lived on Whale Beach Road with her dresser Annie, until she died suddenly in 1970. Annie stayed on in the house, but only survived her mistress for a short time. Soon after her death, the house was demolished, to be replaced by the one I now owned.

"Seems rather a coincidence, doesn't it?" I commented. "I move in and suddenly all her friends start to come around." I'd entertained Gwen and Thelma Scott, and choreographer George Carden amongst others, all of whom had known Evelyn. And I was in show business, too. "I wonder if she's still hanging around," I mused. "If she is, it must seem like a reunion of all her old friends." Another thought struck me. "Did glassware have any significance in her life?"

"She was an avid collector of crystal," Gwen replied. I thought of all the unexplained breakages, my cheap wine glasses and the tumblers that had started life as peanut butter jars. No wonder Evelyn was affronted! It was an amusing theory, but one I didn't take too seriously.

Then David B's mother, Elizabeth, came from England on vacation. She'd been with us less than a week, when she confronted us. "These shoes," she said, pointing to the lace-ups she was wearing. "I can't slip them off without untying the laces, so that's what I do every night. But every morning when I get out of bed, they're all tied up again, with neat little bows. So which of you is playing games?"

Both of us denied tampering with the shoes. We brought it up a couple of nights later when Gwen and Thelma invited us to dinner at their place close by. "That'd be Evelyn," said George Carden, from near the fireplace, his hand resting casually on the mantlepiece. "She always was a meddlesome old bitch."

The wine glass in his hand shattered. It didn't slip from his hand and break on the hearth. I saw the pieces sparkling as they fell.

Everybody laughed and passed it off, but it fuelled a nagging little doubt that David B and I were not alone in our house on the cliff. And so, when I began producing *Exploring the Psychic Mind* for Grundys, I used the subject of Evelyn as a conversational gambit.

One afternoon, I visited clairvoyant Graydon Rixon at his home on the upper north shore, hoping to clinch an appearance by him on the show. I poured it all out to him...the broken glasses, the tied-up shoelaces, the friends from her past, and the accurate description that came from the Tarot cards.

Away from Palm Beach, it all seemed so petty, yet why was it disturbing me? I said as much, when friends suggested I use the experience to turn into a play or TV property. "I'm a writer," I'd reply. "If I wanted to turn my life into a revival of *Blithe Spirit* I'd concoct some manifestations a helluva lot more interesting than these."

"But you're right to be worried," Rixon said seriously. "If she's really around, then she doesn't know she's dead. If the levels and layout of the new house follow the dimensions of her own house, then it's still her property. You've brought her friends in. You're in show business, too, and she'd relate to that. But such a presence can have negative effects. They can be extremely enervating. And they've been known to break up relationships if they favour one partner over another." I suddenly felt extremely vulnerable. I'd been feeling more than usually tired, exhausted in fact, but I'd blamed it on the draining effects of working at Grundy House. Even so, I was still uncertain. "So what will I do?"

"You should consider exorcism before things get nasty."

He walked me to his gate, and as I reached my car, he called the word out again. Exorcism? That word came from horror movies. It had no place in this tree-lined avenue in Pymble. I got into my car.

Immediately, I became aware that the interior was filled with an overpoweringly pungent smell of, to put it bluntly, shit. I jumped out and examined my shoes to see if I'd stepped into dog poo. The soles of my shoes were clean. I examined the floor of the car and looked under the seats. Everything was immaculate. There was nothing but this terrible, sickening odour. I rolled down all the windows and stood in the sun, waiting. After a while, I got back into the car and began the drive back to Palm Beach. Breezes whipped into the car through the open windows and gradually dispersed what was left of the smell. Was this a reaction to that word 'exorcism'?

I flung open the double doors at the entry to the house and stood in the raised foyer. "Hi, Evelyn, I'm back!" I shouted. "Look, dear, you're dead. Do you understand me? You've passed on, but you haven't passed on far enough. You shouldn't be here. Go, for God's sake! Get the hell out of here!"

Was I mad? I stood there, waiting, hearing nothing but the whisper of the ocean against the rocks below. Then I heard a distinct crack from the kitchen. On Elizabeth's last evening with us before she returned to England, we'd had a candle-lit dinner. The candle holder was a sturdy cube of glass. I'd cleaned it of wax, washed it and left it on the draining board. Now, I saw the glass cube lying there in two equal pieces as if it had been a block of butter, sliced cleanly and evenly down the middle with a sharp knife. I examined it closely. There were no jagged edges, no radiating cracks. It had been split exactly in half. And from the sharp crack I'd heard, it had happened right after I'd yelled at Evelyn.

I completed the Grundy special, and its most intriguing feature was when an investigative team, including myself, Carol Raye, a cameraman and a couple of others, went to Leppington on the outskirts of Sydney. While Carol stood closely on camera, we filmed a faith-healing operation by a woman who massaged a man's stomach. Her fingers seemed to penetrate his flesh and emerged clutching what looked like a small portion of bloody entrails.

Afterwards, Carol and I kept her busy with questions, while one of our assistants managed to swipe a cotton swab containing a sample of whatever she was supposed to have removed from the patient's stomach. We had it analysed by the Commonwealth Laboratories and it turned out to be 'of animal origin, probably sheep or goat.'

Perhaps exposing such fakery made me relegate the whole question of Evelyn to nothing but a string of coincidences. I pushed aside what I now regarded as a trivial distraction and devoted my thoughts to a couple of assignments, a TV pilot and a screenplay treatment, both of which brought in money, but never went any further.

Vaguely, though not attributing much importance to it, I noticed that David B. was lapsing in black moods. He seemed restless and morose for no apparent reason, and began taking advantage of the travel perks associated with his job, to fly away to Hong Kong or Singapore on brief week-end jaunts, while I got on with my work. Then he failed to return one Monday and his office rang up to find out where he was. He returned on the Tuesday and sheepishly confessed he'd become 'entangled' with someone else. I pursued the matter like a cop in a TV crime series and under my third degree it came out that each time he went away, he would seek out other men.

"Aren't you happy with me?"

He shrugged and seemed at a loss to answer. Then: "Yes, but you go off into your own little world when you're writing, and I feel left out." He looked around the living room. "And, I don't know why, but I hate this place. I don't feel a part of it."

It was the same old curse of living with a writer. It didn't occur to me then, although it did later, that this appeared to be fulfilling the clairvoyant's prediction about a spirit favouring one partner in a relationship and destructively influencing the other to cause a break-up. Now his unfaithfulness was out in the open, we swiftly grew apart. I was fastidious enough not to want any physical intimacy with someone who was indiscriminately sleeping around, and quite possibly this saved my life as – unbeknownst to us all, the threat of AIDS was just around the corner. I finally asked David to move out. The situation had become untenable and neither of us was happy any more. It had been seven years since we met.

Now I was left in this magnificent house with just a dog and a cat for company. In a valiant attempt at humour, I'd wail to my friends with reference to a famous Hollywood scandal: "I'm rattling around in luxury like Lana Turner, but I don't even have a Johnny Stompanato to stab!"

But most of the time there was the sadness that follows any divorce or separation, be it gay or straight.

I'd forgotten all about Evelyn. One evening, I walked into the living room and my cat Daisy, who had been curled up on the back of an armchair, did a sort of backwards leap, and then began retreating, her wide green eyes fixed upon me. I stood there. I had never seen my cat, or any cat for that matter, behave quite like this. And then I realized her eyes were not fixed upon me, they were staring past me, to my left. I forced myself to turn my head, actually scared at what I would see.

Nothing.

Daisy scooted outside, and after that night seemed reluctant to come indoors. She spent most of her time outside, and eventually just disappeared, never to be seen again.

I lapsed into a sort of pleasant inertia. Was I under some sort of spell? Did everything lighten up because, with the competition gone, Evelyn had me all to herself? There was nothing dark and creepy about the house. It was spacious and sun-filled. The seascape, ever-stirring as it unfolded from the horizon, was a pleasure to the eye and soothing to the ear. I began to go out less, but not I hasten to add for any ghostly reasons. When friends called to invite me down to town for a meal, I'd say: "Look, I'd love to see you, but it's so beautiful here, why don't you come up for lunch at the week-end instead?" I was motivated by the prospect of sitting all night on just one glass of wine, if I drove to town for dinner. There was also the danger, after a good meal, of dropping off to sleep at the wheel on the way back. So I entertained a lot at home.

I remember one week-end, Carol Raye came to stay. As we sat at dinner, the moonlight rippling on the ocean, Carol sighed. "Oh, darling, this is so romantic. Change into Paul Newman immediately!"

"Certainly," I replied, "if you turn into Robert Redford!"

My lassitude extended for the first time in my life, to my career. I lost the urge to seek assignments and instigate projects of my own, and only accepted what I was offered, which didn't amount to much. I was asked to appear on *This is Your Life* three times in a row. The lives in question were those of Bill Harmon, Tommy Tycho and Toni Lamond. "I'm a part of everybody's life but my own!" I wailed jokingly. A fellow guest on Toni's *This is Your Life* was another talented lady, Lorrae Desmond. At the party, following the taping of the show, I found she had been through a divorce and was now living in Narrabeen, which made us practically neighbours. Soon, two suddenly single souls began seeing a lot of each other, and to this day, Lorrae is one of my dearest friends.

About this time, I was offered a trip to London to meet Johnny Speight, creator of the hugely successful British comedy series *Till Death Us Do Part*. Speight had come up with a new concept called *The Tea Ladies* about a pair of elderly tea ladies/cleaners in Parliamentary offices who retrieve government documents and correspondence from waste paper baskets and put their own wildly distorted views on what was going on in the world of politics. It sounded a fun idea. I was given the all-expenses-paid trip in order to Australianise Johnny Speight's scripts – in other words, relocate them to Parliament House, Canberra, and then produce a local version of the series. I imposed only one condition to the production company that hired me – that they'd have a back-up team to help me when I returned.

I was surprised when Johnny Whyte phoned me from London and invited me to stay with him. Relations between us had been strained since the demise of *Number 96* but I was as eager as he appeared to be to restore our friendship to an even keel, so I accepted.

It was a happy decision. With the pressures of *Number 96* now well in the past, Johnny was back to being the amiable, funny guy I knew right back when he replaced me on *The Mavis Bramston Show*. He had moved to a beautiful apartment in Little Venice, an enclave of stately residences on either side of a canal off the Edgeware Road.

I met Johnny Speight in the palatial office of rock music entrepeneur Robert Stigwood, Speight's manager. Johnny Speight represented himself as a salt-of-the-earth rough-as-guts Cockney, an affable version of his famous creation, Alf Garnett. He was immensely likeable, and although it was only mid-morning, he was panting for his first drink of the day.

"Wot d'you see this show as, me old cock?" he asked.

I outlined the concept as it had been briefly related to me, in one sentence. "Great!" he roared, "you got it! They told me you were the right geezer for the job, so come on, let's go celebrate!" And with that, he hauled me off on a day-long pub crawl during which it seemed we hit every bar in London. And when we'd exhausted the bars, we moved on to the clubs, plushy expensive establishments where Speight breezed in like a dustman and was greeted like a Lord. Cohorts of his gathered around. By this time, we were into champagne. Expensive champagne. At one stage, I insisted: "This is my round," and found it cost me nearly one hundred pounds. I arrived back at Johnny Whyte's apartment at some ungodly hour and collapsed into bed. The next morning, I blearily fronted my friend over coffee. "How was it?" he asked.

By that time, the grim truth had hit me. "There are no scripts for me to Australianise. Johnny Speight hasn't written a line. All he's sold to Australia is a one-sentence concept. I'll have to start from scratch."

I put in a call to the production company in Sydney and told them the situation. I reiterated that now, more than ever, I would need a support team to help put the show together while I was writing the scripts. I spent the rest of my time in London mapping out plots and writing pages of sample dialogue for the two tea ladies. I was expecting to have at least one more meeting with Johnny Speight, but although I tried to make contact and left messages with Robert Stigwood's people, I never saw him again. He had probably forgotten that entire drunken day we'd spent together.

I flew home via the United States, planning a few days R and R at the Beverly Wilshire Hotel before facing the mammoth job of starting the Australian version of *The Tea Ladies* from scratch. I was having a wonderful time, spending the Labour Day holiday with my friend Kathryn Grayson and her family. I also spent time with Carmen and Lloyd Pantages, the offspring of the man who founded the famous Pantages circuit and the Pantages Theatre on Hollywood Boulevard, and also with Greta Peck, the ex-wife of Gregory whom I'd met on her visits to mutual friends Joan and Casey Robinson in Sydney. It was Casey who 'discovered' Greg Peck as a struggling actor in New York, and financed him and his wife Greta to come to Hollywood. This catapulted Gregory Peck to success and, eventually, away from his wife, Greta. People often asked me: "Oh, how could she let him get away?" I'd reply: "How could he let Greta get away?" Because Greta was a lovely lady.

Spending time with Greta brought to mind the romantic saga oft-repeated by Australia's doyenne of deportment, good taste and impeccable manners, June Dally-Watkins. Too oft-repeated, in my opinion. In it, Ms Dally-Watkins rhapsodises over the "Roman Holiday" she enjoyed while being wooed by Gregory Peck during the making of that film. I'd always found this intriguing, as I knew Greta and their three young sons were also in Rome while the film was being shot. Naturally, I never brought this up with Greta, except once venturing: "Did you get to see much of Rome?" "Oh no," she replied wistfully, "I spent most of the time at the hotel looking after the children."

I was nearing the end of my brief stay in California when I got a telephone call that devastated me. It was from my old friend Roger.

He told me that Lucy, my mother, had banned anyone from calling me. "But I think you ought to know, your father has had a stroke." I immediately phoned my mother. She told me the facts about my father's sudden collapse and said she'd had great comfort from talking on the phone to Lorrae each evening.

I flew home the next day. It was typical of Lucy. Long the subservient wife of a difficult man, this was her strong independent streak finally showing through. She had shouldered the responsibility of coping with my father's illness but – unselfishly thinking of me – had ordered that nobody spoil my trip by telling me. She had chosen Lorrae with whom to communicate her private grief. And Lorrae had been there for her.

The stroke had almost totally incapacitated my father, both mentally and physically. When I saw him in this state, I felt closer to him than I had in my entire life. It was soon found that any therapy would be useless. Dad needed constant care, and was transferred to a nursing home. My mother amazed me. In complete control of the situation, she told me she wanted their house in Narrabeen sold so that she could move into something smaller and closer to where dad was.

I complied quickly. The Narrabeen house was sold, I found her a small but sunny apartment in Newport, and she moved in. She must have been missing her partner of over forty years, but she never showed it. She was now in control of her own life, but determined to visit my father, source of so much unpleasantness, every day remaining to him. And I drove her there. From then on until he passed away several months later, that daily visit ruled our lives. It was a ritual showing devotion to the man who had once made our lives a misery, and then tried in his own way to compensate. It was his bravery to face the unknown that had brought us to Australia, and for that alone I was in his debt.

While coping with all of this, I withdrew my participation in *The Tea Ladies*. As I feared, no back-up team had been recruited to assist me and I wasn't about to write a season of thirteen comedy scripts, hold casting auditions, and produce the entire show on my own.

I heard a pilot had eventually been filmed in Melbourne, but it went nowhere. Neither did Johnny Speight's version in England.

Wherever I looked there was doom and gloom. Whatever project I'd attempted since the demise of *Number 96* had ended less than satisfactorily. I put on a brave face and hosted luncheons and dinner parties for all the friends who flocked to Palm Beach, my insecurities masked by lots of laughter, good food and wine.

In private, I longed for an end to the negativity, but I was less concerned with my career than my need to meet a significant other.

My track record in relationships wasn't all that good, in my estimation, even though each had lasted several years. I wasn't the promiscuous type. I was happy only when I was in tandem.

There was no doubt about it, I was on a downward roll. That 'old bloke in the sky' had certainly emptied the bucket on me. Or at least, that's what I thought. Unbeknown to me, there was still some of the brown stuff left in there.

19

It seemed, as they say, a good idea at the time. Much, I suppose, like the prospect of a nice, refreshing sea voyage appealed to those booking on the *Titanic.*

The idea for a new soap set in a shopping mall was selected by Channel Ten executives from a number of outlines submitted to them, and after tossing it around amongst themselves like a lot of midgets trying to play basketball, they came to a conclusion widely held in the in the industry about television executives in general, that they didn't have a clue and needed outside help.

Instead of calling a mental health hotline, one of them had the bright idea of reassembling the old *Number 96* team in the hope of conjuring up the magic that had given them the biggest hit in the history of the network. First on board was Bill Harmon, who wasn't exactly the best choice, because, like me, he'd been floundering around since the demise of *Number 96* and had even, briefly, taken over a restaurant on the northern beaches where 'Chilli crab claws' had taken the place of 'top rated show' on his personal career menu. Bill had dreams of success in Australia's film industry, and was reluctant to tie himself to any more TV projects. He consented to helm this new property only through pre-production as far as the launching episode. Then he would withdraw.

First mistake. It wasn't an independent production. It would be totally controlled by the network. And Bill had their okay to jump ship immediately it rolled down the slipway.

Bill called me. Maybe I was the second mistake, and I have to face that possibility. The basic premise appealed to me. Shopping malls, by the late seventies were becoming more dominant in the lives of Australia's suburbanites. And the people who lived in the suburbs and shopped in malls were our television audience. To me, the setting seemed relevant to a show that would reflect Australian life in the eighties, just as *Number 96* had done in the seventies.

Bill and I got together and it seemed like old times. The bitterness that ended our *Number 96* association had evaporated. The enthusiasm that had bonded us almost ten years before came back. We joked and we laughed, like two battered war veterans revitalized by the prospect of a new glory campaign. "Jeezus, look at us!" Bill chortled. "All we need now is Johnny."

And that led to the third mistake. In the after-glow of two pre-lunch margaritas and a bottle of cabernet sauvignon, I uttered the fatal words. "Well, since you mention it, why not ask Johnny back?"

After all, I had recently enjoyed Johnny Whyte's generous hospitality in London, and he appeared to have reverted to his former funny, unobsessive self. Why not? Nostalgia has a way of obliterating the bad times.

Bill and I were there at the airport to welcome Johnny back to Australia less than two weeks later. In the meantime, I had been busy. As Bill said, when the three of us settled down over meet-and-greet drinks: "David's done a wonderful thing. He's populated this whole goddamn arcade with great characters, just like he did on *96*,with a whole lotta plots to keep 'em busy." He slapped his hands on our arms like we were his favourite sons.

"It's just like old times," he growled like a happy bear.

It wasn't.

As was the case with *Number 96*, the network decided not to waste money on a pilot episode. It somehow hadn't mattered with *Number 96* – everything was under the control of Cash-Harmon, and we had taped at least thirteen episodes before the show went to air. In the case of *Arcade*, for that was to be the title of the new series, while a set was being constructed at Channel Ten's Epping studios, nobody seemed able to decide how to actually launch the show. At first, I was instructed to go ahead and write the first batch of half-hour episodes. By the time I'd done four, they'd changed their minds. The show would debut as a mini-series. Different formats require a change of rhythm and pace. I altered my mindset and began fashioning the introduction of characters and the development of the plotlines in a different way. At first, I found this interesting, and while I was working, at least I was being left alone. Bill and Johnny were auditioning a slew of actors and actresses for the characters I'd created, and I was happy with that. For *Number 96*, Bill's choices had been impeccable.

They called me in to look at the videotapes of the finalists. Lorrae Desmond was great in the part she'd read for, the newsagent Molly. Being her friend, I was happy to see she was perfect for the part. I was even happier that everyone else felt the same.

Then I was called to Channel TEN to discuss another change of mind. Now, they wanted to launch the series with a movie-length ninety-minute special. While I was at the studio, I took a look at the set they were building. It was gargantuan – a wide, curving avenue of up-market shops, more like somewhere Ben Hur would go shopping for togas, than a typical local mart of the times. I wondered about the commodities they would have to stock these huge shops with. And I wondered how they were going to populate the wide avenue that constituted the Mall with enough extras to make it look real. It was like a 'Westfield' effort of today, but totally wrong for its time. I had visualized something less elaborate, more contained, much smaller, a narrower concourse with a more suburban-friendly look. What I saw was overwhelming and intimidating, particularly for what was meant to be a cosily-appealing TV series. Imagine if we'd set *Number 96* in The Star Casino. That's what it felt like to me.

I went home nagged by the uneasy feeling that everything was starting to get out of control. Apart from the enormous amount of money they were spending on the construction of the shopping mall, there would have to be other sets, including the homes of all the shop-keepers. In *Number 96,* we'd had four basic sets – two flats that could be dressed as six, plus two shops.

One thing remained constant throughout all the changes – the first shot of whatever version went to air would be a stack of newspapers being dumped outside the newsagents with a glaring front-page headline about a murder. And it was because of this shot I was summoned to the conference room of a major Sydney hotel. It was filled with television executives, senior network representatives who had converged from other states to discuss *Arcade.* Instantly, it became obvious to me that every one of them wanted the glory of having provided input into this new show. They'd all missed out on doing that in *Number 96.* which had come from an independent company. Now, with a network production, they all wanted to have their say and become a significant part of what they already envisaged as another enormous ratings success.

I took my seat and heard the first topic of discussion. Actually, it was the only topic of discussion for the next hour and a half, and it focused on that first shot. The stack of newspapers. Never mind the headline, what was to be the name of the newspaper? The Melbourne people didn't want a Sydney newspaper. The Brisbane guys didn't want any newspaper with a masthead that smacked of Melbourne or Sydney. I can't recall what the Adelaide and Perth reps wanted, but they all began to argue and shout.

I stuck it for fully ninety minutes. I thought: if they're shouting at each other about just one close-up of a newspaper, what other horrors are to come? Finally, I stood up and slammed my hands on the table. I felt like slamming a few heads.

"Gentlemen, if you'll excuse me!" I bellowed. "I'm supposed to be writing the launching episode, to make use of that million dollar monstrosity they're building out there in Epping. I'm on a deadline. And I find this discussion an utter waste of my time!"

With that, I marched out. Possibly this is how one gets the reputation of being difficult. I continued to work on the opening special and the next five half hour episodes. In the meantime, Johnny Whyte recruited some old and some new faces to form a writing team, and began mapping out future episodes at a series of script conferences. I assumed my initial plotlines would be followed and expanded, as had happened with *Number 96*, but by the time I surfaced I found things had already taken a turn for the worse. Some of the plots were now being developed along the lines that signaled the end of *Number 96* – except this show hadn't even started. Johnny had quickly reverted to his dominating, possessive self and would brook no interference. On paper, my original plotlines were already taking off in bizarre directions that involved the characters in ludicrous situations. Whereas I'd gone for human interest, I skimmed through future synopses and found a secret religious cult that hypnotized its followers to respond to the jingle from a 'Mr Whippy' ice cream van. The Chinese family I'd introduced in recognition of multiculturalism, was quickly being involved in archaic Oriental traditions instead of being portrayed as assimilated Australians. The young people in the Surf'n'Ski shop were up to their acne spots in hackneyed storylines that harked back to the 'Beach Blanket' teen movies of the nineteen sixties, and some of the 'up-to-the-minute' slang Johnny had inserted for them to utter embarrassingly recalled the Beatles era. I insisted he put the scripts back the way I'd written them, and we started to bicker immediately.

Things were not going well at the studio, either. A technician's strike had delayed pre-production, and when the taping of the first ninety-minute episode began, it seemed like every destructive gremlin in the nether-world had volunteered for active duty on *Arcade*. The entire production was overwhelmed by that gargantuan set. It made camera angles difficult and dwarfed the characters. Taping dragged through the entire day. I remember sitting in the control room at midnight watching Lorrae do a scene she'd been waiting in full make-up to do since midday. A lethargy settled over the proceedings like a smothering fog, affecting performances and schedules.

Nevertheless, shooting went ahead on succeeding episodes of the series. The set required at least fifty extras daily to give it the appearance of a busy mall. It soon became apparent that shoplifting was going on. The well-stocked shops were beguiling to people required to spend long, boring hours on the set for minimum pay. So much stuff disappeared, security guards were hired to frisk the extras as they left the set.

I began to get late-night calls from actors who hated what the scripts required them to say, dated, stilted dialogue reminiscent of London West End stage productions in the nineteen-thirties. With his status as script supervisor, Johnny Whyte, was up to his old tricks, re-writing scripts to suit his own out-dated standards. After I'd confronted him about the initial changes to my scripts, he now knew better than to tamper with mine, but he was playing havoc with the work of the other writers. Bill Harmon's contract required him only to see the show through to the taping of the first episode, and he had now departed.

I felt like I was seeing the decline of *Number 96* all over again, with this new show on a fast-track to going the same way – except it hadn't even gone to air yet.

When it premiered, *Arcade* sailed like a leaky galleon onto the nation's airwaves on Sunday, January 21st, 1980, and promptly sank. It wasn't as if viewers tuned in and found they disliked it. They didn't even tune in. Maybe it needed the magic of Tom Greer to come up with a sensational slogan like "Tonight at 8-30, television loses its virginity!" As it turned out, "Tonight, television loses touch with the public" would have been more appropriate. Maybe I'd been so manipulated this way and that way in doing the launching episode that the original spark had been lost. Maybe there hadn't been a spark in the first place. I sat at home and tortured myself. Of course, I blamed myself even while acknowledging how the original concept had been bloated and twisted out of shape. I surveyed the horror of it and I compared the absolute ease with which *Number 96* had insinuated itself into the life of Australia's viewing public. Again, I cursed myself for repeating the path I'd laid with *Number 96,* and not accepted a production executive position when it was offered, something that would have given me more of a say in what went on.

But *The Mavis Bramston Show* had cured me of ever allowing full responsibility for a show to weigh down on my shoulders. I wanted to create, I wanted to write, but I also wanted a life and right at the start I'd learned television had the power to insidiously rot you, if you let it.

When *Arcade* went to air, we writers were already weeks ahead in scripts. It limped along until, in its third week, it was axed. The actors were interrupted at rehearsal and told to dump their scripts into a garbage bin and leave the studio. As they left, that expensive set was being dismantled and carted outside to be sold or given away as firewood. *Arcade* vanished with half a dozen stupid storylines still flapping in mid-air like dirty laundry. And nobody gave a damn.

Arcade would enter TV history as the biggest disaster of all time. It has been said that a change of management at Channel TEN was responsible for dumping the show, and that had it been 'nursed' and given more time to develop, the pubic would have caught on. I don't agree. The project was flawed and top-heavy from the very beginning, with too many cooks spoiling the broth. Even with the sadness that so many jobs had been lost, I felt a sense of relief that it was over and done with. And Johnny must have felt the same way, as he quickly fled back to England without even a good-bye. I knew I would never fall into the trap of working with him again. And I resolved to be more careful in future about the projects I accepted.

The only positive results from *Arcade* was that producer James Davern's eye was caught by the performances of Lorrae Desmond and Syd Heylen, and cast them in his upcoming series, *A Country Practice.* It was a deserved career boost for them both.

As for myself, everyone was at me to do 'another *Number 96*' but there was no way I could clone that show – it belonged in the nineteen-seventies. I wanted to do something entirely different. What I came up with was *Canberra Wives*...followed by the qualification: *The Women who Run the Men who Run the Country.*

I thought this concept dealing with the private lives of the movers and shakers in Canberra would be a lot more glamorous and smart than *Number 96*, with the nation's capital substituting for the apartment block. I made sure there were no political parties mentioned, no actual ministerial positions named. It inhabited the abstract world of *Yes, Minister*, which cleverly distanced itself from the politics it was satirising by not taking sides.

The Melbourne production company Crawfords immediately snapped up my concept and visualized it as their new flagship production to follow *The Sullivans.* The script development process with Crawfords was a joy. Each time I flew down, I was welcomed and felt utter friendliness. In fact I was told: "David, we've always wanted you to work with us."

Canberra Wives, conceived thirty years ago, was as quirky as the more recent *Desperate Housewives.* It depicted the domestic trials and tribulations of the wives of politicians, bureaucrats and consular staff, and was meant to be darkly funny, bringing its 'soap' origins smartly up to date. Over a period of several months, involving flights to and from Melbourne where the Crawfords company had its headquarters, my characters and plotlines evolved into a ninety-minute pilot script with which everybody was pleased. No fuss, no dissention, smooth, pleasant, a direct contrast to my *Arcade* experience. A handsomely-bound presentation folio, including my launching script, was circulated to all the networks for consideration.

It seemed to us all we had a potential hit on our hands. Then the big bomb dropped and we all reeled back in shock. Despite repeated assurances that the show would not involve or name any political party nor stipulate any political agendas, every network knocked it back, fearing 'political or bureaucratic repercussions.' One network insider told me: "They loved it, David, but they're shit-scared that if any Canberra identity recognized themselves, or thought they were being depicted in a less-than-flattering way, strange things might start to happen to the network. It could be something as basic as the studio mail constantly going astray, or as complex as a license not being renewed. But any perceived insult would be avenged."

And so it was goodbye *Canberra Wives* and hello to *A Country Practice.* This series had proved a huge success and I was thrilled for my friend Lorrae. I was invited to write two episodes, rather grudgingly I thought, but two eps were better than nothing to an unemployed scriptwriter, so I went along to my first script meeting ready to do my best. The woman presiding over the scripts was the type of person who never quite recovers from that first heady rush of finding themselves adequate. Self important, but obviously insecure enough to fear I was going to move in and take over the joint, she compensated by treating me like an inexperienced hack. I tried to placate her with assurances like: "I just want to stay home and write scripts." Her reply, delivered with a sneer, was: "Yes, well we don't want any of that *Number 96* smut on this show!" This from a creature later associated with *Chances*, a soapie remembered, if at all these days, only for its succession of bare bottoms.

Obviously, I wasn't welcome. Next, I accepted an assignment to 'script doctor' one of the projects being developed under the Government's infamous 10BA clause that permitted tax concessions to people funding movies. Small production companies with big ideas suddenly materialized out of nowhere, and found they could get money with whatever lousy scripts they had at hand from so-called corporate cowboys looking for investments that were an excuse for tax rebates. The flock of turkeys this situation engendered would have fed the entire population of the United States of America on Thanksgiving Day.

My assignment was to 'doctor' a cheap and nasty rip-off of Alfred's Hitchcock's classic *Rear Window*, and it was a typical example of the Z-grade rubbish that was actually getting to pre-production stage circa 1981. It took me one read-through to decide that this script didn't need surgery. It screamed for euthanasia. I tossed in my scalpel and withdrew.

My career appeared to be in freefall. I was getting paid generously for participating in projects that never made it. I had money in the bank, but not the kind of successful enterprise that usually went with it. I had my Palm Beach house. Friends came for lunch and dinner parties. Evelyn had stopped making her presence felt. Let's face it, she had me to herself, whatever that meant. If she was still hanging around, she was keeping an exceedingly low profile, if one can use that term to describe a bunch of ectoplasm. But she certainly wasn't the kind of live-in companion I wanted.

I was lonely. For the first time in my adult life, I had been without a partner for two years. I wasn't interested in playing the field, having one-night stands. I wanted someone to share my life. And there were other sadnesses. My *Number 96* compatriot, Bill Harmon, had been taken by leukaemia. I'd talked to him on the phone while he was in hospital for treatment. "Can I come and see you?" I asked. "Nah…leave it, David. Maybe in a week or two." In a week or two, he had gone. So had my idol, the legendary screenwriter Casey Robinson.

There were upsides on the personal scene. My friends, the parties… and the emergence of my mother, Lucy, as a sort of merry widow. Happily settled in her Newport flat, she blossomed out as a community helper, joining the Red Cross, serving at their shop in Newport and working at the Mona Vale Hospital every Sunday. Free of my father's confining influence, she made friends and was never short of something to do.

Secure in the knowledge that she was going to be fully occupied during the festive season of 1981-82, I took off with Lorrae to spend Christmas-New Year in California. Before we left, I had to organize house/pet sitters. Now that Casey had gone, Joan Robinson would be holidaying in the States at the same time as us. A married couple suggested by friends called in and we made arrangements over a glass of wine in the kitchen. That evening, I was standing in exactly the same spot and happened to look upwards. To my horror, I saw on the flat white ceiling what looked like a drawing of a skull, with lines radiating from the bottom, like what is referred to as a 'chicken neck'. I scrambled onto the kitchen counter for a closer look. It wasn't the kind of mark caused by dampness or an expansion split in the plaster. The skull face seemed etched into the surface of the ceiling, about six centimeters long. I ran my fingers over the surface, but couldn't even detect scratch marks. My peace of mind wasn't helped when a friend I rang suggested it was Evelyn, upset that strangers were coming to live in the house, and reminding me that she was still around….except that was what she looked like now!

Before I left, I stood under this horrible little manifestation and yelled: "Evelyn – if you attempt *anything* to spoil this couple's stay here, I swear I'll bring in an exorcist!"

Evelyn behaved herself, and the house sitters had a lovely time.

Immediately I got back from my trip, I called in a decorator to paint the kitchen ceiling. The job done, he came to me. 'Finished," he said. "But that peculiar mark that looked like a skull gave me a problem. It took six coats to cover it up."

It would be carrying things too far to blame Evelyn's evil influence for the accident Lorrae had while we were in Las Vegas. Wouldn't it?

The only time Lorrae and I were separated was when she went off to lunch with singer Paul Anka's parents at the restaurant they owned. The pavement in front of the restaurant had just been hosed down and had become a film of ice. Lorrae got out of the taxi she'd taken and promptly slipped, breaking her wrist.

The first I knew of this was later in the day, by which time her arm was in plaster from elbow to wrist. With typical efficiency, she had already tried on everything in her wardrobe. "I'll only need help getting into that little black dress, " she told me, "oh – and you'll have to help me do my hair!" Lorrae refused to let the accident spoil our holiday. She was never late once, kept in good spirits, went on every single ride at Disneyland and kept up with our busy social schedule. Kathryn Grayson had us over for Eggs Benedict; we lunched with Toni Lamond who had been living in America for several years and was doing well as an actress/writer, and Carmen Pantages threw a party in our honour, attended by many famous faces from the Golden Years of Hollywood. Lorrae, of course, had to warn the producers of *A Country Practice* that they'd have to write the injured wrist into the series. This was accomplished in the first scene of the 1982 season, by having a loud crash from the bathroom, as 'Shirley' slipped on a freshly-mopped floor.

My return to the empty house at Palm Beach (well, empty if you didn't count Evelyn!) made me long even more for someone to share my life. I began to look through the Personal ads in Sydney's gay newspapers. In doing so, I sealed my fate for the next twenty-six years.

20

Perhaps the slightly negative slant of the ad, while not setting off alarm bells, should have resonated a disturbing tinkle. It started off:

"I suppose it's impossible to believe that an advertisement could lead to a long-term personal relationship…."

I think that's as far as I got, I was so quick to reply in terms of "No, no, no, it's not impossible, because a long-term relationship is exactly what I want!"

His name was Rob Lovell, and he was an English/History teacher at a High School in the Richmond/Windsor area. We began a courtship based on alternate week-ends. I drove to his house in Wilberforce one week-end, then he would come to Palm Beach the next. This went on for several months.

He hadn't come out to his family, even though by then he was in his late thirties. When he did tell them, he felt his alternate lifestyle had to have stability and, yes, dignity. "This has to be for life," he told me. I didn't hesitate. I believed I'd found the person with whom I'd share the worst fears and best joys, someone to look after and comfort, and be loved, looked after and comforted in return. If you get lucky, that sort of relationship is not only a gift, it's a privilege.

"It's for life," I replied.

His family accepted me and became my family. One of his sisters called me her 'second brother.' All the important family celebrations and anniversaries were held at 'our' house. Rob sold his Wilberforce house, came to live at Palm Beach and completed his Master's Degree at the University of New South Wales. Having tired of teaching, along the way he founded his own educational travel company. Maybe if alarm bells hadn't sounded before, based on my previous experience with a partner who befell the temptations of travel away from home, they should have started pealing then. Unfortunately, there were more important distractions. I received dreadful news from London. Johnny Whyte had suffered a massive stroke.

Due to our past disagreements, we had no longer been in touch. A mutual friend, Richard Price of London Weekend Television, telephoned me with the news. Immediately, I wanted to call Johnny in the hospital. Richard said it wasn't advisable. The stroke had caused partial paralysis and speech impairment.

I desperately felt the need to do something for him. All the traits I'd come to dislike in him suddenly seemed unimportant. Johnny, at his best, was kind, funny, generous and hard-working. I recalled the good times we'd had together as I wracked my brains for some way in which I could cheer him up.

I hit upon the idea of recording messages from as many of his friends and colleagues in Australia as I could. I started with one from Carol Raye, whom he adored, then tracked down several other cast members of *The Mavis Bramston Show*. Next, I did the rounds of the *Number 96* regulars, carrying my portable tape recorder anywhere I could reach them quickly. In less than a week, I used a courier service to carry the tape to London, and a few days later, I had another telephone call from Richard Price. He was in tears as he told me what a tremendous effect all the familiar voices had on Johnny. "He plays the tape constantly, and when he's not listening to it, he holds the cassette tightly in his hand and won't give it up." By that time, I was in tears, too.

Johnny appeared to be rallying well under hospital care, but then in a tragic and ironic repeat of the scenario he had inflicted on Arnold Feather, circulatory problems led to the amputation of a leg. In time, as had been the case with Arnold, he was fitted with a prosthetic limb. This enabled him to be sent home to the flat in Little Venice, helped by a carer. He died the following year.

Rob's progress in his new-found career instilled in me a desire for change. I'd lived on the Peninsula for the past seventeen years, the last ten at Palm Beach. I'd had enough of the long drives back and forth to the city, the isolation. Like Dolly Levi, I felt the need 'to rejoin the human race' and seek the stimulation my creative side sorely needed. I sold the Palm Beach house and bought a detached Victorian terrace in its own grounds in Ashfield. It needed work. I personally painted the walls of that three-story house, room by room. I enlisted the help of plasterers and other experienced tradesmen to restore its original features, and for a time it was like living on a blitz site. But eventually, we had a home that was refreshingly different to the Palm Beach house, but one in which we were just as happy.

As I'd hoped, the change was totally stimulating. I recalled that once upon a time - twenty years before, as a matter of fact – I had written two successful novels, *Come to Mother* and *The Love Bite*. Then *Number 96* had intervened.

Now, having had my fill of television, I went back to my original plan. Before you could say Jane Austin, I had completed my 'come-back' novel *Antidote*. A thriller based on the threat of germ warfare, it was a disappointment. Apart from the fact that I was still feeling my way back into the genre, the book was published with about as much enthusiasm and skill as if it had been a pamphlet on the ravages of tinea, and promoted not at all. As a thriller, I'd intended it as a heart-stopper. In reality, it almost caused my own heart to stop. I suffered a minor infarct due to the stress of trying to promote the book without any support whatsoever, while coping with a bad attack of influenza. But as this led to a restorative angioplasty, and there have been no other cardiac problems since, I guess you could say the whole farrago was a blessing in disguise. It certainly led me to dump my then literary agent and find the live-wire Selwa Anthony.

Under her guidance, my next effort *Twisted Echoes* fared much better, with a hardback in London and a subsequent paperback edition in Australia. I went on to write two more novels – *Scorpion's Kiss* and *Hidden Agenda.* In between times, Rob and I traveled the world. Our first trip away together was Egypt. I joined several of his company's group tours, to Europe, Africa and Vietnam, always paying my way because to do otherwise would have depleted the company's profits. Later, we went to Japan, South America, Turkey, Cuba and India, either just the two of us, or in the company of close friends like Lorrae and Roger.

Over the years, I also penned what I hoped were smart, amusing lyrics of the kind I first wrote for the stage revues at the start of my career. I'd always contributed much of Ron Frazer's material in his stage shows, ending with *Pardon Our Privates* which showcased Ron at his very best at the Manly Music Loft for the last time before his untimely death. I also wrote special material for some of Australia's leading entertainers, including Lorrae Desmond, Toni Lamond, Julie Anthony and Donna Lee.

There is also *Careful, He Might Hear You – the Musical*, based on Sumner Locke Elliott's novel about three sisters fighting for custody of a small boy in Sydney during the 1930s. I wrote the libretto and lyrics, American composer Ron Creager – who first came to Australia as Toni Lamond's accompanist – did the music. We presented a 'potted' concert version of the work at the then-cabaret venue, the Tilbury pub in Wooloomooloo one Sunday evening before a packed audience of managements from commercial and subsidized theatre. To perform it, we had an illustrious cast of friends who willingly gave their talents for nothing…Julie Anthony, Toni Lamond, Nancye Hayes, Carol Raye, Rod Dunbar and Bartholomew John. The work was enthusiastically received, and now we had an in-performance video to help us sell the show.

A copy of the video plus the script ended up with the legendary Broadway producer/director, Harold (Hal) Prince. At his invitation, I sent the material on ahead, prior to a planned visit to New York. When I arrived, the warm welcome I received in his office was in sharp contrast to the cold shoulder I'd been given by Australia's self-important little gods of the arts, none of whom had even bothered to return my calls after they'd given the Tilbury preview a standing ovation. The dynamic Harold Prince, who was responsible for such landmark musical productions as *West Side Story, Cabaret,* and *Phantom of the Opera,* astounded me by giving *Careful* unstinted praise. I was overwhelmed. This was the winner of more Tony awards than anyone else, and here he was expressing great enthusiasm for what Ron Creager and I had created. "Sumner was one of my dearest friends," he told me, "and your adaptation does him proud." He said that being an Australia-based musical, it was fitting that it be done there first. "Now, what can I do to make that happen?" he asked, rising from his desk and starting to pace. "I know. I'll write a letter saying how impressed I am with this show, and urging that it be done by one of your companies over there."

I collected the letter the next day. Besides praising the book, lyrics and music, Harold Prince had written: "I've spent a lot of time in Australia over the past twenty years and I kept wondering why an indigenous musical hadn't emerged. *Careful* could well be the one I was looking for. My Lord, I wish I were able to see it done. I'd love to hear how it fares, because I think this is a worthy project, adapted expertly from the novel."

I sent copies of Harold Prince's letter to every commercial management, every independent and subsidized theatrical organization in Australia. Surely, I thought, the support of this genius who'd had such a profound and lasting effect on musical theatre would count for something?

Obviously not. Most of them didn't extend the courtesy of even acknowledging the letter. These days, when they whine about lack of funding, I remember their ill manners and the casual way they ignore years of work. Typical was the lack of response from the then clique-ridden, self-indulgent Sydney Theatre Company. Recently, encouraged by reports of a new regime under the management of Cate Blanchett and her husband, I re-submitted the work. I was telephoned by one of the company's grandly-titled representatives, a girl who proved herself so clueless it was a wonder she managed to dial my number. Right from the word go, my spirits sank. This creature, who was supposed to handle 'literary works', admitted she had never heard of Sumner Locke Elliott, had never heard of his novel *Careful, He Might Hear You*, and had never heard of the classic Australian movie of the same name. She also drew a blank when the name Harold Prince was mentioned. Her lack of knowledge was coupled with an obvious lack of interest, so needless to say, that's as far as *Careful* got with the Sydney Theatre Company.

Rejection from such ill-informed representatives of current theatre, comes as no surprise. After all, every generation breeds its no-brainers and like cream in a jug of milk, vegetables rise to the top of the soup.

Our only opportunity to stage *Careful* came with the offer of a two-week season at the Street Theatre in Canberra. It received excellent reviews from the local press and a good reaction from audiences. Toni Lamond and a supporting cast of amateurs did their best in a production that was less than perfect, understandable in that the director had not only never directed a musical before, he had never even seen one. Ron and I saw the flaws – but that is what an out-of-town tryout is all about. Any musical headed for Broadway has its often painful beginnings in Boston or Chicago. Our out-of-town try-out happened to be in Canberra.

Ron Creager and I always knew we'd have to face hurdles. Would anyone like to try getting an original Australian musical launched in Australia? I have an easier option. Try touring *Fiddler on the Roof* in Palestinian territory. Those who run these things in Australia have become averse to risk, preferring to stage a tried and true old favourite, or a new hit from Broadway or London that has already been acclaimed. Or, the latest trend, a tryout of a new musical based on a proven film title, but totally written and controlled by Americans. We are aspiring to be the off-Broadway try-out venue for off-shore created musicals. Isn't that wonderful? It's great for our wealth of talented performers, but it doesn't do much for us local creative souls. And, of course, there are now the dreaded 'juke box' musicals that feature an artist's or a group's catalogue of familiar hits, embellishing what's nearly always a lousy script linking the numbers.

Ron Creager and I hadn't banked on facing an insurmountable brick wall. However, the joy, as they say, was in the doing. Creating a musical version of *Careful, He Might Hear You*, gave the two of us a tremendous sense of achievement, and we basked in the praise of the one man who really matters in musical theatre, Harold Prince.

Now, the rewritten and finished work sits on the shelf, polished and perfect, ready for the day when some enterprising visionary takes up the challenge.

Fortunately, if rather belatedly, I had reached the stage of maturity in which I balanced any such disappointments with the good things in life. And when I looked around, I found plenty to be happy about; a strong, enduring and loving relationship, a stable home life, robust health despite some ups and downs, and a much-valued circle of friends.

Even the ghost of Evelyn – if you care to believe it – chose to remind us she was still around with a very typical sign.

One evening in our Ashfield home, we were entertaining friends and the subject of Evelyn came up. I recounted the small but strange incidents that had happened at Palm Beach and finished off by saying that obviously our Gilbert and Sullivan diva had eventually found her way to that big *H.M.S Pinafore* in the sky.

The next morning, I was wiping our coffee table, around which we'd been sitting over drinks. One of the pieces was a large block of smoked Venetian glass, with a centre indentation to form an ashtray, but since nobody used cigarettes any more it just served as an ornament. I saw what appeared to be a blonde hair lying across it, and tried to waft it away. It wasn't a blonde hair. It was a hairline crack across the solid block of Venetian glass, and when I touched it the block split precisely into two equal parts.

When our dog died, we decided to move. A big house with a pool was too much responsibility for us when we traveled so much. So I sold the house and bought a wonderful two-level apartment in Darlinghurst, with an enormous terrace circled by a panoramic view of the city. It's one of six residences centred around a lush tropical garden – and nobody knows it's there!

Before going any further, I'd like to include a quote from the celebrated BBC adapter of classic novels, Andrew Davies. When faced with the task of putting Charles Dickens' *Bleak House* on the screen in 2005 he suggested that: "we adopt the technique of the best soaps, with six or eight storylines running simultaneously and a cliff-hanging climax every thirty minutes." This was exactly how we established the structure of *Number 96* all those years before,

One of the rules of soap opera is that nobody is allowed to live 'happily ever after.' If a couple settles down into a blissful married life, it spells doom for their continued existence in the series, because without drama, they cease to be interesting to the viewing public.

I like to think I'm so on the ball, but I missed the message that if soap opera is taken from life, then life is a soap opera and the rule I just outlined still applies. I went through the years with Rob blissfully happy, secure in the knowledge that "this was for life." It seemed like each of us was utterly devoted to making the other happy.

Rob had served for a year in the Vietnam War, but being attached to an educational unit, he was never in an actual combat zone. For that reason, and unlike many battle-scarred veterans for whom memories of Vietnam induce depression and worse, Rob had actually fallen in love with that country. He included an annual tour to Vietnam in his company's itinerary, and always led it himself because he professed to know the place so well. I sometimes jokingly referred to Vietnam as "the other woman" in our relationship. I wasn't far from the mark. As well as falling in love with Vietnam, Rob was also falling for some of its young men.

As I've said before, distance from home has its temptations. It also aids betrayal and makes it easy and undetectable, because it's away from home-base. When the truth finally came out, he admitted to unfaithfulness for the last five years of our twenty-six year relationship.

I couldn't have thought of a better twist to keep the viewers interested in our personal soapie. The split was abrupt, involving for me, humiliation and devastating emotional pain. An entire year went out of my life while I was dosed up on anti-depressants.

After that year, which I don't want to remember, and fortunately couldn't if I tried, I gradually picked myself up, dusted myself off and came to the conclusion I didn't want to be locked in a prison where the bars were hate, anger, bitterness and regret. I looked around and realized I was surrounded by good friends. Life was still going on and the good times were continuing. DVDs released by Umbrella began to put the *Number 96* phenomenon on permanent record. Andrew Mercado, author of the only accurate history of television drama series, *Super Aussie Soaps*, has devoted his talents to helping Umbrella preserve them forever. The release of the first DVD resulted in a sell-out. It also resulted in my realizing the true value of *Number 96*.

It saved lives.

I was asked to be at the launch of the first DVD. To my surprise, the place was packed, and they were queuing for us to sign the DVD covers. During that evening, three guys approached me individually and told me that if it hadn't been for *Number 96* they would be dead. In each case, they'd been young men living in a small country town, thinking that their urges made them freaks, that they were the only ones in the world who felt that way, and they were on the verge of suicide. Along came *Number 96*, and suddenly they saw they were not the only ones, that there were others like them, and there was hope. There have been more encounters like this, with the release of a second, third, and most recently a fourth 40th Anniversary *Number 96* DVD. I have been truly astonished at the interest the show I created all those years ago still arouses. And not only amongst oldies. A young guy who phoned to interview me for a FILMINK website article said he'd viewed the early black and white episodes and found them "amazingly contemporary." I said: "Include that view in your article as a refreshing slant from the younger generation." He did.

The release of these DVDs has attracted critical acclaim never accorded to the show in its glory days. The noted television writer, Michael Idato, summed it all up in his column: "When the first salacious soap opera, *Number 96* had its premiere in 1972, the National Times said it put television back ten years. Four decades on in an era of new conservatism, we should be so lucky. This series is a real prize."

It doesn't stop. On the horizon is a commemorative DVD of *The Mavis Bramston Show*. My past is surging forward into the present and enriching my life.

And so, in true soap-opera tradition, we end on a cliff-hanger. David Sale, always the survivor, is still there, hanging onto that cliff, determined not to let go.

And that's the lovely thing about cliff-hangers.

They make us look forward to the next episode.

www.ingramcontent.com/pod-product-compliance
Lightning Source LLC
LaVergne TN
LVHW041114080826
845145LV00007B/1815

* 9 7 8 1 9 2 2 2 0 4 0 8 0 *